RIDING THE KONA WIND

*Memoirs of a
Japanese American*

Francis Y. Sogi

THE CHESHIRE PRESS
NEW YORK

ISBN 0-9762575-0-5

For information contact:
Mr. Francis Y. Sogi
Kelley Drye & Warren, LLP
101 Park Avenue
New York, NY 10178

The Cheshire Press is an imprint of
MF Book Production Services

Manufactured in the United States of America

Title page illustration: at left the crests of Yoshiemon Sogi (top) and
Nami Shibata (bottom); at right, the name Sogi in stylized Chinese characters.

Contents

List of Illustrations

Foreword

Aᴍᴇʀɪᴄᴀ, ᴀ ʏᴏᴜɴɢ ᴄᴏᴜɴᴛʀʏ, is made up of immigrants from the world over. Starting in 1868, groups of government-sponsored contract laborers and others arrived in Hawaii from Japan. Among those arriving in 1908 was my father, Yoshiemon Sogi, born in 1882, from the village of Soneda, Asakura Gun in Fukuoka prefecture in Kyushu, Japan. From the nearby village of Yamaguma, my mother, Nami Shibata, arrived in 1912 as a picture bride at the age of 18.

A great regret now is that most of the first generation, or as we know them, the Issei, have gone from the scene. With them went unrecorded historical facts and ancestral stories for descendants to read. Before the Nisei, the second generation, leaves this life, let us hope that these pages will encourage each family to keep detailed records and write down its own life story, joys, and sorrows. Let us hope that with each generation, the Sogis will survive, resuscitated with new branches, prosper and spread far and wide. America is still so very young with just shallow roots, while Japan's history goes back thousands of years (it was 2,600 years old in 1941 when the U. S. entered World War II). Perhaps a little Sogi in the year 2500 will be wondering about our forefathers. And proudly, we can point to our family history. We hope that many Sogis will inherit the strength of character of Yoshiemon and Nami Sogi who went through considerable hardships and pain and struggle, enduring and persevering so that their children and those following could have an easier and better life.

A record of great value is also included in this book. It is an oral history of Nami Sogi that is very revealing. It contains the hardships, trials, and tribulations of a young eighteen-year-old bride who left her roots to bravely face a great unknown and uncertainty, going across the largest body of water on this earth to marry a man she did not know. All who read this record will admire the strengths of the first generation of Japanese immigrants who started a new generation to love and respect their elders, and give loyal devotion to the land they adopted. She died on December 6, 1979, after strokes left her paralyzed and infirm and in the care of a very comfortable and nice nursing home in Honolulu.

This recorded history will be given to all Sogi descendants in the United States and Japan and in other parts of the world, wherever they are, in the hope that ties will be renewed and strengthened and that these ties may continue. Let us hope that many a cousin will meet to exchange experiences and stories of many cultures, all going back to the same roots of the Sogi family from whence they had sprung.

In commemoration of our 55th wedding anniversary, this book is the result of encouragement by my wife, Sarah, our son, Jun James, and his wife, Sarah J. Smith. A number of my friends, also, urged me to memorialize my experiences, in introspection and retrospection of my life, people, and society for the benefit of family, descendants, and friends. Not having the sweet insouciance of lettered ease, I have no intention of profiting from this publication, and thus, the self-publishing. If it can serve as a means of raising any funds for any non-profit organization, I will be delighted to contribute this book for its worthy cause.

If all of my relatives and friends who may read this book and find something meaningful in our relationship and understand and appreciate me for truly what I am, I will have served my main purpose in writing this book. I would have liked to include every individual I have met and have come to know, but with limited space, it was not possible to do so. Those who have not been mentioned, but whom I have come to know, hopefully, will understand.

If anyone mentioned in this book is flattered by being included, it was not my intention to do so. He or she was included as an indication of the importance I have placed in our relationship in the context of the situation mentioned. I regret that this book has become quite long and I can only say that it would have been shorter had I more time.

SOGI FAMILY TREE

(Fukuoka, Japan)

Kaemon (88)
Family successor

b. 2/28/1892
d. 12/7/1978

Sayo Kiyotake

b. 10/20/1891
d. 2/28/1984

Yoshiemon
(to HI in 1908)

b. 7/26/1882
d. 5/16/1958

Nami Shibata
(to HI in 1912)

b. 4/16/1894
d. 12/6/1979

Kichiguro

d. 1847

Kichiemon (81)

b. 7/13/1824
d. 7/5/1905

no record of wife

Saki Ota (81)

b. 9/22/1830
d. 9/29/1911

Youemon (78)

b. 5/17/1851
d. 7/9/1929

Iwa Ota
b. 4/18/1863
d. 11/16/1890

Ei Kurakake (87)
b. 1/16/1860
d. 4/5/1947

Yujiro

b. 2/20/1895
d. 12/7/1978

adopted by
Nakadera

(Tokyo)

Asa

b. 5/20/1973

Kintarc Kuratake

m. 3/30/1987

Kichigoro

b. 10/7/1888
d. 12/10/1888

b. = born
d.= died
w.= wed

The characters depicted above make up the Japanese name, Sogi.
Top, *So* (resuscitation); bottom, *ki* or *gi* (tree).

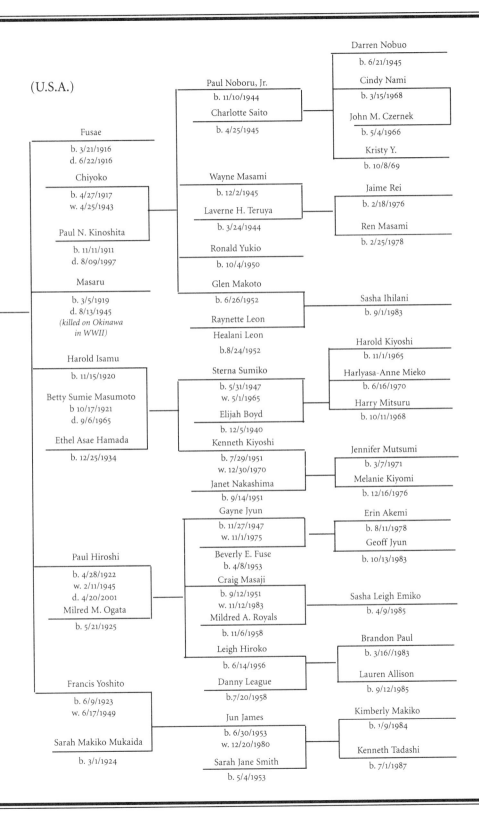

(U.S.A.)

Fusae
b. 3/21/1916
d. 6/22/1916

Chiyoko
b. 4/27/1917
w. 4/25/1943

Paul N. Kinoshita
b. 11/11/1911
d. 8/09/1997

Masaru
b. 3/5/1919
d. 8/13/1945
(killed on Okinawa
in WWII)

Harold Isamu
b. 11/15/1920

Betty Sumie Masumoto
b 10/17/1921
d. 9/6/1965

Ethel Asae Hamada
b. 12/25/1934

Paul Hiroshi
b. 4/28/1922
w. 2/11/1945
d. 4/20/2001

Milred M. Ogata
b. 5/21/1925

Francis Yoshito
b. 6/9/1923
w. 6/17/1949

Sarah Makiko Mukaida
b. 3/1/1924

Paul Noboru, Jr.
b. 11/10/1944
Charlotte Saito
b. 4/25/1945

Wayne Masami
b. 12/2/1945
Laverne H. Teruya
b. 3/24/1944

Ronald Yukio
b. 10/4/1950

Glen Makoto
b. 6/26/1952
Raynette Leon
Healani Leon
b.8/24/1952

Sterna Sumiko
b. 5/31/1947
w. 5/1/1965
Elijah Boyd
b. 12/5/1940

Kenneth Kiyoshi
b. 7/29/1951
w. 12/30/1970
Janet Nakashima
b. 9/14/1951

Gayne Jyun
b. 11/27/1947
w. 11/1/1975
Beverly E. Fuse
b. 4/8/1953

Craig Masaji
b. 9/12/1951
w. 11/12/1983
Mildred A. Royals
b. 11/6/1958

Leigh Hiroko
b. 6/14/1956
Danny League
b.7/20/1958

Jun James
b. 6/30/1953
w. 12/20/1980
Sarah Jane Smith
b. 5/4/1953

Darren Nobuo
b. 6/21/1945
Cindy Nami
b. 3/15/1968
John M. Czernek
b. 5/4/1966
Kristy Y.
b. 10/8/69

Jaime Rei
b. 2/18/1976
Ren Masami
b. 2/25/1978

Sasha Ihilani
b. 9/1/1983

Harold Kiyoshi
b. 11/1/1965
Harlyasa-Anne Mieko
b. 6/16/1970
Harry Mitsuru
b. 10/11/1968

Jennifer Mutsumi
b. 3/7/1971
Melanie Kiyomi
b. 12/16/1976

Erin Akemi
b. 8/11/1978
Geoff Jyun
b. 10/13/1983

Sasha Leigh Emiko
b. 4/9/1985

Brandon Paul
b. 3/16//1983
Lauren Allison
b. 9/12/1985

Kimberly Makiko
b. 1/9/1984
Kenneth Tadashi
b. 7/1/1987

CHAPTER ONE

The First Generation

K ONA HAS BEEN HOME to the Sogis since they arrived from Honolulu in the 1920s. My father, Yoshiemon Sogi, had come in 1908 from a village called Soneda, Asakura Gun, in Fukuoka prefecture on the island of Kyushu, the southernmost of the four main islands of Japan. Nami Shibata, my mother, came from the neighboring village of Yamaguma in 1912. Like many other immigrants, my father had been lured to Hawaii by the opportunity to work on the sugar-cane plantations that were the mainstay of the Hawaiian economy. It was a time of massive inflation and extraordinary changes were taking place in a Japan with poor living conditions. It was a time ripe for thousands of young men and women to leave their homes and villages with dreams of riches to be made in paradise, as Hawaii was seen to be, and to return to Japan with wealth. In effect, there was a feeling of resuscitation and a new life ahead. The Chinese characters for the name Sogi appropriately mean just that: *yomigaeru (resuscitated)* and *ki* (tree). Unfortunately, reality painted a different picture. However, most of the Japanese immigrants remained, enduring lives of hardship and hard, hard work. They sent for picture brides and started new generations of Japanese Americans.

On February 8, 1885, the first group of contract laborers from Japan arrived in Hawaii on the ship *The City of Tokyo*. (A shipment of laborers called the *gannenmono* had earlier arrived in Hawaii in 1868, the first year of the Meiji era.) 1885 was the same year that immigration to the United States from eastern and southern Europe began to grow into a mighty flood, and just one year before the Statue of Liberty raised her torch over

New York Harbor. Conventional textbook wisdom has it that immigration to the United States a hundred years ago was exclusively through Ellis Island. While a great many Americans trace their ancestry through that port of entry, many others came and are still coming in increasing numbers across the Pacific. As with their Atlantic counterparts, passage was difficult and often perilous. Once they arrived, contract laborers worked long and hard to achieve a degree of self-sufficiency.

The official agreement of the Japanese laborers who came to Hawaii provided for payment of $15.00 per month during the term of their contract. Ten dollars were to be paid to the laborer's wife if he was married and if she, also, worked. Then, as now, wage scales differed between men and women. The contract also provided that $2.50 per month would be withheld and turned over to the Japanese Immigration Bureau to secure the laborer's return passage should he decide to return to Japan.

Laborers were required to work 26 10-hour days each month in the field or 12-hour days in and about the sugarhouse. Holidays or days off were on Sundays, the New Year, Christmas, the third of November (a Japanese holiday), and American national holidays. The wording of the contract makes clear the relationship of the contract laborers to their employers. The boilerplate that most laborers signed read:

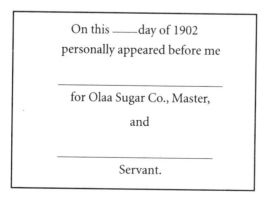

On this ——day of 1902
personally appeared before me

_____

for Olaa Sugar Co., Master,
and

_____

Servant.

When my father arrived in Hawaii, he was following in the footsteps of thousands of other laborers, all on similar contracts. Early newspaper accounts described their appearance as robust and healthy, their demeanor cheerful and contented. Nothing more than routine seasickness seems to have disturbed the passage.

Hawaii welcomed the first Japanese contract laborers with enthusiasm for, if nothing else, the belief was that they would make a potential contribution to the local economy. An article in the *Pacific Commercial Advertiser* is significant. The reporter described the arrival of the early contract laborers as "the most important event that has happened in Hawaii for many years" and dutifully praised King Kalakaua (Hawaii, at the time, was a monarchy) for concluding the diplomatic negotiations that had brought the contract laborers. Kalakaua himself had visited Emperor Meiji in 1881. About 40 years later, however, the euphoria would be dissipated by xenophobic nativism. Congress, in 1924, sealed all American borders, north and south, east and west, when it passed a discriminatory and restrictive immigration law for non-Europeans that was to stand in place until liberalized in 1965.

Between 1885 and 1924, many thousands of Japanese made their way to the Hawaiian Islands, forming the bedrock of what would become the Aloha State's multiethnic Asian population. During this time, ship after ship arrived from Asia, discharging their human cargoes throughout the islands.

My father, Yoshiemon, who had arrived in 1908, was working at the Aiea Sugar Plantation on Oahu when my mother, Nami, joined him in 1912. Years later she reminisced about how she had been a "picture bride": a picture of her future husband had been sent to her in Japan, and marriage arrangements were completed in Japan by registering their marriage in the Family Register before she came to Hawaii.

As was the case with most couples working in Hawaii, my father was considerably older, by 18 years, than my mother. In 1912, when they were united in Hawaii, she was 18 and my father was 30. Before leaving her home in Fukuoka prefecture, my mother, now Nami Sogi, went to Hakata, a port city in the northern part of Kyushu to have her eyes examined. It was there

Nami Sogi

Yoshiemon Sogi

that she first saw the ocean. In an oral-history interview that was conducted in 1975, she recalled: "There were many black spots scattered far away on a blue Japanese mat-like place, and I wondered what they were. I was told that they were boats, and I was to go to Hawaii on such a boat. I was frightened and thought of giving up the idea of coming to Hawaii. Then my father told me it was going to be a bigger boat, so I finally decided to come."

She had all her possessions in one wicker trunk when she arrived in Honolulu. The story of her arrival mirrored that of thousands of other fearful yet pioneering young women who left a predictable life in Japan to embark on a new adventure in a foreign land. My father was in the hopeful, worried and anxious crowd of men who gathered at the immigration station to welcome their new brides. The official at the immigration station kept the marriage ceremony short and sweet. He asked the women to line up alternately with the men and instructed them to complete their marriage vows by shaking hands. How tremendous an impact that simple unaccustomed gesture must have had upon my parents, especially my mother! To a woman emigrating from a country where elaborate bowing rituals defined class and gender relationships, shaking hands as a marriage vow must have made her realize she was in a new situation indeed. She was nonplussed by the incident. Talking about it six decades later, however, she merely said, "The immigration official made us shake hands. That was the marriage vow. Then the husbands took their brides to where they lived on a hack (a buggy)."

In the first few decades of the Japanese presence in Hawaii, the number of men far exceeded the number of women. By 1900, however, about 30 percent of the Japanese in the islands were married, a proportion which compared closely to that of the Native Hawaiians and much higher than that of haoles (whites) and other immigrant groups. By 1908, after my father's arrival but several years before that of my mother's, the Japanese government allowed roughly equal numbers of women and men to emigrate to Hawaii. Official statistics indicate that between 1908 and 1924, 32,000 women and 28,000 men left Japan for Hawaii. Local historians are confident that about two-thirds of the women arrived as picture brides.

The invention of the Kodak camera must have been a boon to the arranged-marriage industry in Hawaii and Japan. It put inexpensive photography into the hands of the masses. Marriage brokers (called *shimpai* in Hawaii) maintained a steady stream of photographs between the Empire of Japan and the Territory of Hawaii to secure helpmates for what had originally been a largely bachelor society. The huddled masses that flocked to Hawaii around the turn of the century were frequently gathered together on wharves for mass wedding ceremonies that concluded with handshakes. In time, public opinion soured, and the Japanese community in Hawaii began to protest the practice. An editorial that appeared in 1912, in the first issue of the *Hawaii Hochi,* condemned the picture-bride industry:

> The most important event in the life of a person is one of getting married, the freedom of choosing an appropriate religious service solemnizing the event should be allowed the individual, if there is freedom of religion and if there is recognition of individual right.

This editorial statement and similar protests led to an end of the picture-bride system by 1917.

My mother was shocked when she arrived at the threshold of her house in Aiea. Nothing had prepared her for the raw conditions under which the bachelors lived. The house for bachelors was an unpretentious shack built with 1 x 12 lengths of rough lumber. It had one door, no windows, a narrow sleeping platform the size of a one-tatami mat raised slightly off the floor, and plenty of mosquitoes. When my mother came to join my father in 1912, they were given slightly more luxurious living accommodations on the plantation. Married people were assigned a house that was a little larger than the accommodations for bachelors. They moved into a house that had a room about 12 x 12 with a backyard about half that size.

My mother rested there for one week before finding a weeding job as a *hoe-hana* (work with hoe) for $15 a month. She soon increased that to $17 a month by working as a *mizukake* (sugarcane waterer). This job involved working on Sundays, too; hence, the bonus.

Still, my parents had to eke out a meager existence as best they could. When my mother arrived, she tried to economize by serving wild vegetables that grew abundantly in the cane fields, thanks to the fertilizer that was used to grow cane. "My husband was very angry at me when I served him wild vegetables," she recalled. "I would go and pick the wild vegetables and boil or cook them with dried fish to make them better tasting. One day my husband got angry and threw down the dish and said, 'Don't mistake me for a rabbit.' He had lived in Hawaii for over ten years, so he was used to better food. Since my home in Japan is a farm and I used to eat only cultivated vegetables, I didn't mind."

THE SOCIAL HIERARCHY

Pacific peoples predominated in the Hawaiian Islands in those days, but the Territory certainly had its rainbow mosaic. Native Hawaiians, Chinese, Portuguese, Filipinos, Spanish, Irish, Germans, and English all contributed to the colorful demographics in the early part of the twentieth century.

Franklin Odo, in *A Pictorial History of the Japanese in Hawaii, 1885-1921,* summarizes the social hierarchy that my parents found when they arrived there:

> At the very top were a few privileged haole owners and managers. In between the owners and the masses of laborers was a group of predominantly haole Portuguese and Hawaiian overseers (*luna*). Next came an ethnically mixed group of skilled workers such as carpenters, mechanics, and locomotive engineers. Finally, there were the field and mill workers, who, for the three decades between 1890 and 1920, were primarily Japanese. The plantation structure, in this broad view, had a castelike quality that encouraged the perpetuation of the image of the Japanese as a completely downtrodden group.

My mother, Nami, recalled that the lunas (Hawaiian for foremen) under whom she worked were white men who would spy on the workers with binoculars and then summarily dismiss the slackers. "When we were dismissed," she said, "we used to feel as though our heads had been chopped off. We were very scared of him." Some of the workers tried to bribe the overseers but my father thought this beneath his dignity. Echoing his samurai ancestors, he would say, *"Bushi wa kuwane do takayoji"* which translates to: "The proud samurai warrior pretends he has eaten by using a toothpick even if he hasn't."

Most of the lunas that my mother remembered were Portuguese and Puerto Ricans who had come to Hawaii earlier. They were mostly water lunas and hoe-hana lunas. The lunas were always mean men. They treated the contract laborers cruelly and threatened them with whips. During the contract period, the lunas knew that workers could not leave, so they did not hesitate treating them in a cruel manner. The threat of the whip, according to my mother, was as powerful as the lash itself. She also remembered the terror of hearing the lunas make whipcracking noises behind them as they called out, "Go ahead, go ahead! work! work!"

Sometimes, the fatalistic *shikata-ga-nai* (it cannot be helped) attitude that the immigrants brought with them from Japan reached its limits, and their accumulated frustrations broke out into open violence. One day, my mother recalled, a group of hot-tempered immigrants from Kyushu got together and beat one of the lunas because he had treated them cruelly. She explained that Japanese people treasure boys so much that they bring them up with special care—more than they do girls. That is why men have pride and won't stand for insults. When one of the men started to beat the luna, the others joined in. The luna received a severe beating, but there was a fellow who joined in last and said, "Let me beat him too." He instructed the others to run away, saying that he would take the blame himself and go to prison if necessary. Since he had no family, he didn't mind going to jail. He contributed a final pounding and said, "I feel good."

The last man did take the rap for the others and was sent to jail. People used to take food to him in prison, my mother remembered, and he would share his food with prisoners of other nationalities, making him a popular inmate.

Hard-Working Immigrants

The Japanese were not the only immigrants to arrive in Hawaii during this time. Just as the 1885 to 1924 period is remembered by mainlanders, particularly Easterners, for the massive influx of people from Southern and Eastern Europe, the same period in Hawaii witnessed the coming of diverse populations from other lands. The first Spanish immigrants had arrived in 1899, the year after Hawaii was annexed as a territory by the United States. The following year, the first immigrants from Okinawa arrived on the *S. S. China*. In 1903, the first Korean immigrants made their way to the Islands and in 1906, Filipinos began arriving. Like the European immigrants who, 6,000 miles away, entered the United States from the east, the Asians who came to Hawaii had visions of a Promised Land (or, as some saw it, a Golden Mountain). Just one week after arriving as a picture bride in 1912, my mother went looking for a job. "We were so ignorant," she said just before her death in 1979. "When we were in Japan, we used to hear stories as though money grew on trees in Hawaii. We were very anxious to earn lots of money quickly and go back to Japan. But when we heard that we would be paid five cents an hour, I was shocked." It meant we would work for five cents an hour, 12 hours a day. There was no social security, insurance, or overtime and only a few days off each year for rest and relaxation. A workday began at 5:00 a.m.

My mother remembered the tribulations of working. "In the mornings we used to get up at 4:00 a.m.," she recalled, "and at 5 o'clock, when the first bell rang, we would gather in one place where we were counted. Then we would go to our working place on the train. In Japan, when we heard that we would be going to work on the train, it made us very happy about coming to Hawaii, but it turned out to be a cane-hauling train. We rode in a boxcar with only a board on the sides, so we were very scared. Some people were so disappointed that they regretted coming to Hawaii. One day a woman committed suicide. We used to go as far as Pearl City to work. One day, on the way, there were several valleys and bridges and this woman jumped from the train. I didn't notice when she jumped.

"I was so scared and trembling but went to see her with the others. She couldn't die, so she cut herself with a knife and died. We were so scared thinking she might appear as a ghost so I didn't want to go to work." With all the ghost stories she had heard in Japan about Hawaii, she became depressed by the actual conditions she faced. Homesickness was not unusual. My mother used to cry after every day's work was done. Feelings of nostalgia were especially painful when she worked on hillsides from which she could see sailing ships that reminded her of the life she had left behind. But she got used to it before long.

"I did *happaiko*" (carrying a bundle) she recalled years later. Happaiko involved carrying bundles of burnt cane on her shoulders and dropping them into the rail car she rode to work. The workers were paid $1.05 for each car they filled. "Because this was better pay than hoe-hana, I worked, but I couldn't continue. It was such a hard job for a woman. My husband worried about me because I talked so much about Japan, and he tried to discourage me from going to work." Unlike my father, my mother was not on contract, and so she was free to return to Japan whenever she pleased.

It was while pregnant and working as a *mizukake* (waterer) that my mother slipped and fell. She suffered stomach pain for three days and three nights. "The baby was born, but he was dead," she recalled years later. "His brain was mushy." Not long afterward, my mother became pregnant again. This time she took extra precautions to be careful, and a baby girl was born safely. They named the child Fusae.

To care for the newborn, Nami stopped doing fieldwork and stayed at home sewing Japanese kimono day and night. It was still the custom in Hawaii for women to wear them at home. One day, however, she was working so hard that she failed to notice that the baby's face was turning blue. The three-month old was taken to the doctor and diagnosed with pneumonia. The doctor prescribed bottle-feeding instead of breast feeding, but it was too late. Fusae lived for only another three weeks.

My mother remembers Fusae smiling at her that day as she went down to prepare dinner. Not long afterward, Nami found her cold. "I should have taken her to a doctor once more, but we couldn't afford the train fare," my mother recalled. "I felt as though as I had killed her." My mother was devastated at the loss of her second child. Overwhelmed by grief, she tried to push away the man nailing the coffin shut for fear that he would hurt Fusae. A dove began cooing early the next morning, and she thought it was their daughter crying "Mother, Mother." After the funeral, our neighbor advised Yoshiemon to hide, give away, or burn all of Fusae's clothing to keep his wife from being aggrieved by the reminders of the daughter who had just flown away like a dove. But Nami found a tiny kimono. "I took her kimono, her nipple with bottle, and a hoe to the grave. I thought of digging the grave up to put the kimono on Fusae. My husband found me standing by the grave. I didn't know what I was doing."

This story was reenacted time and time again in the lives of the early contract workers in Kona and elsewhere in Hawaii. Midwives were available, but her services were a luxury to many of the families. Mother recalls that neighbors used to help each other and experienced the cutting of the umbilical cords many times. It wasn't a good feeling.

"Some women worked until the last moment," she added. "One woman had her labor pain on the train and was rushed to the hospital. We had to give birth by ourselves quietly without any help. I was told by my grandmother that it was a disgrace to moan or cry out when in labor. To fuss, to depend on others, to mention pain is a shameful thing."

My mother's birthing experience was probably like that of many other women in Hawaii during the first two decades of the 20th century. By today's standards, this experience sounds primitive, but it describes more than anything else the love, grit, and determination of the pioneering Issei. Not long before her death in 1979, my mother reflected on how she had, time after time, brought her children into the world:

> When pain came, I would lay an old raincoat on the floor in the corner of a room and put some old clothes on top and use it as a mattress. I would leave a bag of rice in front of me and hold onto it when I needed strength.

Holding on to rice as a source of strength. There is a poem in there somewhere.

In 1990 I was invited to go to the Imperial Palace in Tokyo for the ceremonial enthronement of the Heisei Emperor of Japan. One of the things the new emperor does as part of an ancient ritual is to cultivate a new rice planting, something that his imperial ancestors have done for some 2,650 years. Rice is still the staple food in Japan, and this act is symbolic of the continuity of the Japanese people, a "giving birth" as it were, to new life. In the throes of labor, my mother did not consciously think of these things, but as I think of her holding on to a bag of rice in childbirth, I wonder at the mystery of it all. I don't think my mother ever would have imagined that one of her children, born in Kona, would one day be invited to her ancestral homeland to participate in an imperial enthronement. I say this not out of self-promotion but more as a tribute to my mother and all the mothers of that generation who held on to their rice sacks for dear life.

Hardship was a daily reality for the Issei. The medical-care system was uneven at best. As in the plantation system of the antebellum South or in the company-store setup of mining and mill towns, medical care was paternalistic; it depended on the enlightenment and altruism of individual overseers. Hawaii, at the turn of the century, was still a kind of "third-world" country. The Japanese contract laborers in Hawaii frequently complained that the haole plantation doctors forced them to work even while ill. The Japanese government, seemingly more enlightened on this issue, sent Katsunosuke Inouye as a special emissary to deal with the worsening situation. Inouye was able to negotiate an agreement with the Hawaiian government that led to the assignment of eight Japanese doctors to minister to the health needs of the plantation laborers.

The "handshake" marriage vow, however, did not abrogate the traditional duties assigned to women on the plantations. Even while working as field hands themselves, women were still expected to attend to the domestic duties such as cooking, cleaning, and raising children. It was no surprise that infant mortality rates were high in the early decades of Japanese immigration to Hawaii.

Early Diet and Nutrition

The bachelor workers, for the most part, were fed by mess cooks retained by the plantations. The laborers paid about five dollars a month for breakfast, dinner, and *obento* (Japanese box lunch). The diet for most of the immigrants was simple and low in protein; beef and pork were luxuries. As in Japan, rice was the dietary staple. The early contracts capped the price of rice at five cents a pound, but it was of a variety that lacked the essential vitamin B1. Beriberi, as a result, was not uncommon in those early days.

Mother remembers that beef on the table was cause for a feast. Even miso soup with *iriko,* or small dried fish, was considered a good meal. "I used to pick out two or three fish from the soup and give them to my children," she said. "The children enjoyed them. You can more or less tell what kind of life we lived. When I cooked soup with beef and cabbage, there was more cabbage than beef so the children used to say it was cabbage soup. I picked out all the beef and gave it to the children, so I had no chance to taste beef."

Holidays gave the contract laborers a chance to enjoy special culinary treats. Mother recalls the festive occasions when all the neighbors prepared a potluck feast. On *Gotan-e* ("Shinran's Birthday"), for example, many women worked in the kitchen to prepare *manju* (bean cakes) and other delicacies. The occasion must have attracted lots of women, for Mother said that her children had a special way of finding her in the throng.

"I was the only one who wore homemade slippers, so my children would find me by looking at my feet," she said, laughing. "When I took my children to such occasions when food was prepared, they naturally wanted to taste it, especially the bean paste for the manju. If I gave them a little and there wasn't enough to make even one manju, I would feel badly should someone say that it was because I had given them to my children, so I tried not to take them to such events."

Japanese immigrants were encouraged to bring seeds from their homeland so that they could grow familiar vegetables such as *shiso* (beefsteak plant), *gobo* (burdock), eggplant, pumpkin, and turnip. The Issei pretty much enjoyed the same diet they had remembered at home in Japan. Preparing familiar dishes is one of the ways that all immigrant groups hack out a clearing of stability in the underbrush of wrenching and far-reaching change. The tribulations of plantation life in an unfamiliar land somehow were made more palatable after a breakfast of *gohan* (rice), *tsukemono* (pickled vegetables), and *misoshiru* (miso soup). Hours of backbreaking labor in the fields under the whip of luna overseers could be momentarily forgotten in a lunch of *gobo* cooked with *abura-age* (deep fat cooking). And a luxurious meal of dried fish and fresh vegetables, complete with *shiitake* (mushrooms), brought together workers and family for a convivial evening of shared experiences in a strange, new country.

Probably the most popular maxim of the Issei in Hawaii and on the mainland was *shikata ga nai.* Whether translated as "it can't be helped," "you can't do anything about it," or "keep a stiff upper lip," the message it conveyed was clear. Don't rock the boat and do your duty. Centuries of Confucian training in Japan, combined with the need of adapting to a new country, helped create this attitude. Harsh economic realities were at play, too: workers who depended on the plantation overseers for their meager sustenance would not be overeager to bite the hand that fed them.

But this does not imply that the Issei were a slavish, passive lot. Like the African American spirituals of the old South, the songs my parents and their fellow workers sang to each other in the fields, called *holehole bushi,* nurtured their souls and bodies for the grueling tasks at hand. Singing in Japanese, they wove around themselves a close-knit musical net that helped sustain them through long hours of work on the plantations. More than half a century later, my mother remembered one of the songs they used to sing on days when the workers would pool some of their savings to create a makeshift credit union called *tanomoshi-ko* (mutual financing association). About 10 or so workers would get together and deposit three or five dollars each month. "And this was very big money," she recalled. "The one who bid the highest interest would get the month's collection. Sometimes it was only one dollar a month, but we tried not to take it in order to earn the interest. People who needed money badly were willing to bid a high interest offer. So the person who waited until the last received lots in interest. When we got our tanomoshi-ko money, people used to sing a song "Shall I go back to Japan or go to Maui?" She hadn't sung the song in more than 50 years, but my mother had no trouble in remembering it:

Joya kuwa kireta shi	Our contract is over
tanomosha toreta, yukoka	I got my tanomoshi money
Maui no Spreckelsville	Shall I go to Spreckesville in Maui?
Hore hore pari pari	*Hore hore pari pari*

Pari pari was the onomatopoetic sound of peeling off the old leaves of the sugarcane stock. Everybody used to sing songs like this because the luna overseers didn't like the workers to get into long-winded conversations that would slow the pace of work and reduce output. Just like the background music provided on assembly lines today, a communal rhythm actually increases output. My mother said, "The luna encouraged us to sing because we would be working with the rhythm of the song." Another song my mother remembered was:

Nihon derutokya yo	When I left Japan
futa oya sama ni	I told my parents
kane wo okuru to yuute deta ga	I'd send them money.

Other songs took advantage of the luna's inability to understand Japanese. They expressed deep frustrations at the working and living conditions in the plantations. One such holehole bushi went as follows:

Dekasegi wa kurukuru	The workers keep on coming
Hawaii no tsunami	Overflowing these Islands
Ai no Nakayama	But it's only our beloved Nakayama
kane ga furu	Who rakes in the money

While such work songs provided release for the workers, they were not the only entertainment they enjoyed. My mother remembered that itinerant kabuki players used to visit, though she never went to see them because she couldn't afford the 50 or 75 cents per show. But the performing arts had been a familiar staple of plantation life since 1893, when Yoshijiri Iwamoto from Yamaguchi began performing *ukarebushi* songs for workers celebrating the end of their contractual obligations. In the days before movies, radio, or television, traveling musicians and storytellers provided plantation workers with ties to their homeland. All of this came to an end when my father completed his obligations to the plantation.

By the time my mother was 23, she had already given birth to three children. Her third child, Chiyoko was born when father worked in the sugar mill. By then, the family was on the way to saving some money. Since my mother was unable to work in the field any more, my parents decided to use their hard-earned savings to buy a store in Honolulu. A relative of my father persuaded him to turn over half of their savings so that he could procure a store for them. Unfortunately, he was a dishonest man and absconded with their money.

"My husband was a very honest person," my mother said later. "We trusted others, believing that others were the same as he." Of this experience, my husband said: "It was all right, we did not cheat. We were cheated."

Returning from Honolulu after this incident, my parents took what was left of their savings, bought a quarter acre of land with an old house in Kaimuki, and moved from Manoa, where their first son was born. "My husband worked as a carpenter, and I raised vegetables," my mother recalled. "I pushed the cart my husband made for me and sold vegetables from Sixth Avenue in Kaimuki to as far as Waikiki, where a fountain was located. I used to leave my daughter Chiyoko at my neighbor's home and left my baby son Masaru in the hammock at the house."

After living in the Kaimuki area for several years, their second son, Harold Isamu was born. During this time an old friend from Fukuoka who lived in Kona urged the family to move to the Big Island of Hawaii.

INVESTMENT IN THE FUTURE

The Issei immigrants believed in hard work, a strong disciplined family unit, the importance of ownership of one's own land and home, independence, perseverance, obligation, and the education of children. They stressed the importance of the past and the need to plan for the future with optimism. Saving was an important part of their planning, as well as constant vigilance against waste. Hence, the second generation fared well, especially in Hawaii. But the Nisei required dedication and effort to forge ahead in the face of the challenges, adversities, and discrimination they encountered.

CHAPTER TWO

First Stirrings of the Kona Wind

T HE SOGI FAMILY MOVED to Captain Cook on the Big Island of Hawaii in 1921 from Kaimuki on Oahu, with the assistance of my mother's cousin's family, the Yanagis. While there, Hiroshi, the third son, was born. About a year later, father learned of a classmate from Fukuoka, a man named Ushijima, who lived in Keopu. Through his urging, the family moved to a 14-acre old farm in Lanihau, next to Keopu. They were close to the Ushijimas, who had adopted two children, Chikayo and Tsukasa, from the Kobayashis of Kainaliu, and who assisted us in settling down in this farm. We lived in Lanihau for the next 18 years.

After World War I, the mood of the nation turned inward. The American public refused to follow Woodrow Wilson's lead into the League of Nations and instead turned the Democrats out of the White House in 1920. It was the first presidential election in which women across the nation could vote, and the first election in which, at least officially, office-seekers could not bribe potential voters with a drink at the local saloon because Prohibition was enacted in 1919. For all its outward looseness and high living, the Roaring 20s were a decade of suspicion and outright hostility on the part of nativists who wanted America's ruling class to be white, Anglo-Saxon Protestant (so-called WASP). Nativist sentiments became so strong that, in 1924, Congress slammed shut the Open Door by halting almost all immigration to the United States. The flow of Japanese and other Asian peoples to Hawaii was prohibited by law, bringing an end to the era that had begun with the arrival of contract laborers in 1885. It was in this context that the last of the seven children was born to Yoshiemon and Nami Sogi. Though named Yoshito. I am legally known today as Francis Y. Sogi. I was born on June 9, 1923, the year of the *Inoshishi* (boar), soon after the family moved to Lanihau/Keopu, a hamlet in the northern part of Kona.

Kona! What memories that name evokes. Lush green mountain slopes, sparkling blue waters where winds tossed about forming the Kona wind with the robust fragrance of roasting coffee wafting through the lee side of the island. My home was in a small town, a hamlet, a haven where common goals could be reconciled with rugged individualism. A nurturing place where sons like Masaji Marumoto and astronaut Ellison Onizuka grew up and achieved national and international fame, firsts in the country in their respective ways. Masaji was the first Asian American to graduate from Harvard Law School and to be appointed Associate Justice of the Supreme Court of the Territory and then the State of Hawaii. Ellison was the first Japanese American astronaut.

Kona has incredible scenic views on the gentle slopes of Mt. Hualalai and Mauna Loa. The scenic view today adds considerable value to property, but had no value in the early days. Today, there is a strong demand for properties with ocean views. There were many properties with such views, but when I grew up in Kona, it was just another property overlooking the ocean.

Kona is the area from where the famous Kona Wind blows and from where it travels in the northwesterly direction, along the island chain onto the vast Pacific Ocean. This is the wind I rode, and on which many of us from Kona have been carried forward to all parts of the world. On the opposite and east side of the island is the city of Hilo, the county seat of the Island of Hawaii. To the north, there is Kohala, known for the famous Parker Ranch, the largest privately owned ranch in the country, once owned by the Richard Smart family, and in recent years known for resorts that were established along the coast on the leeward side of the island, just south of Kohala. To the south, there is Kau, bordering the volcano area of the active Kilauea crater that has been continuously erupting and pouring out hot lava since 1983. This has added considerable land area on the coast as lava flowed into the ocean, and has been attracting many tourists to the area. This is just south of the renowned Black Sand Beach that was created by wave action of thousands of years upon black lava cinders. Close by is what is known to be Mark Twain's tree, along the highway. Mark Twain visited the island of Hawaii and stayed awhile close to the southernmost point of the United States. The continuous flow of lava has caused "vog", not smog, to form over Kona, creating a haze and disturbing the ecosystem of the usually clear blue skies.

The District of North Kona includes the lands known as Kealakehe and Honokohau. I lived and grew up north of Keopu in Lanihau. Up along Mamalahoa Highway, on the slopes of Mt. Hualalai going south from Keopu, small villages line the highway, leading into the town of Holualoa where there were garages and service stations, a hotel, a theater, a school and churches. At the corner of Mamalahoa Highway and Hualalai Road, the famous Kimura Store that sells native lauhala goods is located. It is managed by Alfreida Kimura Fujita and her mother who is in her 90s.

Next, while heading south, we come to Keauhou, Kainaliu (where Teshima Restaurant, a well-known and beloved place for Kona-ites, the locals, is located and thriving) and where Mrs. Teshima in her late 90s continues to work daily. Honalu, Kealakekua, Captain Cook, and Hookena are the towns to the south of Kainaliu.

Along the oceanfront, there are the villages of Kailua and Keauhou along the Alii Drive with resort hotels interspersed in between, such as the former Kona Inn, King Kamehameha Hotel, Kona Hilton, Keouhou Beach Hotel, and Kona Surf. To the south and along the coastline we see Honaunau, Keei, and Napoopoo where there is a white monument on the one and only piece of land owned by Great Britain marking the spot that memorializes Captain Cook who discovered the Hawaiian Islands and died after a battle with the natives over a misunderstanding.

Mainland Americans, especially those on the East Coast, who have a more Eurocentric outlook, may find it difficult to understand the flavor of life in Hawaii, which is our first multicultural state in America. The Pacific Rim looms large in our national consciousness and I reflect on how much of my life has been spent along the way raising Asian American consciousness to mainstream Americans. On the surface, this can be quite schizophrenic.

THE DOMINANT SOCIETY

As I look back on those days in Kona, I realize that for the first 18 years, Kona was my whole world. I had no knowledge about even the other islands in Hawaii, let alone any other part of the world. Likewise, I had neither desire nor ambition to travel anywhere. At that time, of course, I also had no idea of the great historical events that were going on around me. Like children everywhere, I was too busy getting to know the people, places, and things around me in Kona. Though rural it was a kingdom of my own and there was plenty to absorb.

The Lanihau/Keopu area's demographic composition of the residents was somewhat unusual, when compared to the rest of America. It is not on the map of the United States. The Japanese immigrants were the dominant society and constituted most of the population of the area. There were a few other ethnic groups, such as Korean, Filipino, Chinese, Hawaiian, and Portuguese. One of the two schools and churches was for the Japanese community.

In such an environment, I felt very proud and confident living among "my own kind" without feeling any prejudice or discrimination in school or in the community. It is the same form of security that those in the dominant society in America feel among themselves. We looked alike and lived a life similar to everyone else, and we acted alike, coming from a common culture and heritage where no one stood out, except for the very few other ethnic groups. We lived in our own dominant society and it gave us confidence and security as it gives to those in the dominant society in America today.

Besides this unusual social makeup of the community, the very essence of farming was similar throughout the world, except we did not have the vicissitudes of changing seasons and cold weather. Like all farmers in America, we were true capitalists, taking great risks in operating and managing a farm and being at the mercy of weather and market conditions. A farmer's work never ends, and there was always something to do from dawn to dusk, seven days a week. Farming was not for the timid, and it required determination with stubborn rugged individualism to forge ahead and meet the challenges faced by farmers. Individualism was the key to the character of a farmer. It was a great feeling of confidence living in such a community knowing that we were as good as anyone else.

By the time I was born, our family lived in a wooden, three-bedroom house. There was an eat-in kitchen with a table for seven. The roof was really a large sun deck covered by a platform upon which the washed coffee beans were spread; it had wheels that could be rolled out for coffee drying on sunny days.

The sight and smell of coffee processing was a most vivid memory in my childhood, for our whole family life centered around the harvesting and bagging of the red coffee beans that were the staple crop in Kona. I can still see my father pouring sacks of beans into a hopper that fed the coffee grinder he made himself. The grinder separated the beans from their red skin. The skin passed to the rear into a dump and the beans went into a wooden vat filled with water. The grinder never crushed the beans. When the tank was full, we climbed into it as in a winery. We trampled the beans with our feet to wash off the sticky fluid. A motorized conveyor belt carried the washed beans up to the rooftop platform where someone would use a wooden rake to spread them out for drying. Even during periods of sunny weather, it would take four or five days for the beans to dry completely. When they were dried, they were pushed into a hopper through a hole in the roof that led to a chute that poured the beans into burlap bags down below, about 60 pounds each.

Young people today probably will find it hard to imagine growing up in a home that doubled as a coffee-processing factory, but it was a matter of course in Kona. We lived close to the land and depended on the neighbor-hood for mutual support although each farmer was independent, tough, and stubborn in his determination to provide for his needs. Our closest neighboring friend, the Ushijimas, were also from Fukuoka. In addition to their small coffee farm, they raised cows, pigs, chickens, and other animals that provided us with milk and meat.

Our immediate next-door neighbors were the Hayashidas below us and the Marutanis above us. The Hayashidas had seven children, including my classmate Saburo, as well as Kiyoshi, Masao, Fusako, Toshio, and two others. Because our properties adjoined each other, the Hayashida children usually passed our house on their way to school, so we usually walked together up a narrow footpath for about a mile to the main highway next to the Nakahara store. Up the hill from us, Mr. Marutani had remained a bachelor for many years, so it was a festive occasion when he finally got married. I remembered his wife as being very attractive and we used to tease her husband that he did not deserve such a lovely spouse. We always enjoyed visiting the Marutanis on New Year's Day for Mr. Marutani always served sake (rice wine), even to us ten-year-olds. The Marutanis had three daughters: Hiroko, Matsuye, and Mitsuye. Hiroko and Matsuye have passed away. Mitsuye is now Mrs. Walter Oshima, who, with her husband and rel-atives, own and operate the Oshima Store in Kainaliu. Their son, Michael, a graduate of Brown University, is now a lawyer in the prestigious law firm of Arnold and Porter in New York. There was, also, a younger daughter in the family.

Other nearby neighbors included the Fukumitsus with their 11 chil-dren, including my classmate, Gilbert, and his brothers Yoshio, Sadao, Yutaka, Ralph, Koichi, and their sisters, Kikue, Yukie, Matsue, Sumie, and one other. The men of the Fukumitsu family were handsome and were good musicians. Next above them was the family of their relative, Masaichi Matsumoto.

Further up toward Mamalahoa Highway, I remember the Nakahara family especially because they operated a store and a small movie theater.

The theater was nothing like the elaborately decorated movie palaces that dotted the American landscape during the 1920s. It was really a garage and storage area that the Nakaharas would use from time to time to show the films they would obtain from Japan. The films were all silent, but they were accompanied by a *benshi* who would narrate the story by speaking, singing, or crying and emoting all the roles. These occasional films provided a rare opportunity for outside entertainment. Radio broadcasting was in its infancy in the 1920s but no one in the area had radios. Since we had no electricity, either, the only sound entertainment device I remember was the old hand-cranked record player. We worked and studied by the light of kerosene lamps, with the brighter white-gas lamp used on special occasions only until we moved later to our seven-acre farm on Mamalahoa Highway, the main highway in Kona.

Masamitsu Onizuka had worked at the Ota general store before marrying Mitsue from Hilo, the big city 100 miles away, and starting his own country general store a few hundred feet north of the Nakaharas. The store is still there, although somewhat inactive after the death of Michi a couple of years ago. The Onizukas had a daughter, Shirley, and two sons, Ellison and Claude. Ellison was the first Japanese American astronaut who was pushed into national and international fame. On his second outer space flight, unfortunately, the Space Shuttle *Challenger* exploded and the entire crew died. There are several monuments in his honor at Konawaena High School, Kona Airport, and Little Tokyo in Los Angeles.

The Komo family also operated a store nearby, about half a mile south of the Nakaharas. It was a small general country store with a gas pump out front. The Komos had a daughter, Fusae and three sons, Hideo, Satoru (Clarence), and Kenneth. Hideo, who never married, ran the store for many years after his father passed on. In recent years, it appears that Kenneth has been operating and managing the store.

Even though these country general stores in Kona served our immediate needs, they were really just colorful local corner stores. When we needed to make major purchases, we would go to American Factors in Kailua, located along the pier. In addition to being a large retailing emporium, it also handled all export of coffee and produce as well as cattle from the local ranches, such as those run by the Greenwells, Stillmans, and Hinds. The small local stores also got their supplies from American Factors.

Those who have never lived in a farm in Kona might not be able to imagine how the economic system generally worked based on the cycle of planting and harvesting coffee. Most farmers did not have a regular cash flow, unless they raised vegetables and fruits and sold them. And so we bought our tools, fertilizers and other necessary supplies on credit from stores in the neighborhood. Most families produced their own food supplies, except for items imported from Japan like rice, soybeans, dried codfish, shoyu and other food products not available in Kona. When the coffee harvest was complete and the coffee was ready to be shipped, the first shipment was for debt service, so the first price usually would be lower than the off-season price. This system kept the farmers almost generally in debt to the creditor stores. At best, the farmers would break even and it was difficult to manage to improve beyond the minimum required.

However, as time went on, the coffee farmers started to sell their surplus coffee to other sources so this garnered a better price for them. Thus financed, they were able to grow other produce that the stores did not bother to purchase. Also, we children would work at odd jobs during the off-season, like the job I had unloading lumber for American Factors, working under the National Youth Administration program; and on weekends at Kona Inn. Slowly, the farmers began to better themselves economically.

LIFE ON THE FARM

We lived below Mamalahoa Highway on a 14-acre farm, where I was born, until 1937 when I started high school and moved to the seven-acre farm on Mamalahoa Highway across from the Nakaharas and Doctor Seymour, and a few hundred feet south of the Onizukas. By then, our economic situation had improved considerably. Our parents labored long and hard under difficult and unimaginable conditions during their early years in this country so that the second generation, Americans of Japanese ancestry or Japanese Americans, as we are commonly referred to, would not have to go through the same hardships as they did. This may have been a part of the culture they brought with them from Japan. As the farmers became somewhat self-sufficient, they began to become conscious of the importance of education. Like immigrant families everywhere, the Japanese in Kona concluded that the best way to help their children would be to give them self-help tools like education, either vocational or academic.

We had nine pairs of hands on our farm to tend the 14 acres of coffee and vegetables until Chiyoko and my two older brothers, Masaru and Isamu, left for Honolulu to seek employment. This left my brother Paul and me, together with two Filipinos from the Philippines, Eugene Viloria and Puerto, to whom we provided separate living accommodations. Eugene was known as Henyo and he was a vital and permanent part of the family while Puerto was an itinerant worker who traveled to do other work during the off season and returned to our farm during coffee season. Henyo was a jovial fellow with no unpleasantness of any kind. He enjoyed strumming on his guitar and ukulele and was an accomplished musician by Kona standards, singing mostly in the Filipino language and a number of Hawaiian songs. I learned to strum the ukulele from him and also picked up some Ilocano, the dialect of the province in the Philippines from where he came. This was the second foreign language that I learned from Henyo while attending grade school at Honokohau School.

Although he was a farmer, Henyo was a skilled craftsman and taught and helped us weave fishing nets, both the Hawaiian style of conical throw-nets and the floating nets *(tate-ami)* with linen cords. He carved his weaving awl with a knife out of a single piece of bamboo and one end was sharpened to a point to pass through the opening of the net as it is woven. He fashioned the other end like the letter U to hold the nylon cord. It was about eight inches long and two inches wide. The throw net was of a conical shape and held together at the vertex that was bound together with cord to form a hardened grip, which is held before throwing it into the water as fish are sighted. As the net lands on the water, it sinks immediately since it is loaded with small pieces of lead. The size of the opening of the net is determined and woven depending on the size of the fish we were interested in. The cord or nylon was not large, but was strong enough to catch any size fish that might be around relatively shallow waters and tries to escape after the net lands around the fish in the water, trapping it in its circular form.

The vertical *tate-ami* was woven in a somewhat similar way except it was rectangular and about six feet wide and about 25 feet long. On the top end, there were round pieces of wood. Ordinarily, the wood from the *hau* tree, light and porous like balsam wood, was cut into six-inch round pieces to keep the net afloat vertically in water no more than six feet deep. At the bottom of the net the lead pieces were tied on to keep the net upright. Once the net was laid across an opening or encircled an area, we would splash the water during the day, or use lighted torches at night. With the excitement, the fish would try to escape and be caught in the net by their fins or gills. This was the easiest method as we were almost guaranteed to catch a number of fish that were small but very delicious. The net was usually stained with kukui tree sap which was of a dark brown hue and that contained a preservative substance that prevented the net from deteriorating quickly notwithstanding constant exposure to salt water.

Along the ocean beyond the old airport in Kailua-Kona in the Honoko-hau area in the Princess Liliuokalani trust lands, there were several ponds, inlets, and coves where we would go net fishing and poling from the shore line at least two or three times a month with great success. We never returned home empty-handed as no one else fished in these areas, except our family with Henyo who was an expert fisherman as well as an excellent cook. In the ponds that were privately owned, one or two attempts with the net would give us enough fish to last a week and we never took more than we and our neighbors, the Marutanis, Fukumitsus, Hayashidas, and Ushiji-mas, with whom we usually shared our catch, could consume. We went on these fishing forays for a day or part of a night with the family when coffee was not in season. At times, we camped out in a well-covered cave formed by volcanic rock. Henyo would cook the fish we caught during the day with local beach vegetation for flavoring. There was a sandy cove where our family enjoyed a private beach with plenty of fish to be caught at our leisure. Paul and I would dig the sand on the beach and burn a little fire, douse it and cover it with sand and sleep over it to keep us warm for part of the night watching the stars flying across the skies with the gentle Kona winds blowing about us.

In addition to pole fishing, which was for sport and enjoyment, and netting for the catch, we did spear fishing underwater and from the shoreline. Off the coast of Kona there are high cliffs and especially in the Honokohau area the fish would come floating on the surface as if to sunbathe and sleep, and hence their name *netabo* "the sleeper." As it floated, we would use a spear on a long bamboo pole from the rocks above and spear them.

Pole fishing was not fun at all for me as it required patience and it was time-consuming. My father enjoyed it immensely as it was quiet and peaceful sitting on the rocks with water washing up and down the sides of the cliffs and stones. We would throw old breadcrumbs that attracted the fish, and we would select the type of fish we wanted and let the hook and line, which was leaded, sink to the depth where the desired fish were swimming. There were all kinds: *papio, ulua, uhu, kupipi, hage,* and at night, *menpachi, aveoveo,* and others, all edible and delicious. At times, the desirable fish was nowhere around, and we would lower the hook and line to the bottom of the ocean and the sure catch *hinalea* would be there, but no fisherman would admit that he would come home with only hinalea although it was fine when broiled. Since our fishing expedition regularly proved successful, my mother usually preserved the fish with salt and dried or pickled in vinegar.

Many happy memories of our fishing expeditions along the Kona coast remain clear to me. I can still smell and taste the fish that were so delicious when cooked in soy sauce with ginger and other condiments, like the menpachi, a large big-eyed red fish, or papio or ulua. Even today, I prefer fish from the Pacific Ocean to those caught in the Atlantic. Some time ago, I learned that a fish diet offers substantial benefits. Salmon, sardines, and mackerel have a type of oil that is healthy and highly recommended in health reports. Even fish bones, when cooked crisply, can be chewed and consumed for calcium.

When I returned to Kona after many years, Henyo had married and raised children, one daughter, Roselina, and two sons, Eugene, Jr. and Albert. All three have children of their own and are living a good life in Kona. Eugene, a spitting image of Henyo, worked with Aloha Airlines at Kona Airport and Albert is with Hawaii Planing Mill.

My father was a man of few words and had a very low boiling point. As he grew older and we grew older, he could no longer dish out corporal punishment which was freely and summarily meted out or dispensed at his own whim and fancy without recourse or appeal. This was quite a common practice in Kona at home and at school. There was traditional Confucian discipline and respect for parents and authority without question. There was nothing democratic about our younger life, but it may have been a saving grace as we knew exactly where our boundary was located and any venture or transgression beyond basic rules resulted in retribution that we felt not only physically but also remembered long enough not to repeat the offense. Authority lay in our parents and they were the prosecutor, judge, and jury, tempered of course with a considerable degree of compassion. The fear of authority and retribution was coupled with the cultural element from Confucianism that all children must respect elders, because they are more learned and wiser, having lived longer.

It was an accepted practice for parents and teachers, at least during my grade-school days, to punish misbehavior or infractions of rules or mischief with a 12-inch ruler on the knuckles, or with a belt on the rear of the wrongdoer, as my principal did at Honokohau School. A slap on the cheek on the face or pulled ear was also not uncommon when we argued with the teacher or our parents. Though I was mischievous, being the youngest in the family, I was not subjected to much of my father's punishments. Living on a large farm had its advantages. Whenever father wanted to punish me,

I would run off on the rocky area over which he had difficulty running and therefore he could not catch me. As time passed, he would cool down and I escaped punishment. Mother always told us about father's short-temperedness and said that she was also subject to some abuse in her younger days, but she had made up her mind very early in marriage, especially after the children came, that she would never leave him because she would not want to subject the children to the same fate that she was thrown into when she had to cope with an unloving stepmother after her mother passed away.

Like all Japanese families, and perhaps in other cultures in Africa, the wife or mother usually managed the household finances and the education of the children. The husband or father was the provider and he concentrated on his work for his future, and on weekends spent time with the family. Whatever a father does is for the good of the family ostensibly, such as devoting a great many hours to work. He is responsible for the family unit. An employee of a company in Japan, for example, devotes his entire life to that company, for it looks after the welfare of its employees and he, in turn, provides for the needs of his family. Society is the responsibility of the government. With this system of responsibility for the three different sectors of life, family, employment, and society, there is no need for charitable giving in Japan as we know it in the United States. In hindsight I am thankful for this cultural practice because my mother was very shrewd and tight with money and did everything possible not to waste anything, especially food. There were five children in the family and whenever anyone left food on the plate she would say, "There are many children in other parts of the world who are starving, and how can we waste such wonderful food?" She would usually end the meal eating the leftovers. She also used other tactics to convince us not to waste any food. At times, she would say that wasting food would result in *bachi,* a term meaning "curse." She may have succeeded to some extent as I still have a feeling of guilt when I waste any food and think of the many people throughout the world, especially innocent children, starving for lack of food. I have tried to pass this on to my grandchildren, Kimberly Makiko and Kenneth Tadashi.

With my mother handling everything in the household, including not only family finances but also the financial management of the farm, we were able to improve our financial position considerably. My father was a fine carpenter and had steady employment during the off season, and my mother was a creative seamstress, sewing all of our clothes and farm wear from work shoes to rain hats and raincoats, resulting in considerable savings.

The medicine man came around once a month and he would leave non-prescription medicine for use until his next visit. The next month we would pay him for the medicine that was consumed. It was a consignment sale, a common practice in Japan.

Because of, or in spite of, these years, life thereafter was relatively easy insofar as work of whatever kind is concerned. Throughout my professional career I have worked long hours and at no time did I feel it a drudgery or that the work was too heavy or difficult. The stamina I developed in Kona has kept me going and enabled me to devote 70 hours or more a week for long periods of time when my work had demanded it during the early years in my profession. I have always felt that one should do something productive or contribute time and energy for the benefit of society. Every day should represent progress in learning or creative thinking. Rest and relaxation are important in life, but idleness is wasteful.

CHAPTER THREE

School Days

L ooking back, apropos to my Year of the Boar, when I was born, my first recollection is my first day of school at age 6. I started classes at Honokohau Elementary School in 1929. That first day of school remains vivid in my mind because I had the first inoculation of my life. The first shot in my arm was such a new experience and a painful one, and I can still recall the rash it caused. However, I also have pleasant memories of my early grade school classmates and I get to meet some of them from time to time in different situations.

Saburo Hayashida, who lived below us, was a classmate through high school. Saburo later moved above the Ota Store and the family eventually moved to Honolulu. Saburo opened a watch-repair shop in Aala Park and retired. Masao, his younger brother, was a class below me, and there were two younger brothers below them. The last time I saw Toshio was when we were all on leave together in Chicago during WWII. Harold Kiyoshi Sasaki from Honokohau continued into high school with us and then worked as a chef at Kona Inn. After volunteering for military service during the war, he later settled down in Kona and owned and operated the '76 Chevron service station in Kainaliu, across from the Aloha Theater. I remember him as short-tempered, but he has mellowed. Walter Sur, another classmate, who lived in Honokohau, went through Konawaena High School and part of the University of Hawaii with me. We spent a great deal of time together growing up in Kona and even worked part-time together at Kona Inn, though I stayed there longer than he did. I remember him as being good in math. With the coming of war, we went our separate ways and I did not see him again until some time later. The last time I saw him, he had lost his voice.

A number of other classmates dropped out of high school to work on their family farms or to do other work in Kona. One of them was William Keanaaina, whose family ran a slaughterhouse below the Greenwells, north of Honokohau School. Others who left school early included Helen Pahee and Hideo Goya. As I reminisce about my early days in grade school, I think about one element that has appeared throughout my life: challenge. In every situation, whether in studies, sports, or career achievements, I have always felt that there is a challenge to be confronted and overcome. The Army, ironically, might have been the only situation where this challenge did not exist too seriously for me, except to become a commissioned officer.

In academic studies, there was another challenge, my classmate, Stanley Imada. He and I always vied for better grades whenever we were in the same class from elementary grades through high school. His brothers went to the University of Hawaii and they did very well there. They lived close to the school and everyone in the family became successful. Stanley was bright and alert in class and someone to compete with in studies, though he never participated in team sports. The oldest sister, Hanayo, managed the school cafeteria at Konawaena for many years. The oldest brother, Richard, became a successful real-estate broker in Honolulu, and his slogan was, "Open the Door, Richard." Tom, the second oldest, also did well in school and worked at the Veterans' Administration after his military service. Stanley joined the U.S. Postal Service in Honolulu after college and loyally remained with it until his retirement.

Other classmates of Honokohau Elementary School I remember well are Haruko Nakamatsu from Keopu, who became a nurse after graduating from Konawaena and later worked in New Jersey. The sport of fencing was of great interest to Haruko and at which she became quite adept. She was Sarah's maid of honor at our wedding in New York City on June 17, 1949. Haruko married Hisashi Yoshihara and died quite young after an asthma attack. Shizuko Uda lived across from Walter Sur and went through Konawaena with me. Later, she married a mainlander and raised a family in California and now lives in Long Island, New York. I remember her as a plump and jovial girl with a sweet smile. Sarah and I visited Shizuko in May 2004 in Long Island at her home with her daughter where she has lived for many years after World War II. Toshiko Isomoto, very quiet and shy, was born and raised in Honokohau with her two brothers, but we completely lost contact with her after Konawaena. Yoshiko Kurosawa, another Honokohau classmate, lives in Kona with her family.

I took an active part in sports, becoming captain of the volleyball, softball, and basketball teams. We had little interschool competition, though there was a rivalry between Honokohau and the Holualoa Elementary School. Holualoa was a K-8 school, similar to Honokohau, but in a more affluent and semi-rural area that boasted a regular theater with seats, stage and screen, and a screening room. The Holualoa kids came from families that took cars and bicycles for granted.

Hard as I tried, I could never spruce up our softball team enough to defeat Holualoa. Our rivals, however, later became classmates at Konawaena High. I remember those junior high school battles against the likes of Allen Iseo Nakamura, Shigeo Kimura of the Hualalai Garage, Gilbert Hakoda from the Hakoda Store, and George Ikeda from the Ikeda Garage across from the Inaba Hotel. George Ikeda was killed in action in Europe while serving in the U.S. Army with the 442 Regimental Combat Team. The Ikedas were related to the Inabas by marriage. George's younger brother later became a lawyer and worked for an insurance company on the West Coast. There was also a sister. The Inaba family was a large one with many boys, including the late Minoru (my teacher at Konawaena), Goro, Yoshio, Norman, Futoshi, and Yoshiharu. Minoru lived to age 98, keeping very active in the community. He was a legislator and an athlete in high school, one of the first graduates of Konawaena High School in 1925 and one of the organizers of the Kona Historical Society.

After moving to Kona, my mother handled all family finances, including the purchase of food and goods for the farm as well as the sale of products from the farm. In those days, there was no bank in our area in Keopu or even in Holualoa or Keouhou. The nearest bank was all the way down in Kealakekua. No deposits, no check writing privileges, certainly no cash machines as exist in the modern era. How my mother managed her money was a mystery, but there always seemed to be cash around to pay for everything we purchased except for the farm supplies, which were purchased on credit and paid for with coffee or in kind. She probably kept the cash in a tin can in the house, which was dipped into to pay the medicine vendor, and other itinerant peddlers who came to sell various things. For other goods we ordered many things through the Sears Roebuck mail-order catalogue, especially during the New Year holiday season when it was our custom to have new things to greet the New Year. This was also the time to give respect to the equipment that gave us service during the past year, by placing symbolic fruit and *mochi* on the equipment, a typical Shinto practice. Our home had a small Shinto shrine in our living room, as did many Japanese farm homes, and mother always observed this practice.

We had locks in our house but they were never used. No strangers ever came around, and the neighbors could be trusted. I am aware of no burglaries during my life in Kona. This sounds incredible to those living today, but we all lived then with a sense of security and freedom from the anxiety that besets people now, especially in the big cities. This sense of security in a location where we represented the dominant society greatly contributed to our well being as we were growing up in Kona.

For relaxation at home, we would either read or listen to records. We subscribed to the Japanese newspaper, *Hawaii Hochi,* which had a Japanese and an English section with cartoons. Some of the cartoons were in serial form, which we followed religiously, looking forward each week to see what happened to Slim Jim, Dick Tracy, Felix the Cat, Annie Rooney, Flash

Gordon, and Dagwood. My parents also subscribed to one Japanese maga-
zine for their reading pleasure. Among the many Japanese records we had
were *Naniwa-bushi* and martial music, which I enjoy to this day.

FIRST JOB

When I was 14, I got my first job unloading lumber working for American
Factors for pay. The store received its cargo from the freighter SS *Humuula*,
operated by the Inter-Island Shipping Company, in the port of Kailua.
Twice a year, a cargo of lumber would come in. The freighter would anchor
offshore and extend a long rope to shore for unloading the lumber. The
lumber would be tied into a bundle and offloaded into the water and I
would ride the bundled lumber raft and pull it back to shore using the rope.
It was cheap labor but easy money because it was fun and the work was not
difficult. We did need a social security number and I obtained one fairly
simply. Ordinary cargo was unloaded from the SS *Humuula* by means of a
barge or outboard motorboat that made numerous trips to the freighter
and unloaded on the pier.

Cattle shipped from Kailua, however, came via a different route, either
through the port at Kawaihae, about 25 miles north of Kona on the Kohala
coast, west of the Parker Ranch. These ports had corrals in the water that
forced the cattle into a narrow area where they were tied by their horns and
pulled to the boat. In Kailua, there was no corral, so the animals were
driven along the highway from local cattle ranches and chased into the
water. There, cowboys held them at bay until each animal was tied to the
small craft to be hauled onto the SS *Humuula*. I remember seeing cowboys
on horseback chasing after the mavericks that would break away from the
herds. The "water" cowboys of Hawaii had to be more skillful than the
"land" cowboys of the American West, for they had to make sure the cattle
kept their heads above water lest water get into the cows' ears, killing the
animal. This unique method of corralling cattle seemed to be peculiar to
Kailua and Kawaihae, so it became a tourist attraction in later years. It was
quite a sight watching the cattle being loaded onto the SS *Humuula*. The

small craft would maneuver alongside the larger one, towing ten cows, five on each side, tied by their horns. The SS *Humuula* would lower a large canvas "waistband," which would be placed under the animals' bodies, then hoisted above into the vessel's holding area for the overnight voyage to Honolulu.

The term "steerage class," in which I traveled from Kona to Honolulu, probably originated through this practice of shipping steers to market. First class comprised the private rooms out of sight and stench of the cows. Steerage class passengers paid much less for the passage, but they had to endure an open area on the same level with the animals with their foul stench and no sleeping facilities except for benches and wooden slatted floors.

Working as a young cargo handler for American Factors opened my horizons a bit, but throughout my teenage years, work on the family coffee farm occupied most of my time. Kona was still basically an agricultural area, and coffee was by far the one and only staple crop until macadamia nuts came later as a successful Kona product.

Schooling took a back seat, however, for the three-month coffee harvest season was scheduled from September through November, which was our school summer vacation. Vacation time in Kona, however, meant long, grueling hours on the farm. We worked from dawn to dusk, seven days a week, to tend and harvest the crop. Sometimes we started as early as three or four in the morning to wash the coffee and transfer it to the rooftop platform for drying. We wanted to finish this before sunrise so that we could begin harvesting immediately after breakfast at the break of dawn. When the season was over, it was good to get back to school in November, for the school year offered a period of less strenuous regimen.

Kona coffee is considered a gourmet coffee that can command a high price today because of the care lavished upon its harvesting and processing. Only the red or ripened coffee beans are picked by hand off the branches. We never allowed the beans to grow overripe, turn dark and purple, and fall to the ground. Over and over again, we returned to every tree during the three-month harvest season, plucking the beans when they were at the peak of their red maturity. Still, not all Kona coffee was of the same quality. The Lanihau and Keopu coffee farms nearby were blessed with unusually rich soil, creating taller, fuller trees. Farther north, however, as in Honokohau, the trees grew in rockier soil, so were scrawnier. Where I lived, we sometimes had to use ten-foot-tall ladders to pick the coffee beans. We also used a homemade hook with which we pulled down the high branches full of red berries. However, with the advice and help of the Hawaii Agricultural Extension Service, the farmers were taught to prune the trees allowing new growths. In doing this, the resulting trees were shorter and fuller, not requiring ladders, and increased the harvest. Insofar as harvesting is concerned, Kona coffee is still harvested in a similar manner to maintain its quality and reputation as a gourmet coffee

Such was my life during my days in elementary school. Our parents believed in hard work, a strong disciplined family unit, the importance of ownership of one's own land and home, and the education of children. They stressed the importance of planning. They said: "Today, be ready for tomorrow, this week for the next and so on, and always be prepared for the future." In emphasizing the importance of preparedness and education they did all they could to give their children as much guidance and education as family circumstances permitted.

Konawaena High School

By the time I entered high school in 1937, the family finances had improved somewhat, largely due to my mother's acute management, a situation typical of families in Japan. We were able to move up to a seven-acre farm across from the Nakahara store. Our next-door neighbors were the Kikumoto family with Paul Itsuo and his younger brother. Below them lived the Nakayamas, whose oldest son Harry rode a motorcycle to his job at Kona Inn in Kailua, along the ocean front, where he was a waiter for many years. Our neighbors to the north were the Nagaos, with Masayoshi and two younger sisters. Immediately north of them and across from the Onizuka

Store lived the Seymours with a son and a daughter. Dr. Seymour, a physician, practiced in Kealakekua.

Our new *mauka* (upper) house had three bedrooms and a dining room. It was built from 1 x 12 lumber raised slightly on stilts. We had a separate house for coffee processing and there was no need for the movable roof. Our helpers, Eugenio (Henyo) Viloria and Puerto, lived in the coffee house. Despite generally poor economic conditions during the 1930s, and quite desperate situations for many mainland farmers, we were able to improve our situation. The seven acres gave us enough to manage and spend extra effort in vegetable farming. Life was much easier, giving the young people more time for recreation. This was very important as we entered high school, for it allowed us to participate in extracurricular activities such as after-school sports, clubs, and social functions. I commuted to high school every day in a green school bus that was driven by a high-school graduate who had remained in Kona. The bus stopped in front of my house every morning at 7:39 and took about 45 minutes to pick up students from the Honokokau and Keopu areas. Although Konawaena High School was only about 15 miles south of Lanihau, it took the better part of an hour to arrive there because of winding roads on mountain slopes, though gentle, that had to be negotiated at 25 miles per hour. Other students at Konawaena came from Holualoa, Keauhou and Kainaliu from the north, and Kealakekua, Captain Cook, Napoopoo, Honaunau and Hookena from the south, arriving in other school buses or even by private cars. By the 1930s, motor vehicles in Kona were becoming less of a novelty. Though it was a far cry from today's two- and even three-car families, the proliferation of motor vehicles indicated that even the rural outbacks of the Hawaiian Islands were entering the modern world for better or worse. Traffic was heavy when another car passed by on the two-lane highways

The bus for Konawaena came at 7:39 a.m. and left school at 4 p.m. in the afternoon for the return trip, giving us a chance to participate in after-school activities, to study in the library, or to hang out in local stores.

Even now, I can remember in detail the winding road from home to school and back each day. If our driver had kept a list of his itinerary and pickups, here's what it would look like: from Honokohau there would be Toshiko Isomoto, Yoshiko Kurosawa, George Sasaki, and Stanley Imada; from Keopu, there were Masayoshi Nagao, Takeo and Kazuo Ota, Saburo, Masao, Fusako, and Toshio Hayashida, my brother Paul and myself, Paul Itsuo Kikumoto and his brother, Hatsuko Nakayama, as well as Kyuichi Matsumoto, Clarence Satoru, Kenneth Ryuso Komo, Ralph and Gilbert Takeo Fukumitsu, James Takuma, Michie, David, and Richard Komo, Haruko Nakamatsu, and Kazuma Ichishita. There was another bus that picked up the students from Holualoa and those from Keauhou. Others from Kainaliu were not provided any bus transportation as it was walking distance to school—of about three miles! The Holualoa students included those from the Moris, Onakas, Nishimuras, Kimuras, Kurashiges, Joses, Nakamuras, Yokoyamas, Nobrigas, Gouveias, Chos, Springers, Smythes, Kawakamis, Kanekos, Okanos, Sagarangs, Kongs, Seos, and Teshimas.

A classmate wrote in the Foreword to *Ka Wena O Kona* (our school annual) two brief paragraphs that express more than anything else the sense that we were, even then, aware of what was going on in the larger world. The Foreword reminds us that we were racially integrated, too, in an environment that didn't make a big issue out of a situation that we took for granted. Here's what it said:

> Today, in spite of the murderous and devastating warfare that is being waged elsewhere in the world, student life in the United States continues uninterrupted. At Konawaena, too, we are carrying on the traditions of American life. Here, we are a typical American high school group, wherein students of many races mingle to weave the rich multicolored tapestry that we call democracy. It is said of man that he lives an experience three different times—first, in anticipation; second, in participation; and third, in retrospection. It is hoped that this 1941 *Ka Wena O Kona* will be of value in helping us to achieve that third phrase of our school experience of the past year.

That introduction, probably written by Helen Ikeda, the yearbook editor, is quite profound in many ways. For one thing, it reminds me that even on the extreme west coast of Hawaii, then an American territory for only 59 years, we already thought of ourselves as being typical Americans, no different from our peers in a thousand small towns on the mainland. Literally on the opposite side of the globe, we still were quite aware of the war raging in Europe, which was the "world." Asian culture certainly permeated the Hawaiian Islands more so than any other part of America, but our school still lifted up a Eurocentric outlook to us. All of the landed gentry, primarily Europeans, sent their children away to private schools and we seldom ever saw them in any of our common, or daily functions or activities.

Our principal, Ernest De Silva, a man of Portuguese ancestry, underscored this worldview in his farewell message to us, also published in *Ka Wena O Kona.* He wrote, in part:

> A peace loving nation is grimly beating her ploughshares into swords and methodically toughening her every sinew to meet what appears to be a gigantic struggle to determine whether liberty and intelligence shall prevail among men or whether the ruthless militarism of modern Europe shall mark the course man shall take. Exactly in what manner we shall act is still an undecided question, but through the web of confusion and indecision that is spread over much of our thinking today we see an important American decision. It is a decision to oppose with the full weight of the will and courage of the American people any force which endangers the American way of life: a way of life which is becoming a religion with us. May this yearbook serve to remind you of the things you have learned regarding the American way of life and the important role which every American school plays in preserving these great principles of American democracy which we are now arising to defend for ourselves as well as for those who follow us.

Mr. De Silva's tone might sound a little bombastic by today's standards, but it underscores an attitude that seems to have been lost in today's confusion over values and national goals, especially in the public-school system. Most Americans of my generation grew up in an era in which the public-school system was revered as a uniquely American institution that was meant to simmer students from a myriad of backgrounds in that great "melting pot," a term which is now out of date in our modern multicultural society. As would be apparent at the outbreak of World War II, that "melting-pot" attitude did not apply to Asians, especially to the Japanese on the West Coast. But, unbeknownst to mainland folks, thousands of miles away from "Middle America," we at Konawaena High School pledged allegiance to the Stars and Stripes as definitively as anywhere else. Despite our American viewpoint, though, we still preserved our local heritage. Our "Alma Mater" is quite different from any mainland school song. Here's how it went:

> Hail, Konawaena, pride of Hawaii, we thy children sing
> Daughter of Pele, Mauna Loa cradled, make us worthy of thy name.
> To thee, oh jewel of the Konas, jewel within the island jewel
> We, thy loyal sons and daughters, pledge our lives, our hopes, and aims
> May the light of truth you've kindled, burning bright as Pele's fires,
> Lead us on throughout the ages, hail, Konawaena, hail to thee.

Konawaena High School was quite a large complex, with facilities for 599 students and about 25 faculty and staff. The main school building was situated high on a slope atop a hill. At the base was the lower playground, serving as the athletic field for track, baseball, football, and any other outdoor activity. Below the athletic fields were the teachers and the principal's cottages with ranch lands beside them. On the tier above was the gymnasium and single tennis court; facing the hill and to the right of the gym were the agriculture and music buildings. Higher up was the roadway leading to the administration building and parking area for the buses; higher still were the main administration and classroom building.

I can still remember in exact detail the physical layout of the main building. To the extreme left was Pyun Sun Pyun's chemistry lab, where we made palmolive soap with palm and olive oil, then Jeannette Skinner's biology class, Mr. Nishimura's social science classroom, Ina Moon Pyun's English class where we were required to memorize 32 stanzas of Thomas Gray's "Elegy Written in a Country Churchyard," and Janetta Peterson's typing room, next to the library, where we were often reminded by Mrs. Peterson that we should "speak clearly, if you speak at all and carve every word before you let it fall." Mabel Trooien was our librarian. In the center of all this was the principal's office, occupied by the mustachioed and stately Ernest De Silva. There was Ernest Griswold, the superintendent of schools for the district, whom we nicknamed "Egg Head" because he had a receding forehead and was balding in the back. I remember Kenji Goto, the school administrator, who also taught bookkeeping, for his Spencerian penmanship, so meticulous, precise, beautiful and orderly. Annie Akamo was the school secretary and Miss Ako was athletic director for girls. Above and to the left of the administration offices was Seventh Day Adventist Albert Vestal's school shop with its ripsaw and other carpentry tools. To the immediate right was the cafeteria, under the able management of Hanayo Imada, my classmate Stanley Imada's sister. We could buy lunch at the cafeteria for five cents. The students helped out in the cafeteria on a rotating basis; at least once a week where we got a free lunch in exchange for our work, not counting the food we could manage to consume while on active duty. Cafeteria duty was not unwelcome to most of us, since it presented a chance to have a "lavish" hot Western meal, even though it was just corned beef and cabbage or stuffed cabbage for a nickel, followed by an ice-cream sandwich or Popsicle for another five cents. The latter might contain a wooden stick offering a freebie. The last building to the right housed the grade school and classrooms for Minoru Inaba, Daisy Kurashige, Frances Fox Challenger, Arthur Song, and others.

My first day at Konawaena was not quite as traumatic as my first day at

Honokohau Elementary School. Still, I felt all the anxiety of a new experience opening before me. The area around Konawaena was more urban than Lanihau, Honokohau, and Keopu: many more homes in town, a post office, bakery, garage, and so on.

On my first day at the big school, I was assigned to Homeroom 9-21. For the first time in my life, I was in a classroom with the so-called Big Town students my brother had warned me about. As I looked around, I saw no familiar faces from Honokohau, no one from Lanihau or Keopu. Many of the other students had old friends. I could only sit silently as they laughed and joked with each other before the class was called to order. The roll was called alphabetically, and by the time the teacher got to "S," I was somewhat petrified that I had difficulty responding "present" or "yes" as the others had done. To me, this was a classic case of a small fish in a big pond. I had been the leader of this, the captain of that, all through my days at Honokohau Grammar School. At home, praise flowed lavishly for my intellectual achievements. But another, more pleasant memory, remains of that first day of school in 1937. I remember looking across the room and seeing a fellow classmate. I had no idea who she was or what her name was then, but I do remember making a mental note that she was a nice, pleasant girl. Later, I got to know her and learned her name was Makiko Sarah Mukaida, known to her friends as Maki. As I write this, I can say that she is still a nice, pleasant person, and much more. She is in some respects definitely more equal than others. "Maki" has been my wife for 55 years.

That first year at Konawaena was not a resounding success for me. For one thing, I regret not having taken a shop course in basic carpentry, as was required for freshmen. It would have been a natural for me because my father was a true artisan and carpentry was his forte. He worked on many construction projects and was really very good at what he did. He made everything at home and I assisted him for as long as I can remember. I did report to shop class the first day of school. The starting bell rang, but two seniors, Hiroyuki Mori and Yoshiharu Inaba, took their time by ambling into the class a few minutes late. Albert Vestal, the shop instructor, was furious. He spent five minutes in unleashing pure vitriol on the two tardy students. He yelled that his six-year old was smarter than the two "stone-head" late arrivals, and so on. I had never witnessed such an outburst, especially not at school. Promptly after class, I trotted over to my advisor and asked to transfer out of this shop class. My advisor consented, and I was placed in the only other available class at that time, advanced music. Had I persevered and taken the shop course, I would have been able to learn valuable skills I could have used later on in fixing up our home in New York, to say nothing of learning something of human relations in the process.

Maybe it was a kind of punishment for my timidity, but the music class was a disaster of a different sort. I didn't have to worry about being terrorized by a militaristic instructor. Up until then, I had had very little exposure to music except the Japanese *naniwabushi* and songs learned at church or elementary school. The *Aloha Oe* represented pretty much my peak musical experience before high school. I knew nothing of notes, had never even known they existed before Miss Day's class. I was asked to select an instrument and had no idea what kind of instruments existed. I selected the trumpet only because a trumpet-playing friend happened to be in the class. He was Herbert Texeira, one class ahead of me at Honokohau and the third child of Honokohau's principal, Anthony Texeira. I soon learned that Herbert was no better than I was, but at least he could read some notes. So, over the rest of the semester, I expanded my musical repertoire to include bugle calls for reveille and taps. Easy stuff. I could play them from memory before long. When we played together as an orchestra, I feigned my trumpet parts but the simple notes I could handle without too much difficulty. Beethoven and Mozart were still a long ways off for me but were required composers in our music appreciation sessions.

Thus did I struggle through my first year at Konawaena. In retrospect, it seemed simple, but to a 14 year old from a very rural area, it was overwhelming. I made friends gradually. Most days, I took an *obento* from home instead of spending five cents at the cafeteria. David Yanamura did the same. We ate together in the gymnasium where it was quiet and open.

For the rest of high school, David and I became closer friends; we played together quite a lot and we both enjoyed tennis. I took up the game after starting to work part-time on weekends at Kona Inn in Kailua, owned and operated at the time by Inter-Island Shipping Company. David was one of the buddies who helped get me through the trauma of high school. And, of course, there was that young woman I spied on the first day of class, the one everyone called "Maki."

HIGH SCHOOL SPORTS

The class of 1941 was a large one, with my fellow students coming from the northern and the southern tip of Kona, mostly by school bus. A few of the students came from more prominent families by Kona standards, and were chauffeured to school in private cars. Kaoru Kajiwara, for example, worked for Judge Thompson and lived with him in a large white house in Captain Cook. The Judge dropped Kaoru off at school each day on his way to the local court. Haruko Okimoto also came by car. Her father worked for the school and the family operated the Okimoto Hotel. A few even drove their own cars to school, like Herbert Ushiroda, whose family owned a store at the bottom of the road from the school, at the intersection of Mamalahoa Highway. Herbert was a rascal and the bane of the teachers in all the classes. He operated a garage in Kealakekua for many years and is today a stroke survivor and father to six, "three boys and three sons," as he puts it.

My Konawaena High classmates were really classified by whether or not they participated in sports. Basketball, baseball, and track were the three principal sports in which we competed with other high schools. Football and tennis were intramural only. We were not fully helmeted or equipped to play football on an interscholastic level. I preferred tennis, and played on our intramural team regularly. The best net man at school was Harry Manago, whose family owned the still successful Manago Hotel and popular restaurant. I remember his fine stroke and his mean serve. In his later years, he would travel the world over with ship cruises every year. Among the teachers, math/chemistry teacher Pyun Sun Pyun was the best tennis player. He played regularly after school. Other tennis players included the Mormon missionaries, young kids right out of college, who wore straw hats and always had a tie and jacket. They usually stayed in the Kona area about two years then rotated back to where they had come from. David Yanamura was my regular tennis partner and we spent many hours after school playing on the court next to the gym. It was not in the best condition, but it was better than nothing, so it served our purpose well. I began playing tennis after starting to work at the Kona Inn, which had two courts for guests. I used to spend hours watching them play, and one day my coworker Philip Suzuki gave me a racket. It was almost brand-new but he didn't like it because the grip was too small. This racket was my passport to the court, though I never advanced beyond a certain level because I never took formal lessons. As a result, I never unlearned the bad habits I picked up. As with anything, not only tennis, a small investment in lessons would have paid out big dividends later on. Be it sport or subject matter, it is always best to learn from a professional or from someone who knows the sport or subject well.

Ignorance is not always bliss. It is like going off on a wrong road without realizing it. My mother always told me: "It is the shame of the moment to ask, but the shame of a lifetime to be ignorant." I also found out that those who ask questions are liked because it flatters the person being questioned. By associating with those "in the know," one can learn by the old Socratic precepts of learning through conversation and dialogue. In the days when there were no written records, learning took place through the process of conversation, each knowledgeable person imparting what he or she knew verbally.

If empires are won or lost on the playing fields, I guess it's appropriate to talk about athletic events while reminiscing about sports at Konawaena High. Baseball was our most serious competitive sport, however, and our teams were really strong during my four years at Konawaena. In 1941, my senior yearbook reported that "the Wildcats, under the tutelage of Mitsuo Fujishige, again remained as champ of the Big Island junior interscholastic league for the fourth consecutive year." The Wildcats, along with Hilo High's Vikings, even went to Honolulu to represent the Big Island in the annual interscholastic prep tournament. Our archenemy, especially in my senior year, was Honokaa High School. Honokaa had a star baseball player by the name of Sumio Nakashima, one of those small but wily players who was a good shortstop and base stealer. Throughout the games, we kept an eye on him because he was always the deciding factor. He was not a long hitter but he was a sure hitter and always got on base, like our coach, Minoru Inaba, a former star of our baseball team. Once on base, Nakashima usually managed to score a run with his skill in stealing bases.

Basketball, however, was the most popular of the three sports. Our archrival on the court was Hilo High. Hilo had a good coach who produced many good players who went on to become varsity stars at the University of Hawaii. The basketball games were always cliffhangers, and though we usually lost, it was an occasion for the whole community to come out at night to rattle the opponents with frying pans and other noisemakers.

My late brother, Paul, was a star shot-putter and discus thrower on the track and field team, which held its own with any other school on the island. He was also a star boxer who was defeated only once, by a Hilo pugilist.

All in all, the sports teams that Konawaena produced held their own in interscholastic competitions. Besides the ones mentioned above, my classmates who clearly excelled in sports included Kats Matsumura, Ben Tanabe, the late Yasuto Saito, Ben Arcamo, Harry Manago, Edward Sagarang, Ted Kong, the late Tom Iori, Iseo Nakamura, Ritsuo Uchimura, and Packard Harrington. Packard came to Kona from Farrington High School in Honolulu, where he'd been a football star. These classmates formed the backbone of the school teams that competed with other schools of the Big Island of Hawaii.

EXTRA-CURRICULAR ACTIVITIES

For those students whose mental abilities were somewhat more developed, Konawaena High offered a range of competitive and other activities that included the debating team, the *Wildcat* (school paper), and *Ka Wena O Kona* (yearbook album). Our debating stars from our class of 1941 were Nelson Hada, Helen Ikeda, and Kaoru Kajiwara. All three were blessed with a good gift of gab. Our leading journalists included Maki Mukaida, Helen Ikeda, Mitsue Kaneko, Doris Adachi, David Yanamura, and Teruo Yoshida, who passed away, but had written the book *Mongoose Hekka*. There was many a discussion as to whether people in Kona ate *hekka* using mongoose or not, but it is very doubtful that they did. There were enough clubs and activities to satisfy the interests of all students. Some students participated in the Girl Reserves, YMCA, all with the goal of getting along with others and developing leadership, a part of education that is often neglected.

Not knowing anything better, I was happy with the education I received at Konawaena. It was certainly much better than anything I had during the first eight years of my schooling. At Konawaena, I had to catch up in many areas, but it was exciting and I did enjoy high-school life with new things on the horizon every day. I also received private tutoring from Mrs. Skinner, who took an interest in me. We spent many hours after school to prepare me for college and advanced learning. She was the only teacher who seemed to show interest in me in this way.

The class organizers back then were the organizers of our reunions. The late David Yanamura, Mitsue Kaneko, Ronald Mitsuo Yoshida, the late Taketo (Mike) Kawabata, Ben Arcamo, Stanley Imada, Helen Ikeda, Harry Manago and others in Honolulu always led the group on Oahu. In Kona, there were a loyal cadre of Konawaena supporters, the late Yash Deguchi, Gilbert Takeo Fukumitsu, Terumi (Colbert) Nozaki, Rochelle Onaka Ashikawa, Hazel Muraki, Aiko Ikeda Watanabe, the late Sadao Oishi, Masaru Nagatoshi, Tatsumi Oue, Nelson Hada, the late Kiyomi Ashihara, Doris Adachi, Satsuki Morihara Motoki, Nancy Higashihara, and Setsuko Nakagomi. After fifty years, our friendships still remain mellow and on-going.

Graduation at schools in Kona took place in August, not in June, as is traditional in most of the other schools in Hawaii due to the coffee harvesting season. This schedule enabled the students to work in the coffee fields during what was our summer vacation from September through November.

Exposure to Outside World

In addition to the four dollars a month I earned from National Youth Administration (NYA) correcting algebra papers for P. S. Pyun, our Algebra teacher at Konawaena High, and doing yard work at Honokohau Elementary during weekends, I also worked at Kona Inn, a plush tourist hotel in Kailua. The job was offered me by my neighbor, Harry Nakayama, who had worked there for many years. Walter Sur, my classmate, also worked with me when the tourist trade was busy. Even in the 1930s, tourists usually came by chauffeured limousines from Hilo, which had both an airport and boat docks. After touring the volcano area on Friday afternoon, the tourists would arrive at the Kona Inn in the evening and leave on Sunday. On Saturday evening, there would be a Hawaiian program with a luau, hula dancing and other entertainment. It was a night out for everyone, even the local landed gentry and ranch owners who would dine as a group, sometimes with many at one table. Standard fare for the luau was dinner with choice of suckling pig, beef, or turkey as the main course. Many times, I was assigned to serve such large tables and I was able to remember who had ordered which dish. My little mnemonic technique was to associate the diner with a cow or pig or turkey and look for features in his or her face that resembled the animal or bird. This was necessary because on a busy Saturday, we were required to serve 20 to 25 guests at one sitting. Kona Inn considered itself a classy hotel of high quality, and it was, and we were not permitted to write down any order. I never told my customers how I managed to remember so many orders. Of course, being young, I had a very good memory.

During the days, I did other work at the hotel. Compared to the grueling and time-consuming work in the coffee fields, this weekend work was quite easy. I also relished the opportunity to expand my horizon by meeting mainlanders and some of the "upper crust" of Kona. Frequent guests were Errol Flynn, Francis Brown, George Ii Brown, Doris Duke, who at that time hung around with Sam Kahanamoku, and other glamorous beach types from Honolulu. This whole scene impressed me a lot. It exposed me to formal dining and service and a style of living that was foreign to me.

David Smyth of Konawaena was the night clerk and doubled as a bartender. Being a neophyte to the work of bartending, he was asked for a Tom Collins. He excused himself and returned and said: "Tom Collins is not listed in the telephone book."

Among the cooks, there was also a Chinese baker who came early in the morning to bake muffins, bread and pastries for breakfast. His muffins were especially delicious, even though I used to see him wiping the sweat off his forehead with the back of his hand and continue to knead or mix the dough with the same hand.

Walter Sur and I bunked in at the employees' quarters in a separate cement building on the Kona Inn grounds. One day word got around that there appeared to be a great deal of personal interaction going on between the limousine chauffeurs and female personnel of Kona Inn at the employees' quarters. Walter and I shared a room in the same building and, while it was built with cement, for better ventilation the walls between the rooms did not extend to the ceiling of the building. We could stand on a chair or someone's shoulders and peer over into the next room. At first, what we saw and heard was novel and exciting. While we tried to sleep late at night, the drivers and their lady friends would be quite active in the rooms next door. Out of normal adolescent curiosity, we had to take a look, of course. It was quite an experience for us youngsters to watch naked bodies rolling on the bed, and listen to moaning and sighing; it was something we had never witnessed before. As I said, working at Kona Inn exposed me to a style of living that was entirely foreign to me.

Working at Kona Inn also gave me a chance to sample a whole new style of cuisine. Sunday buffet was a special event for the so-called Kona society as they gathered on the open dining area facing Kailua Bay. They were the Greenwells, the Hinds, and the Stillmans. They were considered the "landed gentry" of Kona, and the Greenwells with their English heritage were even referred to as the "blue bloods." Though they might be ranchers, cowhands or cowboys, they did own the land and had cars and wealth that we coffee farmers just did not have. We never mixed with them socially because they were a world apart. The buffet was truly a five-star spread with all kinds of salads, local fish, fruits, cold cuts and bread. I worked in the pantry after the dining room closed to help prepare for the following day's buffet lunch, while I served as a waiter during the day.

Our class, 137 strong, graduated from Konawaena High School on August 14, 1941, and I was Sarah's escort to the Senior Ball, one of the rare occasions when everyone dressed up in his or her best outfit. Since first noticing Sarah on that memorable first day at Konawaena, I had frequently ended up working with her or being placed next to her at lunch or social gatherings. It appeared, almost, that we were meant for each other, though much to my surprise and chagrin, I learned later that she had another young man in mind. Fortunately, he went away to Mid-Pacific Preparatory School in Honolulu.

Graduating from Konawaena was really a major watershed in my young life. Kona had been my entire world for 18 years. I had no knowledge, desire, or ambition even to travel to one of the nearby islands. Suddenly, in the fall of 1941, all of this was going to change. At Konawaena, we studied geography and learned that there was a much bigger world outside Kona, even beyond the great city of Hilo on the windward side of the Big Island, where one could go to the Kress 5 and 10 cent store. Little did I realize how over the next 50 years, the world would shrink with the speed of travel becoming faster and the Kona wind carrying me to lengths and breadths I knew not where or how far.

FLASHBACK: REFLECTIONS ON CHILDHOOD

In grade school, I was the leader all through the eighth grade and felt good being the leader of the team in sports and in other events, as I thought

I was better than most. In high school, the situation changed drastically. I was no longer the recognized leader in sports. There were many more able basketball, volleyball, baseball, and football players from all over Kona. I was good in softball but it was a nothing sport and it counted for naught except in local community leagues. David Yanamura and Harry Manago were much better tennis players than I. Kats Matsumura was excellent in baseball; Ben Tanabe and Yasuto Saito and Ben Arcamo were super in basketball; Ed Sagarang was a champion boxer in his class. I tried out for boxing because I did punching-bag tricks at home for many years but this was my speed and I never entered a ring in competition to knock-out an opponent as did Paul, my brother, who was in the same class as I was. Minoru Inaba did much to help me become a star but it was not in the cards. Thanks to this experience, though, I am now able to play most sports, even purely for exercise.

At first, this sudden change in my perceived standing among peers hurt me, but it forced me to immerse myself in studies and intellectual pursuits, which I did for four years in high school because Honokohau Elementary School was as backward as any public school in the United States can be. For this reason, I considered dropping out of school and going to work to become economically independent and help my parents deal with the perennial debt they incurred by operating a coffee farm that required hard work and long hours. My parents dissuaded me from dropping out, and I continued in high school but it required a great deal of catching up because the kids from other areas had attended better schools and they lived in villages with stores, garages, hospitals, libraries, and bakeries. They included the kids from Holualoa and nearby, such as Allen Iseo Nakamura, Gilbert Hakoda, Roy Murata, David Cho, Rochelle Onaka, Mitsue Kaneko, and Hazel Muraki; the kids from Kealakekua, such as Tatsumi Oue, Shizuo Uchimura, Kats Matsumura, Hazel Muraki, Helen Ikeda, the late Haruko Okimoto and Makiko Mukaida; and those from Captain Cook, such as Yash Deguchi, Doris Adachi, and many others.

One advantage of which I was confident of was the fact that I could memorize many written materials, long or short, with ease. I memorized all 32 verses of Thomas Gray's "Elegy Written in a Country Churchyard" as required by all in our English class, and to this day I am able to recite a few verses and remember distinctly the message that comes from the poem, with its opening lines, "The curfew tolls the knell of parting day." As William Wordsworth said: poetry is the spontaneous overflow of powerful feelings recollected in tranquility. A good example is our national anthem.

In the other subjects at school, such as algebra, geometry, logarithms and calculus, there were supers like the late Mike Kawabata, a veteran of the 442nd RCT, David Yanamura, a crooning karaoke maven, Ronald Mitsuo Yoshida, and Stanley Shigemitsu Imada, my elementary-school competitor. Tamio Otsu, another classmate, was a known leader as our class president and later the student-body president in our senior year, while I was the treasurer. Nelson Hada was our recognized orator and participated in many debate contests with Helen Ikeda, Tamio Otsu, and others.

During my high-school years, I began to wonder in my moments of retrospection and introspection where I fit into the scheme of things. Where do I fit among friends, peers, and others that I found myself inter-acting with, within this huge world of Kealakekua where our high school was situated? I came to the conclusion that I was an individualist and could not fit into team sports so I had to select sports where I was able to control the situation and be solely responsible for the consequences. As a strong believer in individualism, I did not want to depend on others, if at all possible, nor ask for favors, as this will give rise to an obligation. As a result, I began to develop a psychology of my own and analyzed others based on their actions and reactions, always following my mother's teaching. She would say: "Other people are your mirror." She meant that other people act by reacting to what I say and what I do or as I act. I carefully examined other people's body language and telltale signs of approval or disapproval. Of course, most of those with whom I came into contact during my high-school days were Japanese or Japanese Americans. Most of them were still deep into their cultural baggage and had not assimilated into American life as a whole and we represented the dominant society in Kona.

Despite the fact that my parents had lived in Hawaii for 30 years or so, there was another dynamic at work, family tradition. Though my parents by now had given up any thought of ever returning to live in Japan, there was a plan to send me there to enter a military academy and pursue a military career, following a family tradition of my mother's who had a relative of fairly high rank in the Japanese Imperial Navy. I cannot imagine how different my life would have been had the decision been made to outfit me for a career in the service of the Emperor.

Looking back into my past 12 years of school life and my life at home with my parents, we were always reminded that, as immigrants, each generation should achieve greater things and do better than the previous generation. This can be accomplished only by being better than others and in pursuit of excellence. Only time will tell whether this will be true. Our parents believed in hard work, a strong disciplined family unit, the importance of ownership of one's own land and home, and the education of children. In emphasizing the importance of preparedness and education, they did all they could to give their children as much guidance and education as family circumstances permitted. This is what I left to face the outside world riding the Kona wind, wherever it took me, not knowing where it might lead me.

CHAPTER FOUR

Serving My Country

T HERE WAS AN UNSPOKEN expectation that I would attend the University of Hawaii. This is not an unusual situation among new immigrant families who realized that education is the ticket to upward mobility and success in a society like that of America that has no fixed nobility. With this expectation in mind, I concentrated on my high school studies, but my plans did not become real until after I passed the college entrance examination.

ON TO COLLEGE

So it was that, in the fall of 1941, I prepared to continue my studies by entering the University of Hawaii in Honolulu. For some unknown reason, and without prior arrangement, Sarah and I were the only classmates headed for the University who happened to be on the SS *Humuula*, the same boat that carried cattle from local ranches. This time, the boat was headed from Kona to Honolulu with human passengers as well. It was an overnight ride. When I got to the embarkation point, Sarah was already there with Tom, her second older brother, who was accompanying her to Honolulu. They were riding first class while I was in steerage class, where the cattle were also loaded. The voyage, which began after nightfall, was uneventful. There was no food service or service of any kind for that matter and so the only way to pass the night and the rough sailing was to go to sleep on a hard wooden bench. Arriving in Honolulu the following morning, I was met by my brother Masaru, who took me to an apartment in Kakaako, at 944 Cooke

Street, where my sister Chiyoko and brother Harold were also staying. Brother Paul remained in Kona with my parents. The new apartment was not Park Avenue, but it was quite comfortable, with enough room for each one of us plus an area for me to study. It was clearly an improvement over life in Kona, although anything was a bit better than Kona at that time. Sarah lived with her brothers, Bennett, Tom, and Sam, and her sister, Emi, at 1944 Dole Street, where they had a house. That house was within walking distance to the University of Hawaii which Sarah also attended.

Freshman year at the University of Hawaii was exciting, with new challenges and a complete change in scenery and outlook. For the first time in my life, I was in a situation where time was pretty much my own, except to attend class at the University. The only hardship was ROTC, which started early in the morning at 7 a.m. and continued for an hour. Wearing the required neatly pressed and snug-fitting khaki uniform for the ROTC class was a new experience and pleasure for me.

Now, suddenly, I found myself in a world increasingly ruled by commercialism and mass-produced objects. The break from Kona to Honolulu was more than just a geographic one. It marked the beginning of a new way of life for my classmates and me. The transition was eased by having some old friends from Konawaena around me, classmates like Walter Sur, Ronald Mitsuo Yoshida, Tamio Otsu, Allen Iseo Nakamura, and Mike Taketo Kawabata. We hung around together and occasionally went into town for lunch and to play pool. My freshman courses included Economics, Japanese, Survey, English, Government, and Speech. Speech was required of most of us from Kona and the other islands.

A WORLD AT WAR

Just as tension was increasing over the possibility of war between Japan and America, my mother decided to make a return visit to the old country, setting out in that fateful year 1941. She made the journey partly to rekindle ties with kinsfolk and old friends, but partly as a religious pilgrimage. She confessed that, for years, she had hated her stepmother until she finally understood certain teachings of Buddhism, which she had discovered with the help of a priest in Kona. "If it weren't for my stepmother," she recalled as an elderly woman, "I wouldn't have had to come to Hawaii and suffer this much. I really hated her."

With the help of her priest, Mother set aside her bitter memories, instead recalling her grandmother's instruction: "Something in your fate has brought you two together as stepmother and stepdaughter. You must understand her." So in essence Mother returned to Japan seeking reconciliation, but her stepmother already had passed away. She did, however, enjoy a warm reunion with her large family and then set out on her return trip in what was surely the last ship to sail from Japan to Hawaii. She recalled that the security inspection was extremely strict. After returning to Kona, she decided to go to Honolulu to help my sister Chiyoko with her dress shop. She sailed on the SS *Humuula*, which had taken me to Honolulu four months earlier. She arrived on the morning of December 7, 1941, at about 6:00 a.m., an hour before Japan's attack on Pearl Harbor.

I was an early riser and I remember studying at my desk after breakfast that morning. It was about 7:00 o'clock on Sunday, December 7, 1941 of the first semester of this freshman year at the University of Hawaii. The radio was on and I listened as I was studying. Suddenly, I started to hear explosions and anti-aircraft guns being fired in the distance. A bulletin came over the radio that there was a massive maneuver going on. Then, the announcer said: "This is the real McCoy! This is the real McCoy!" and he repeated it over and over again. Reports flew thick and fast. It was reported that the Rising Sun mark was spotted on the airplanes and were identified as Japanese. Pearl Harbor was being attacked by Japan. Soon, sirens began shrieking through the streets. I heard a bomb or anti-aircraft explosion in the nearby residential area of Makiki where Sarah lived. I learned later that the whole block at McCully and King Streets, across from where Sarah and her family lived, was destroyed by one of our anti-aircraft shells.

The initial Sunday morning raid on Pearl Harbor on December 7 soon proved to be the only one, though there were many false rumors of Japanese parachutists landing in Manoa and other areas of Oahu. It was also reported that an enemy mini-submarine had gotten jammed at the entrance of Pearl Harbor to prevent any vessel from leaving.

The traumatic days of December 1941 soon calmed down into a wartime condition that included martial law, drills, Red Cross coffee and doughnuts, and all the other familiar routines of World War II America. Unlike the mainland, of course, Hawaii had experienced military attack first-hand. After Pearl Harbor, more than 120,000 Japanese and Japanese Americans in the western states were ordered to move into American concentration camps. Measures that drastic did not happen in Hawaii, except to a few, because of its large Asian population.

With decisions being made thousands of miles away in Tokyo and Washington, my idyllic lifestyle in Kona was beginning to vanish for all time. Anxiety and uncertainty had returned. My Japanese cousins, uncles, aunts, grandparents and other relatives were now our enemy.

I continued studying. That evening, I heard a call on the radio for ROTC students to report to the Armory, which was close to the apartment where I lived. I walked over, reported in, and was assigned an M1 rifle with a clip of six bullets. We were ordered to keep the bullets outside the chambers of the rifle at all times unless specifically authorized to load. Our unit was called the Hawaii Territorial Guard. It was made up of all ethnic groups although it was heavily Nisei. No thought was given initially to ethnicity or race. We were all simply pitching in to do our duty in this moment of extraordinary crisis.

My unit was billeted at Aliiolani Elementary School in Kaimuki and assigned to guard the electrical and water pumping stations around the Kaimuki and Kapiolani areas in the eastern part of the city. We did this in four-hour shifts for just over six weeks until January 19, 1942. Then we were abruptly assembled in the middle of the night and told that those of Japanese ancestry could no longer serve. The United States government had deemed us untrustworthy. Specifically we had been designated by Selective Service as enemy aliens (category 4-C), even though we were United States citizens serving our country in uniform. Paradoxically, Nisei who already had been drafted into full-time Army service, or who were members of National Guard units (as opposed to the Territorial Guard) were retained in uniform and eventually reconstituted as the path-finding 100th Infantry Battalion.

Many in my unit were bitterly disappointed by our dismissal. I took it stoically. I was naive, to say the least, about the possibility of discrimination at work. The act of standing guard had become monotonous and, when nothing happened, guard duty seemed less and less worthwhile. At any rate, we had no choice but to return to civilian life. The University of Hawaii had reopened, but I was in no mood to resume school in mid-term. A classmate from Konawaena High School was working as secretary to the construction superintendent at the Kahuku Airport on the northern tip of Oahu. Through him, I got a clerk's job working the swing shift, from four to midnight. The pay wasn't all that good but it gave me a chance to save some cash. As essential defense workers, we could get an unlimited amount of gasoline, a major perk in an atmosphere of strict rationing. I worked at the construction site a few months and then took a job as mail clerk in a Big Five corporation, Castle & Cooke. I got this job through my acquaintance with the corporate secretary of the company, a man named Leslie Deacon, who was to become known and liked for helping many younger Japanese Americans during the war. I worked for Castle & Cooke for six months before returning to school in the fall of 1942.

By this time, both Japanese aliens and American citizens of Japanese ancestry were being relocated from the West Coast states to the desert and mountain camps. The threat of relocation hung in the air around us in Hawaii. I vividly remember FBI agents coming to our house to search for weapons, radios, items of Japanese culture and any material they deemed subversive. We didn't protest, having been taught by our parents to obey authority. All of us lived under martial law and a strictly imposed nighttime blackout. We blacked out the windows of our home. We painted the car headlights black on the upper half and installed a small hood so the lights would not shine upward and be visible from the sky. As the year 1942 went by the hysteria about Japanese descendants somewhat subsided without the mass internment in Hawaii that many people had feared.

In the Japanese community, there was tremendous emphasis on displaying loyalty to the United States. Those of us still in school felt uneasy about being civilians in the midst of the war effort, even though we had been turned out of the Territorial Guard through no choice of our own. The breakthrough in our status came with the reopening of the Army to the Nisei. The first recruitment in Hawaii was for the famous 442nd Regimental Combat Team. Many of my school friends volunteered, as did my brother Harold. I already had interrupted my studies once, and I decided to continue at the University of Hawaii for the time being. Soon my 442 friends had left for training at Camp Shelby, Mississippi.

The initial emphasis on the 100th Battalion and 442nd Regimental Combat Team was part of a high profile propaganda campaign to offset the damage done to the American reputation by the internment of Japanese Americans in concentration camps and to reinforce the idea that World War II was a battle for democracy and against fascism. Thereafter recruiters came looking to fill a more specific need. The United States military had almost no one who spoke, read, or wrote the Japanese language. It was simply not something white Americans knew about or had studied before World War II, with the exception of a tiny handful of people. So in the wake of recruiting for the 442nd, the Army issued a call for people to engage in translation, interpretation, interrogation and anything to do with the Japanese language. Intense fighting was in progress, but there was little doubt about the outcome, which meant that the American army would be occupying Japan sooner rather than later.

MILITARY INTELLIGENCE SERVICE

I volunteered for the Military Intelligence Service (MIS) on February 3, 1944, along with my oldest brother, Masaru. The small, seemingly isolated Kona community played a special role in the MIS, because the recruitment cadre had two well-known figures from Kona. Foremost was a Harvard law school graduate, Masaji Marumoto, who had grown up in his father's store in Kona. He had moved to Honolulu to attend school and had graduated from McKinley High School with the class of 1924. From before the war, Marumoto had played a key role in minimizing the distrust, then winning the trust, of the American intelligence agencies and the FBI. He was widely connected in both the Japanese and haole communities, and he had served as the first chairman of the Emergency Service Committee (ESC), the group formed under the martial law government of Hawaii to maintain a positive relationship between the Japanese community and the rest of society.

By the time of the MIS mobilization, the threat of mass internment had passed, and Marumoto was induced to help spearhead the MIS, provided he was allowed to enter initially as an enlisted man. He insisted on completing Basic Military Training. This was especially remarkable not only because of his high status, but because of the fact that he was nearing forty years old and had a twisted foot, resulting from a childhood accident. The second prominent figure in the MIS recruitment was Kenji Goto. He was my high school teacher at Konawaena High and eventually became the administrator of the Japanese community's hospital in Honolulu, Kuakini Hospital. Given the eventual importance of the MIS in United States military history, I again think of the Kona wind. What force emanated from our tiny community that churned up such key people when an unusual type of skill and mindset was needed?

The MIS training was like a long outing with family and friends in other ways. We had been drawn from the same ethnic group and the small, tight-knit society of Hawaii. My brother Masaru and I both joined MIS. Between the two of us, his decision was more difficult than mine, because he was the oldest son. My parents expected him to carry on the family tradition and look after them, as was done in Japan. While working for defense contractors in the Pearl Harbor area, Masaru had saved enough money to buy a house in Palolo Valley, the next valley over from the University of Hawaii, so the family could be together. Mother and Father were saddened

to see us go off, following Harold's departure with the 442nd, and this was
compounded by Masaru's special obligations to the family. We left behind
our brother Paul, who was disqualified for service because his right shin-
bone had been infected when he was young and operated on. He was not
incapacitated by the operation, however.

So many school friends joined MIS that it sometimes seemed like a
uniformed extension of the University of Hawaii. I cannot begin to recite
them all, but among them I must mention Richard Kosaki and Ralph
Miwa. Richard had been student-body president at McKinley High School
in 1941 when the bombs fell. He was the freshman class president at the
University and eventually became student-body president. Ralph, an excellent writer, had contributed feature articles to the University newspaper
and, like Richard, was active in student government.

Dick, Ralph and I had shared our schoolboy dreams of what we might
do after gaining an education, talking often about law, medicine, and aca-
demia. At the time I had no clear goal of my own, so the MIS came as a welcome escape. Before we left, Ralph's mother took me aside. She thought of
me as a veteran sailor because I had crossed the channels from the Big
Island to Honolulu. She asked me to look after him because he had never
been away from home and never been on a big ocean vessel. I assured her
that I would look after her boy, both crossing the Pacific and afterwards in
the Army.

LIFE IN "REPPLE DEPPLE"

We spent our first ten days in the "Repple Depple," or Replacement Depot in
Wahiawa on Oahu. This was a temporary military installation with wooden
barracks for bunking only. The mess hall, showers, and toilet facilities were
all housed in separate, temporary, buildings. There was no hot water and it
was not easy taking cold showers every day. We completed preliminary
paperwork, took IQ tests, and received uniforms that were several sizes too
large. I can still recite the Army serial number they gave me, 30107581. We
were classified in different divisions that indicated our language proficiency,

the most proficient being classes A-1, B-1 and C-1, who took an abbreviated six-month course. The rest of us, the A-2's, B-2's and below, took a nine-month course. I was placed in D-2, which put me near the top of the second tier of students, and assigned to the nine-month course.

I made up my mind to excel. Sitting in those cold barracks at the Repple Depple, it occurred to me that challenges and competition had dominated my life. I always had a competitive spirit, wanting to perform better or excel in sports or gardening or schoolwork. I had been constantly told to be the best at whatever I did, be it shining shoes, carpentry, or whatever. "Always pursue excellence and go the extra mile" became my motto. I never moped about a setback in competition. I seemed to have a natural feeling that everything would work out for the good of the whole in the long run. Optimism sprang eternal. The Japanese have a word for this, *akirameyasu*, which has to do with accepting one's fate because it is inevitable. It is a kind of reverse fatalism that I must have learned from my Buddhist parents.

ON TO MINNESOTA

After about ten days in the Repple Depple, we left for Camp Savage in Minnesota. This was my first trip to the mainland. We traveled five days by Victory Ship to Oakland and another five days by the Southern Railway to Minnesota, with a stop in Needles, California. The train was either too hot or too cold, and even before we reached our destination, many of us had the sniffles. Camp Savage was about twenty-five miles southwest of Minneapolis. It was in a farm area with no towns or villages nearby and only a few scattered places to eat. We learned that the MIS camp had been located here because the heavily Scandinavian population had never been exposed to Japanese Americans. They had no preconceptions about us. We were well treated and traveled freely and comfortably around the region on pass. Similarly, the first training station of the 100th Battalion was in Wisconsin at Camp McCoy. However, they had subsequently been sent, along with the 442nd, to Camp Shelby, Mississippi, where they got a first-hand look at deeply ingrained prejudice against African Americans.

Facilities at Camp Savage were not ultramodern by any means. It previously had been a government home for indigent old men. The classroom was small but adequately heated by a potbellied stove. About twenty students were assigned to a class, two per desk. My deskmate for nine months in Savage and Fort Snelling was Hideo Tominaga, originally from Honokaa, which is on the opposite side of the Big Island from Kona. Many members of the class were connected to Hawaii in some way, often to the university, but some of our classmates had come directly from concentration camps on the U.S. mainland.

Our teachers in Camp Savage were either civilians or non-commissioned officers, including Masaji Marumoto and Kenji Goto from Kona. By this time they had completed a six months course and been promoted to Staff Sergeant. School went on from morning until nine every evening. We studied *sosho* (cursive writing), geography, grammar, *kanji* (Chinese characters), tactics of the Japanese military, and translation of Japanese manuals into English. Military subjects were all in English and conducted by Army personnel, with exams each Saturday. There were no difficult concepts or analysis to tax the brain, and high scores came easily.

The first several months were bitterly cold. Sub-zero weather was something we had never experienced in Hawaii, but we all survived. We enjoyed the new experience with snow and welcomed the arrival of spring in Minnesota. There was much to do outdoors: hikes, bivouacs, and trips to the countryside. Except for the temperature, it was like being in Kona. There were no houses for miles around, only fresh clean air. In June of 1944, around the time of the D-day invasion in Europe, the MIS was moved to Fort Snelling, which is about fifteen miles north of Savage, close to the headwaters of the Mississippi River. The main buildings at Snelling were all permanent brick structures, including a chapel, field house (larger than a gymnasium), officers' club and quarters, an NCO club, library, tennis courts, Olympic-size swimming pool, and golf course. There was a large parade ground on which we held our military drills and paraded once a week, or more often when brass from Washington or elsewhere visited us.

Wooden barracks housed the service personnel at the other end of the Fort.

Our social life was taken care of by the USO and the local YWCA, which arranged dance parties at the YWCA facilities in Minneapolis every Saturday evening. Students from the University of Minnesota came in large numbers, and many dates among the partygoers resulted. On Wednesdays, there was usually a dance at our field house, which could accommodate more than a thousand people. At one of these parties, I met a third-generation Norwegian woman from St. Paul named Erna Hustvedt. She was slim and well proportioned, with shapely legs and red hair propped up high over her head. We danced, and I found her to be good company. She was both well spoken and well mannered. We dated, played golf together on our Fort Snelling golf course, and during the summer went swimming in one of the ten thousand lakes Minnesota is reputed to have.

My horizons were widening. That summer I went to New York City for the first time in the company of my deskmate, Hideo Tominaga. This was my first time in the place that would so influence my future. We visited the sister of a Nisei friend and stayed at the Paramount Hotel on Times Square. At the time the Paramount was home to Billy Rose's famous Diamond Horseshoe nightclub, so my excitement of staying in the hotel was heightened. I immediately liked the sheer size and impersonality of the great city. While so obviously different from faraway Kona, there seemed to me to be a crucial common denominator. Rugged individualism was the order of the day in both New York and Kona. I thought, "This is the place for me."

People from Hawaii are good at making friends and good at networking. Ralph Miwa's brother had friends in LaCrosse, Wisconsin, the Nelson family. We paid them many visits. We also went to Chicago often on the train, usually on the "Four Hundred," which was the number of minutes it took from Minneapolis to Chicago.

At a big servicemen's nightclub outside Chicago, in Evanston, Illinois, Ralph and I sat down at the bar but were not served. This in itself was not really a problem, because it gave us a chance to enjoy the scenery without having to spend any money. Our good fortune ran out when the bouncer approached us and told us to leave. Having come from Kona, I had never experienced discrimination or racially based prejudice. We asked why but he did not explain, so we left. Ralph was visibly affected by this treatment, but the fact was that I was not. I did not feel hurt nor did it negatively affect me in any way. Possibly pure innocence and naivete had something to do with it, and possibly my ability to rationalize.

On reflection, after all these years, it is the only incident I can think of in which I experienced open discrimination. I do not remember any slight or ill treatment owing to the fact that I was Japanese in appearance. If such things occurred, I probably pitied the perpetrator for his ignorance and inadequacy, but did not otherwise react. I firmly believe that my upbringing in Kona, where the dominant society was made up of Japanese, helped me build this strong sense of security, pride, and inner self-esteem. These qualities gave me and, I think, others from Hawaii a kind of "Teflon" coating. We Hawaiians tend to see the brighter side of things and not the negative, dark side. We tend to see, and bring out, the good side of people. I realize that our experience was much in contrast to Japanese Americans on the United States mainland, and I think we came out differently as a result. But that gets ahead of my story.

Graduation and Teaching Career

We graduated from MIS in November 1944, after nine months in school. I was looking forward to overseas duty but was sidetracked by the Army's need to expand its Japanese language capability. After having done well in school, as I had been determined to do, I was selected to become an instructor. I was promoted from Private First Class to Staff Sergeant and given a pay raise of about a hundred dollars a month.

I was assigned to teach Japanese grammar, even though I had never mastered it, let alone taught it. As is the case with all languages, it was purely a matter of memorizing, which came easily for me. I kept one or two lessons ahead of the students. This taught me a valuable lesson, which is that the best way to learn a new subject is to teach it to someone else.

Nami Sogi during World War II, with three-star flag representing her three sons in the U.S. Army

My brother, Masaru, had left for overseas duty right after graduation. I did not know where he was going or what his assignment was to be, nor did I hear from him. More than ten months passed. On August 13, 1945, two days before the war ended, I received a call from a Western Union operator in Minneapolis. In a cold voice, she told me that Masaru Sogi had died on Okinawa. The message was delivered as impersonally as a notice of parcel-post delivery. I learned later that the official telegram had been hand-delivered to my parents in Hawaii by the Department of the Army. Masaru was flying into Okinawa with nine other language interpreters from Hawaii. Those were the last and most desperate days of the empire of Japan. The lights on the airfield were turned off because a kamikaze suicide attack was occurring just as they were landing. Masaru and his comrades died when their airplane crashed into a mountain.

His death was a tremendous shock. I was caught totally off-guard. It was an even greater shock for my mother, who had great expectations for her oldest son. Thankfully, my brother Harold survived the bloody military campaigns of the 442nd Regimental Combat in the European Theater and returned home safely to the family.

The war ended two days after Masaru's death. With victory over Japan, I was faced once again with the question of what to do with my life. I had been in service over three years, and many of the people around me were planning to return home to resume their education. My interest in studying law was reviving. I ran into several people who were my role models, such as Masaji Marumoto, now a Judge Advocate officer; and Major John Aiso, head of the MIS, who was to gain great prominence in Los Angeles after the war.

But the person who really gave me an insight into law was a man in my class, Taro Suyenaga. He pointed out that law provided the opportunity to mold an argument or formulate a theory to advance the cause of a client. Medicine, on the other hand, was usually a matter of following the same prescribed treatments over and over. I began to look at law as offering a broader spectrum of creativity than medicine. I was about to commit to the law school idea when the Army asked if I was interested in going to Japan for a year as a commissioned officer. This was a fateful proposition. I thought this was a once-in-a-lifetime chance to meet my relatives in Japan and see how they were faring in the aftermath of such a terrible war.

A Commissioned Officer

Although I was then a Staff Sergeant to be commissioned a Second Lieutenant, I had to go through basic combat training, something I previously had avoided. Master Sergeant Francis Motofuji and I were selected from the faculty to go to Fort McClellan in Anniston, Alabama for six weeks of basic training. I got a new serial number—0936634. As noncommissioned officers, Francis and I stayed with the cadre that ran the training program, so we were relieved of such duties as Kitchen Police and cleaning the barracks. We reported to regular military training of the most basic type and attended lectures. Time went by quickly that winter of 1945-46, although I remember a particularly bitter cold spell in February and March that required an overcoat and mufflers, even in Alabama. The cold was especially painful out on the firing range. We had to take turns attending the targets behind the pits. If any group or platoon did not pass the firing-range test, all of us behind the pits had to go back in the bitter weather to set the targets back up for the repeaters on Sunday. No one failed.

As a result, we slept in on Sunday and then went to church or to the canteen for pancakes and coffee. While MIS had been predominantly people of Japanese ancestry, this was a mixed group. I began making acquaintances with such names as Donald Helm, whose family had been in the shipping business in Yokohama, Japan; George Moore, a mid-westerner; and several Jews, including Stanley Falk and Stewart Scheuer, with whom I would keep in contact over a lifetime. Upon completion of basic training, we left by train for our return trip north, boarding at Anniston and transferring at Birmingham.

This was the first time we realized we were in Jim Crow country. Everywhere we saw two sets of toilets and signs segregating the blacks from whites. As typically occurred for Asian Americans in the South, by some unexplained code we used white facilities. As we boarded the train, Francis Motofuji and I noticed that one car in the train was almost empty except for a few black passengers. We preferred sitting in the car with the African Americans because it was not crowded. When we showed the conductor our orders, he told us to move to the next all-white car, which was much more crowded. We were being treated as white, although the conductor did not know what to make of us. I began to realize why the Japanese Americans on the west coast were considered enemy aliens and placed en masse in concentration camps in violation of our U.S. Constitution.

Upon receiving our commission back in Fort Snelling, we were quartered in the BOQ (bachelor officers' quarters), which had roomy and much more private living quarters and a separate dining room. The recreational facilities were better, and even the arrangements for entertainment were handled differently. We no longer had to go to the YWCA or the field house where young ladies were bussed in from the city by the USO or similar organizations. Instead, we now had a social director who arranged for smaller group functions, usually with coeds from the University of Minnesota or working girls from Minneapolis and St. Paul.

We had volunteered for duty in occupied Japan for a year, so all of our preparation at work went towards that end. Late in May we took the train for Fort Lewis in Seattle, Washington, with Donald Helm and his classmates, all newly commissioned second lieutenants. We rode the Great Northern Railway route, up mountains and down through beautiful valleys, the continental divide and through the Glacier National Park. When we finally arrived in Seattle, we stayed for five days. I remember seeing the famous comedian Joe E. Brown play the great white rabbit in *Harvey*, which I have never forgotten.

CHAPTER FIVE

Occupation of Japan

F EW EVENTS WERE to have such an effect on me as my service in Japan, but my youthful awareness then could usually be measured in days and weeks rather than months and years. When we sailed out of Seattle on a Victory ship, a card game started right away. Nominally I was in charge of a company of soldiers, but I only went downstairs once daily to holler at the sergeant in charge over the roar of the engines, "Is everything okay?" Otherwise our floating circle of officers interrupted our card game only long enough to eat and do some light calisthenics. I would remember if I had lost money, so I must have at least broken even.

Other than the card game, the trip was devoid of tension. There was nothing to fear. My main goal was to find my relatives in southern Japan, but I knew that wouldn't happen right away. After nine or ten days we arrived in Yokohama harbor, the port city of Tokyo. From there we were trucked to temporary quarters at an army base called Zama, where we waited a few days for assignments. On the fourth day of July 1946, I departed for the Allied Translation and Interpreters' Service (ATIS) of General Headquarters, Supreme Commander of Allied Powers in Tokyo. ATIS was housed in the old NYK Shipping Line building, and many of the ATIS personnel were from Fort Snelling. In addition to translations, we handled domestic intelligence by collecting and collating information and disseminating it to field units throughout Japan.

Because I had not been involved in combat, nothing had prepared me for the devastation of Tokyo. Enormous areas were still leveled as a result of saturation bombing, even though the war had been over nearly a year. Construction was flimsy and temporary. Although people were no longer going hungry in large numbers, many needed more to eat than they were getting.

Early on I developed a habit of giving away rations to the Japanese, and I looked for other little ways to help as time went on. For all the suffering I witnessed, I should say I encountered no bitterness on their part over losing the war and no resentment of the Occupation. Their thoughts had turned to figuring out how they were going to rebuild and move on.

We worked on the lower floors and lived upstairs. The Army's female civilian employees were quartered across the street in the old Kaijo building. There was no air conditioning, so the place was steaming in summer. The women would rush home after work and disrobe quickly with the windows open. Promptly at five o'clock, the young officers in our building rushed to their quarters upstairs, closed the doors, and took turns spying through powerful naval binoculars. I learned later that some of the women across the way were peering back with binoculars of their own.

Our other summer recreation in Tokyo was golfing at the prestigious Koganae and Abiko golf clubs, then operated by the Army. The royal families played these courses, and today the memberships cost $2 million or more, if they can be purchased at all. As officers, we all had privileges at the motor pool and requisitioned Jeeps and three quarter ton trucks to travel on weekends. We often went to hot springs that not too many military personnel knew about—such places as Kinugawa, Nikko, the area behind Nantaizan, and Kisarazu in Chiba.

If we stayed in town, we went out to the Red Cross Club near the present Diet Building. We also went to the Mitsui Club for officers in Mita, and others that were not so pretentious but certainly adequate. If you stayed around the billet, you could always find a card game or some other form of gambling.

The more enterprising members of our group did business in the black market. We each had a regular weekly ration of cigarettes and liquor but hardly enough to do any serious reselling. Those with friends in the

Tachikawa Air Base would fly down to Hong Kong and return with cartons of liquor, tobacco, and sugar, which were all scarce in Japan and much in demand. With the additional supply, some of our men did fairly well.

COUNTER-INTELLIGENCE CORPS

After a month at ATIS, I transferred to the Counter Intelligence Corps (CIC). I moved out of NYK and into the school quarters in Kanda or Kudan-shita, the location of a place where the once-feared Japanese Army *Kempeitai* had been headquartered. The *Kempeitai* was a secret security police and the closest thing Japan had to a Gestapo. Shiro Amioka and I and about twenty other officers went to school there. Shiro and I did well, with average scores between 95 and 100. We were mindful of our performance because we believed good scores would lead to an assignment at the CIC in Tokyo, which was considered the plushest duty in Japan. The Tokyo CIC was close to General Headquarters, directly under the G-2 Section of General Charles A. Willoughby, the highly respected top brass of Army Intelligence in Japan. In addition to all the lifestyle amenities, being stationed in Tokyo CIC meant that a second officer and I could share a Jeep at any time of day, night or weekend. By pulling strings, we could also get commissary privileges, like the married officers had, and be able to buy provisions for weekend trips. With our high average scores, Shiro and I made plans to live the good life in Tokyo for the balance of our army careers.

When our assignments finally came, we found to our chagrin that we were being sent to CIC Headquarters in Sapporo on the northern island of Hokkaido. Being descended from a family from Hawaii and southern Japan, I had only a vague idea of where Sapporo was. Today its image has been glamorized somewhat as a winter wonderland, dating particularly to its being the site of the 1972 Winter Olympics. It does have dry, powdery snow that is great for skiing, but it is literally the coldest and closest place in Japan to Siberia. Hokkaido is brutally cold and in the 1940s it was not many years separated from a kind of frontier status.

Shiro and I were heart-broken. We mentally retraced our thirty-day stay at the school. We were no cardinals of virtue, but neither could we recall any serious bad conduct. Why were we being banished to the waste-land? Not having any choice, off we went north, where we learned quickly the answers to our question.

Sapporo, Hokkaido, Japan

Of Japan's four main islands, Hokkaido is the most remote. Until the drive for modernization in Meiji Japan (1868), Hokkaido was populated almost exclusively by the indigenous *ainu* people. By the time of the Occupation, it was extensively populated by Japanese but was not as densely populated as the rest of Japan. Its southern tip lies just north of the central island of Honshu, where Tokyo, Osaka, Nagoya and other great cities are located. To the west from Hokkaido is the convergence of China, Russia, and North Korea. To the north is a long north-south island known as Sakhalin, and to the east is the open Pacific Ocean.

The principal city of Hokkaido is Sapporo, which is in the upland over a large protected notch that faces the Asian mainland. Next to Sapporo is an *ainu* colony, and next to the *ainu* was a city called Asahigawa. My friend Shiro and I settled down into a four-story building in Sapporo, and in that one building we had offices, a dining room, a recreation room and sleeping quarters. We were centrally located, being close to the Sapporo Railroad Station and also the Grand Hotel, the only hotel then in operation.

Although initially our hearts were not in the Hokkaido assignment, we pragmatically went along with SOP (standard operating procedure) and performed whatever work came our way. An Army Major was in command and right below him was Captain Shigeru Tsubota from Hawaii. Master Sergeant "Bud" Mukai was our top non-commissioned officer. The rest of us were CIC agents of varying types.

I did all kinds of investigative work and whatever else assigned by G-2 of General Headquarters. From these assignments we quickly learned that Hokkaido was not really a frozen wasteland but rather a place teeming with widely varied people and different, often clashing, interests.

For geographic reasons, it was a re-entry point for troops of the Japanese Army, and redistributing them and re-integrating them into a civilian economy was one of the enormous challenges of post-war Japan. Many of these troops returned to home soil from Russian Siberia and Korea and others from Sakhalin. The demographics were further complicated by the fact that many of the Koreans were from North Korea and had been working as slave labor for the Japanese Army in Sakhalin. In the aftermath of war, they too had gotten only as far as Hokkaido. After a few days of surveying this scene and engaging in fieldwork, Shiro and I became completely engrossed in our work. We threw ourselves into our assignments, taking on many cases and constantly writing reports for G-2 in Tokyo.

THE NEW WAR

The big picture emerged fairly quickly. In a world weary of war, we had been taken north by a new conflict. The outline of the Russian bear appeared in the fog, foreshadowing the Cold War. With Japan and Europe prostrate, the two great powers left standing—the Union of Soviet Socialist Republics (USSR) and the United States—struggled to define a new balance of power. The Yalta conference of 1945 had acknowledged two spheres of influence, one American and one Soviet. In 1946, Winston Churchill had made his famous "Iron Curtain" speech in which he described Soviet repression in Eastern Europe. Now Shiro Amioka and I had been stationed just below the far eastern tip of the Soviet Union, the Sakhalin Islands.

Originally controlled by Imperial Russia, Sakhalin had come under Japan's domination as a result of the Russo-Japanese war of 1905. In that war, Japan emerged as the first Asiatic country to defeat a white country in modern history, a victory that sent a shock wave through the West. The Sakhalin boundary had been in chronic dispute and after the war of 1905 was set more or less in the middle of Sakhalin along an east-west axis. In the closing days of World War II, the USSR, most prominently including Russia, launched a military campaign that recaptured the entire island, as well as a chain of small islands to the east, the Kuriles. Accordingly the USSR nearly touched the northern tip of Hokkaido.

Lest there be doubt about the drift of events, the Army newspaper in Tokyo was constantly writing about the difficulties the Occupation forces were having with USSR personnel on the Far East Commission, which represented the victorious Allied powers in Japan. Back home in America, the fear-mongering of McCarthyism was beginning to haunt the public imagination, calling into question the loyalty of many Americans who were liberal in their views, or who had participated in liberal or radical groups that had been popular in the 1930s.

The tilt of our investigative work was determined accordingly. The rightist credentials of the Japanese Army were accepted at face value, and almost anyone connected with our erstwhile mortal enemy was considered trustworthy. Little to no effort went in to investigating Japanese Army personnel. Virtually all our effort was aimed at monitoring left-wing, radical, and communist activities in Hokkaido. Our standing orders were to investigate and report any indications of left-wing movements of any kind.

The four or five of us with language ability devoted much of our time to gleaning information from Japanese returnees from Russia, North Korea, and Sakhalin. Every Japanese who returned to Japan after the war was required by law to report to the Japanese police and give his name, address, and where he had been. The names of these returnees, then, were given to us by the police throughout Hokkaido. Based on a prioritizing of this list, we called the returnees in for questioning. We asked them standard questions, which had been given to us, to determine as much as we could about the area from which they had returned as well as the people with whom they had associated. What did they remember about the local Communist party? What relationship did they see between local communists and the new Russian occupiers? What did that suggest about the intentions of Russia? Given the fact that we had been engaged in a horrible war with Japan, it is remarkable how overnight the Japanese became our eyes and ears in our investigations. We would ask, "What did you see? What did you hear?" The Japanese would dutifully attempt to answer. A typical interview lasted thirty to forty-five minutes. If the returnee seemed to have information about the Russians, the interview ran longer.

Because of the interest of CIC in political activity was nearly indiscriminate, this generated a lot of work and no small amount of confusion. For example, I witnessed an early meeting of an organization that was to dominate the politics of Japan for the rest of the century. It was a meeting of the Liberal Party, which later merged with the Democratic Party to form the Liberal Democratic Party of Japan. The meeting also attracted a number of ethnic Koreans, as you shall see. The event took place in Sapporo in a second-floor room with sliding *shoji* screen doors and a floor covering of traditional *tatami* (straw mat). Forty or fifty people sat on cushions facing a podium. When I entered, the receptionist let me through only after I identified myself with my CIC badge.

I sat at the back. The main speaker was the Minister of Communication, a man named Hitotsubashi. He was a little way into his prepared speech when he used the words *hanto jin,* which means "peninsular people." Because these words substituted a location for a country, it was a colonial reference that denied Koreans their national identity. (They are more properly called *kankoku jin,* or people of Korea). Before I realized it, someone stood up to the left and then to the right, until fifteen or more people were challenging the speaker. Someone shouted, "How dare you call us Koreans by that dastardly name." Cushions started to fly in all directions and people were pushed around. *Shoji* doors fell down in the mayhem. In a few minutes the place was in a shambles. The crowd dispersed when the police arrived. It all happened so suddenly that any two persons who might be asked to relate what happened could not have possibly agreed to anything except that the cause was the use of the derogatory term for Koreans.

I submitted a routine one-pager to the CIC suggesting it was a passing incident that would not be repeated. However, I was instructed to investigate further, and I found it necessary to meet with the head of the Liberal Party of Sapporo. His name was Dr. Hideji Arima, a medical doctor and one of the leading specialists on tuberculosis at the Imperial University of Hokkaido. I visited him one evening at his home and interviewed him at length. He told me about the strong feelings that existed between the Japanese and the Koreans as a result of Japan's subjugation and occupation of Korea for many years. As part of a vein of history little-known by people in the West, Japan's colonization of Korea began as a result of the 1895 war between China and Japan, much of which was fought on Korean soil. This was reinforced by the 1905 war between Russia and Japan, which again was fought in Korea. Japan had annexed Korea in 1910 and thereafter exploited its resources and people. Accordingly the outburst at the meeting had its own history and logic and had nothing to do with left-wing sentiment. This satisfied headquarters, and it was the end of the incident.

Next I was assigned to investigate the labor union movement at the coal mines in Hokkaido. The situation was particularly serious at the Yubari Mines. It was winter and snowing heavily. The temperature dropped below zero for extended periods. Under such conditions, it was impossible to travel either by Jeep or train. The only alternative was to employ a small armored tank called a weasel. The CIC had ready access to several upon request to our friends at the nearby 7th Cavalry. The weasel would be loaded on a flattop to Yubari Station, and from Yubari Station we could travel to the mining area. We did this a number of times to check on the labor movement and to make sure that labor unrest did not pose any serious problems to either the military or to economic development.

Suspicion does not make for efficiency. One of my assignments was to check on a woman who was said to be agitating local residents about the Occupation. No one seemed to know her name or exactly what she looked like. In such situations, we called in the local chief of police and asked for his cooperation. We told him that this person may be a left-wing agitator. After some time, we got a name and address from a reliable source and passed the information on to the police, asking them to put the woman under surveillance. On a weekly basis, the police gave us precise reports of her movements from the time she woke until the time she went to bed, including such information as when she went to the public bath. After several weeks, the woman complained about the way the police called her in every day to ask questions about her movements. It turned out that the wrong person was being questioned. I eventually would leave Hokkaido without locating the real agitator, if indeed she ever existed.

DEALINGS WITH THE RUSSIANS

Being stationed in Hokkaido I began to see that the world was not only made up of American and Japanese influences. The world was an incredible brew, and we were challenged to learn about its exciting complexities. In Hokkaido we found a Russian language teacher. She was part of a small group of settlers known as White Russians, whose sentiments lay with opponents of the Communist Revolution of 1917. She offered to teach us Russian, and a few of us studied with her for six months. Classes were twice a week at night for about two hours. We found the Russian language rather simple. It was based on the Cyrillic alphabet of thirty-four letters. Each had a distinct sound, enabling us to pronounce every word phonetically. Our two years of language study at Ft. Snelling made it relatively easy for us to pick up a new one, and so Russian was merely a matter of memorizing sounds and words. As a result of the course, most of us could read the Russian newspaper and carry on simple conversations.

In addition to these Russian residents of Sapporo, there was a contingent of Russian officers stationed there representing the Russian Mission in the Occupation of Japan. Our instructions were to keep an eye on their activities. One night, one of my fellow officers and I invited two Russian officers to a Japanese restaurant for dinner. To equal the rank of our Russian counterparts, we were promoted for the evening to Lieutenant Colonel and Major. I was no longer Second Lieutenant Sogi but Major Sogi. Our Russian language ability at that time was nil but they spoke reasonably good English.

The four of us met at the appointed time in the evening. As the meal went on, my colleague started to eat more and more because the Russians were so non-communicative. During this period of the Occupation, the only Japanese whiskey available was called Nikka Whiskey. It was not at all that good, but at our age and experience, it didn't matter that much. We were drinking Nikka Whiskey straight, and at a pretty fast pace. We started toasting them with "*kampai*" (Japanese for "bottoms up"). They would respond with nothing more than a *clink* and "*dorink*" ("drink!"). I must say they were disciplined. Whenever we asked a question or made a statement, they would merely nod or grunt. And they were seemingly unfazed by drinking an enormous amount of whiskey. We kept thinking that more Nikka would make them relax, but after so many *kampais* and clinks and *dorinks*, we were much more affected than they were. We gave up.

COUNTER-ESPIONAGE

Our work in CIC also involved undercover assignments. One CIC team, consisting of two of our agents, lived among the Japanese in civilian clothes. This was effective in obtaining all kinds of information, but it had its occupational hazards. For example, at one point an agent fell into a love relationship with a woman who was the subject of the investigation, and he had to be transferred.

I myself became involved in undercover work as a result of a routine questioning of a returnee from Sakhalin. The returnee and I were sitting in my office, separated only by a two-foot-wide wooden desk. I started the interview as usual by asking his name, address, and family situation. Before I could go further, the interviewee said, "You probably know everything about me."

At first I thought he must be kidding. He was slightly nervous and fidgeted in his chair. For a moment I was lost for words as I looked through my information sheet. He rescued me by volunteering, "I will tell you all about myself and what I am doing."

"Why don't you start from the beginning?" I replied.

He said the Russians in Sakhalin had sent him and another person to Hokkaido to gather information about the U.S. Army. The Russians had leverage over him because he and his family had gone to Sakhalin when it was occupied by Japan. His family had wanted to resettle in Hokkaido after the war, but they had not gotten out. He subsequently was pressured to work for the Russians, while his family was effectively held hostage.

He and another Japanese man had come in on a small boat. The second man had worked for the weather bureau in Sakhalin and was an expert wireless operator. Together they were supposed to gather and relay information to the Russians. As they approached the northernmost tip of Hokkaido at a place called Wakkanai, their boat tipped over. They managed to swim to shore with a radio and other transmitting apparatus in a box sealed so tightly that it floated. They buried it and marked it with a wooden stake.

This was quite a revelation, and I immediately contacted CIC headquarters in Tokyo to pursue it further. I was dispatched to the Weather Bureau at Ohtemachi in Tokyo and confirmed that there was indeed a weather station at Sakhalin, though they could not verify the name of the employees. Next, I went to G-2 headquarters at SCAP (the Supreme Commander of the Allied Powers) in the Dai-Ichi Building. There I got a clearance to compromise the team and use it to transfer misinformation to the Russians. One motive was to scatter a little dust in the spying eyes of the Russians. A second motive was to protect the relatives left in Sakhalin by the Japanese nationals. The Russians expected to hear something, and we intended to fill the void.

First, we had to retrieve the box the two men had buried. To help me search, a warrant officer was assigned to accompany me by train to Wakkanai. We walked about three miles along the shoreline before locating it and digging it up with a pick and shovel. Fortunately, the warrant officer was a strapping young man weighing over 200 pounds. Being his superior officer, I had him carry the sixty-pound load back to the railroad station at Wakkanai. When we examined the equipment later at CIC headquarters, we saw that it was all "made in USA" wireless equipment, including a transmitter, batteries, and other devices. The box was waterproof and the inside was dry.

Our plan was for our short-wave operator to set up the equipment at his house with the wiring concealed under the floor. The transmitter and other equipment would be kept in a box for safekeeping, to be removed only during the evening when messages would be sent. The messages were to be encrypted, first by writing them in Japan's phonetic language, *katakana,* with a number assigned to each character. The message would be converted to groups of five digits. Finally, we added the agent's code number, which was subject to change by instructions from the Russians. All of this would then be transmitted in Morse code.

Although the 11th Airborne unit's radio operator stationed in Wakkanai might intercept the transmission, no one would be able to decipher it. Even if the message was decoded, by then the agent's code number would have been changed. We therefore arranged for the person whom I had originally interviewed to gather some information for us, while remaining alert for others who might have been there doing work for the Russians.

It was not long before we discovered another man who seemed suspicious. He lived in Asahigawa, about a two-hour train ride from Sapporo in the middle of Hokkaido, where the *Ainu* had settled. So as not to arouse the interest of the local police, we did not ask him to come to the office for an interview, which was usually arranged by the local police.

We played the real undercover role here. Another agent and I, wearing borrowed civilian clothes, took the train to Asahigawa to interview the subject at home. After some questioning, he admitted that he, too, had been sent by the Russians in Sakhalin to gather information on U.S. Army troop movements. He was a radio operator and showed us the transmitting equipment he had. It was the same type that the other team brought with them. We asked our new spy to accompany us back to Sapporo that afternoon. He agreed but asked if we could wait at the railroad station since his neighbors would become suspicious if they saw two strangers staying at his place until the next train.

We returned to the station in sub-zero weather. Our borrowed raincoats were hardly sufficient to keep us warm, though we were fully clothed with long johns and woolen underwear. To keep from freezing, we took refuge in a nearby restaurant that had a charcoal *hibachi* going. Since we were occupying two seats in a narrow space, we had to order something to eat. We managed to stay there all morning slowly sipping tea and eating cookies and the like, but at lunchtime a bunch of workers came in and the proprietor asked us to leave unless we were having lunch. We ordered lunch and ate it slowly in order to pass another two hours or so. The workers ate quickly and left, so before long we were alone again. I kept awake reading whatever Japanese magazines were lying around. My partner drifted off to sleep. When more customers came in, the proprietor prodded him to wake up. Although a trained CIC agent, my partner had never before done undercover work. As he stretched and began to wake up, he said, "Okay, Okay." Everyone looked at him, then at me. With those two American words, he had given away our cover and we lost our place of repose. We had to spend the next very cold hour waiting in the unheated railway station. Fortunately, our suspect showed up as promised and the three of us returned to headquarters.

We learned from this Asahigawa agent that his partner lived in a mining town about three hours northeast of Sapporo. He also told us that his partner had $20,000 in U.S. military scrip that was being used by the Occupation forces in Japan. The money was stored in a suitcase stashed away in the man's attic. We subsequently learned that the scrip was counterfeit, that it was being printed by the Russians on a printer stolen somewhere in Germany, and that it was being used by Russian agents in U.S. Army locations around the world.

To pick up this Asahigawa man's partner, we needed the cooperation of the Japanese police. I contacted the Chief of Police at Sapporo police headquarters, with whom we had worked closely in connection with our operation. Explaining the mission, I requested that someone accompany me to interview the individual, with the stipulation that neither his family nor his neighbors be disturbed any more than necessary.

CIC agents usually traveled in a plush train car of our own, but obviously we had to forego its warmth and comfort and take a regular Japanese passenger train. Again, I borrowed civilian clothes from Yoneji Goto, a Japanese American civilian employed by the Army whose wife operated the gift shop at the Grand Hotel. Mr. Goto had also been an instructor at the MIS School in Fort Snelling. I even changed my glasses from military silver rims to a more Japanese-looking local product for the mission. To be even more a part of the local scenery, I took along two rice balls wrapped in *nori* (seaweed) and filled with *ume* (pickled plum) and *takuwan* (pickled turnip). These were in my left pocket. In my right pocket, I took my CIC snub-nose three-inch barrel six-shooter, as required by regulations. Also, by regulation, the gun's chamber was empty. Rules about firing the pistol were quite strict. Whenever we fired a shot from the allotted six bullets, we were required to report to headquarters when it was fired, where, and under what circumstances it was necessary to use it.

Since it was a long way to the mining area, we started out early enough so we could return the same evening without sleeping over. It was the afternoon rush hour, when people were going home from the city or changing trains in Sapporo to different points in Hokkaido. For instance, those who went to the fish market at Otaru usually changed trains in Sapporo. Most of the travelers were carrying personal articles or foodstuffs on their backs. With the chief of police leading the way, we boarded the train but it was standing-room-only. I of course didn't want to attract attention to either myself or the Sapporo chief of police. However, just as the train was about to pull out, a woman came running in with a square can on her back fully loaded with seafood. As she pushed her way in, she jammed the corner of the can into my ribs. My immediate reaction came out in English.

"Ouch!" I yelled.

People looked at me for a moment just as the people in the restaurant had looked at my partner when he said, "Okay, okay." I looked away in a mixture of fear and embarrassment, and the chief of police and I moved away from the entrance area. Thankfully, the incident passed without further complication. If there had been surveillance, I would have given away my cover. After a few hours, we were finally able to sit down. We decided to have our dinner. I pulled out my rice balls, cold and dry by then, but still tasty with the *takuwan* and *ume* inside. There was nothing to drink, but the rice sustained me for the evening. We finally reached our destination and took a cab to the suspect's house. At the suggestion of the chief of police, I said nothing during the entire visit. Over the customary tea, the chief identified himself and casually carried on a conversation with the suspect. When the suspect realized he had been found out, he agreed to cooperate with us. He was quite surprised when the chief mentioned the suitcase in the attic. Reluctantly, he retrieved it and it was indeed full of military scrip. I confirmed the amount and put it in my pocket. Subsequently I turned it over to headquarters and the problem of counterfeit scrip was taken out of my hands. I imagine that it went up to a high level in the military, since the scrip was obviously spread around the globe and undermined the integrity of financial transactions.

We learned that the two agents were supposed to watch for movements of the United States military in Hokkaido. We fed them some misinformation on the subject, stretching the truth as to how large a force we had and how mobile it was.

This was not an isolated incident. Prior to my departure, CIC turned up a second team of Japanese who likewise had come down from Sakhalin and were working under duress for the Russians. Their assignment was to inform the Russians about the movement of military cargo. They had no more real commitment to the Russians than the first team, but they feared for the welfare and safety of the families they left behind. We similarly set them up with a system of misinformation. Our show of concern for their families almost felt like social work.

I must say the CIC's preoccupation with the political left reflected an intense fear of Communism that I never shared. It was true that the Russian army was nearby, and the Communist party had some following in post-war Japan. But I never saw them as a major threat, either to security or to the political establishment. Neither did most Japanese. Realistically, there were local communists who had their own genuinely held views on restructuring conservative Japanese society. The truth was that Japan needed to be shaken up. On another level there was the Communist Internationale, the Comintern, which was run from Moscow. There was little evidence of the Comintern at work, which left us with the homegrown variety of Communists. Our discoveries of agents, scrip, and transmitters were exciting to me, a youth from Kona, but did not reveal anything fundamentally threatening to the future of the free world. Alas, I was never to be the subject of a Hollywood movie.

What mattered most were the reconstruction of Japanese society and the future of U.S.-Japan relations. In this regard, I saw that the expensive lifestyle of Occupation forces formed a barrier between the Japanese people and us. Our unit's railroad car was a case in point. It was fully heated and equipped with toilet facilities and sleeping quarters and was far superior to anything civilians were using. At our request, it would be attached to any engine going anywhere in Hokkaido. We could park in a rail station or rail spur for any length of time.

As we went from place to place in the dead of winter, with sub-zero temperatures and snow on the ground, we felt guilty. From our half-empty cars, we would see the Japanese trains packed to the hilt, with people packing heavy loads of personal belongings or food that was being taken to market. Food was scarce in Japan at that time, though farm products were rather plentiful in Hokkaido, as were Hokkaido salmon, Wakkanai scallops, and Kushiro *kegane* crabs. But things were certainly hard for the defeated Japanese people, and the victorious Occupation forces operated from a position of privilege.

Because officers were in short supply, I doubled as a mess officer for our unit. As such I was in charge of all the food and supplies for the headquarters. Ice cream and other foodstuffs, as well as light bulbs and cigarettes were especially in demand. For a gallon of frozen concentrated ice cream, the 11th Airborne would give us three gallons of regular ice cream. I could use two gallons for the mess hall and give the third to local residents to obtain information, leads or other types of cooperation. Cigarettes also helped a great deal.

Although some Japanese resented the Americans, the Occupation was not an opportunity for wholesale pillage of the defeated nation, as frequently has been the case throughout human history. With the tone set by General Douglas MacArthur at SCAP, many Americans realized it was important that Japanese traditions and culture be preserved and revitalized.

I must admit that many of us were sympathetic to the plight of the Japanese and we did what we could to help the local residents in any way we could. In this connection, other Japanese Americans and I had a special vantage point and a special role to play. With our sense of relationship to a defeated people, we realized more than ever before how human beings around the world have the same basic needs, wants, fears, and aspirations. When we saw someone struggling or hungry, it occasionally dawned on us that there we were, separated from that experience only by our parents' immigration to Hawaii. It was a lesson that would serve me well over the next few years in Japan and for the rest of my life.

We of Japanese ancestry were in the best position to win over the good will and trust of the Japanese. I personally tried to do everything possible to go the extra mile. In addition to my official duties, I spent extra time getting to know the Japanese, talk to them and associate with them. Through such contacts, I tried to impart the practice of democracy to the Japanese and encourage the Americans on the scene to facilitate the rebuilding and democratization of Japan.

I often simply gave away my rations to people I thought needed them. I also became a supporter of an orphanage, and at Christmas I sponsored a party for the children.

On any given weekend, fellow CIC members and I would be out hiking or skiing with Japanese friends. Maruyama, which was to become the site of the 1972 Winter Olympics, was merely a hill. There was no ski lift, so we walked up on boots with seal skin hair facing down, which kept us from slipping. On one occasion, we hiked up a mountain with Japanese friends for three hours, lunched at the top in bright sun, then skied down in forty-five minutes in virgin powder snow, following our local expert.

Some of my friendships in Japan were to last a lifetime and spread from generation to generation. Dr. Arima, who had introduced me to the Liberal Party, continued his warm, open conversations with me. He was a true Christian who spawned an entire family of doctors. Two of his three sons were doctors and his three daughters married doctors.

When his second son, Jun, was married in the winter of 1947, I was invited to the wedding. I drove the bride and groom from the church to the reception in a Jeep, which was difficult for Mrs. Arima to get into while wearing a formal Japanese wedding kimono.

Dr. Arima eventually ran for the House of Representatives and served a number of terms. He ran for the governorship of Hokkaido but fell short in the vote. He nonetheless served in the House of Councilors until he passed away. Eventually the entire family moved to Tokyo with the exception of Jun, who remained with the Medical School of the University of Hokkaido. Our friendship continued across time and distance through Dr. Arima's children, grandchildren, and even great-grandchildren.

Visiting Relatives in Fukuoka

Much of my one-year tour of duty had gone by without seeing my relatives, my original main motive for going to Japan and a source of anxiety for my family in Hawaii. Finally, in February of 1947 I took a leave from CIC and flew south to Fukuoka on a military transport, thanks to one of the many connections CIC had with the American military government.

Fukuoka is the name of both a major city and a prefecture with large rural areas, from which many of the immigrants to Hawaii were first recruited. When I landed in the city, I lodged at the military billet, a local Japanese hotel. There I met my classmate from MIS training, Donald Helm. We had a brief but grand reunion, catching up on what happened to those who had been commissioned with us and had come to Japan with us. Jim

Cahill, Stewart Scheuer, Stanley Falk, and a few others had been sent on to Korea, which had the reputation of being the worst assignment in the Far East. Donald had been scheduled to go there, but because of his family's prewar connections in Yokohama and his relatives there, he ended up in Fukuoka. Another Snelling graduate, George Moore, had become the personal interpreter for General Robert L. Eichelberger, the Commanding Officer of the 8th Army. (An aside: The General's patch was two white figures, representing a weight lifter's dumbbells, on a red background. The nickname that we in the lower ranks gave it was "a pair of dumbbells in a field of red tape.")

Soneda Village, Fukuoka

The most remarkable reunions were yet to come. The families of my mother and father lived in two outlying villages that adjoined one another. I visited my father's family first, arriving in my second lieutenant's uniform, my six-shooter in my pocket, bullets removed. My father's younger stepbrother lived with his three sons and his mother (my step-grandmother), then eighty-nine years old, in an old thatched-roof farmhouse with a barn and outhouse.

The Sogi family greeted me, but it seemed difficult for them to realize that one of their own relatives was the "enemy" and now part of the U.S. Army Occupation Force. Because of my step-grandmother's advanced age, she particularly did not realize the meaning of all of this. As a result, there was not much talk about either the war or the Occupation.

I stayed over one night in the Sogi house, which was unheated except for a small brazier with two or three pieces of charcoal. Everything was scarce. Again I saw these were extremely hard times for the Japanese. As farmers my relatives fared better than some, simply because they grew their own rice and vegetables, though everything was rationed and regulated. The only way to survive the cold night was by taking a hot bath in a steel tub with wooden slats inside.

I learned that Seigen, the oldest son in the family had gone to the

Kaemon Sonogi in 1947. Back row, left to right: Kaemon, Yoshikazu, Hideto and child Yoshihiro. Front row, left to right: Sayo (wife of Kaemon) and grandmother Ei

Yoshikazu Sonogi family. Left to right: Chizuko, Kumeji, Ayako, Yoshiko, Yoshikazu, Takahiro, Yoshihiro

Pacific War and was killed in action, leaving behind his wife and a son. My cousin, Yoshikazu, the second son, succeeded his deceased brother by marrying his surviving wife Yoshiko and adopting his son, Yoshihiro.

When I said good-bye, my aged step-grandmother kept saying that I should not do such a foolish thing as leave home and I should stay with the family. The most I could say was I would stay in contact, and I have. I can report that cousin Yoshikazu subsequently had two more children, both college graduates, now living in Tokyo and Osaka. His other brothers live nearby in Asakura. The oldest, adopted son lives at home with his wife and will eventually take over the farm.

Yamaguma Village, Fukuoka

Next I visited my mother's family, the Shibatas, who lived over a hill in the second village, Yamaguma. I was greeted by several relatives, led by Takumi Shibata, my mother's younger brother, who was by now head of the household. Several of my mother's sisters and one of her half-sisters also were present. The welcome was less than warm. I later learned that they were seriously surprised by my U.S. Army uniform, even though they had seen pictures of me and gotten news about me in letters written by my mother. It so happened that the Kyushu area had lost the largest numbers of sons and husbands in the Japanese Army in the Pacific War. Four of my Shibata cousins had been killed in the war.

The atomic bomb blasts had gone off in southern Japan. I also was reminded of the fact that their villages lay in the path of where the American army had projected the invasion of Japan. As I became familiar with the landscape, I recalled that during the latter part of 1944 and early in 1945, we MIS personnel at Fort Snelling all responded to long questionnaires from the Navy and Military Intelligence in Washington concerning the eastern coast of Kyushu. We were asked to give any information or pictures we had of the terrain, landmarks, weather, and shoreline.

We had a lot to talk about. Mother had two brothers and seven sisters, all living close by. When she visited them before the war started, all seven

Nami Sogi's brother, sisters, nephews, and nieces, 1947

Nami Sogi's three sisters, nephew, and relatives

sisters had settled down together on the *tatami* floor. They had giggled like teenagers and talked far into the night. I could now imagine this scene readily. My mother had been only eighteen when she left her sisters for Hawaii, and she was forty-one on her return visit.

During my stay, I began probing into family history, for the first time consulting the village registries that served as a record of people's lives. Up to this time I had known more about the Shibatas than the Sogis, and now I saw why. My father's life in Japan was not that happy. His mother had died, and his father had remarried. To my considerable surprise, I learned my father had married for the first time at a young age, probably arranged by the family. The register showed this marriage taking place in 1902, and it dissolved the same year. Thereafter I assumed these were the reasons he left Japan for Hawaii.

The most surprising news was about my Uncle Tamotsu, my mother's youngest brother. Following a family tradition of military service, he had been selected from among high school graduates and assigned to an elite naval flight-training program called *Yokaren,* where he served in the Third Class. He then was assigned to the Sasebo Naval Base, the third of the four major naval districts in Japan. After successfully completing his intensive training, he was selected as one of more than seven hundred naval pilots to participate in the attack on Pearl Harbor. His assignment was to the aircraft carrier *Kaga,* one of the four carriers that formed the core of the attack fleet. Each pilot was assigned a specific target, based on the Japanese Imperial Navy knowing exactly the location of each vessel in Pearl Harbor as a result of regular reports from a naval intelligence officer assigned to the Japanese Consulate in Honolulu. This man would visit a restaurant in Aiea, above Pearl Harbor, and as he sipped coffee he studied the movement of ships, reporting his observations to Japan on a daily basis.

I am told that Uncle Tamotsu was assigned to bomb the *S.S. Arizona.* Depending on the location of each target, either a torpedo or a bomb was used. Because the *Arizona* was anchored alongside the repair ship *Vestal,* it could not be torpedoed, so bombs were dropped on it from above. Tamotsu successfully returned to the *Kaga* and returned to Japan. My relatives showed me three medals he had received from the Emperor.

I thought back to how I had been studying in my room in Honolulu early that Sunday morning when the air-raid sirens started wailing. I could never have imagined then that my own uncle was piloting one of the planes that was raining bombs down on the American fleet in Pearl Harbor. Because Mother had just returned from visiting in Japan, Uncle Tamotsu was probably quite aware of her presence in Hawaii, though not the exact location.

For nearly half a century after this revelation, I tried to verify the story of Uncle Tamotsu through sources other than my own relatives. Whenever the war or Pearl Harbor came up with Japanese, I would relate the story, but without result. Then, one day, in the late 1990s I was having lunch with two gentlemen in New York from Kawasaki Heavy Industries, which had produced armaments during the war. They arranged for me to meet with one of their senior executives, Admiral Yoshida, who had joined Kawasaki in an advisory capacity after he retired as a staff officer with Japan's Self Defense Force. Admiral Yoshida said Uncle Tamotsu was almost undoubtedly assigned to the *Kaga* or one of four other carriers that participated in the Pearl Harbor attack. He referred me to Takeshi Maeda, chairman of a group of former naval officers called the *Unabarakai* that included a number of the survivors from the Pearl Harbor attack. Maeda telephoned me at my hotel while I was staying in Tokyo. When I mentioned my name and my Uncle Tamotsu Shibata's name, there was a sudden silence. Apparently, he was surprised. He took my name and telephone number, then abruptly hung up. Not long thereafter, he called back and arranged to meet me at the hotel. Maeda said he had been assigned to the aircraft carrier *Kaga* with my uncle after graduating from the same Third Class of the *Yokaren* naval flight school.

Subsequently he published a book detailing his Third Flight Training Class in the Japanese Navy. Both he and Uncle Tamotsu were Flight Petty Officers, Second Class, and had graduated together. According to Maeda, Tamotsu was a skillful and dedicated pilot, and also a quiet man who kept to himself. The two had gone through intensive training in different parts of Japan, but their home base was along Lake Kasumigaura in Ibaragi Prefecture, close to the Pacific Ocean, beyond Chiba Prefecture. The title of

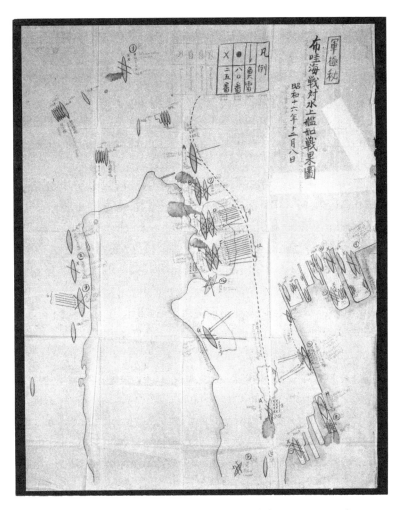

Map of Pearl Harbor, Hawaii, carried by Tamotsu Shibata on December 7, 1941

Takeshi Maeda's book derived from the fact that as the pilots left from their home base, they would face Mount Tsukuba with their planes and pay their respects as they took off. The training was intense. Accuracy was their prime concern. Mr. Maeda claimed some of them could drop a bomb into a large factory chimney. To become familiar with the situation and terrain at Pearl Harbor, the training took place in South Kyushu in a coastal area that resembled Pearl Harbor.

In the decades following the war, Maeda has been active with other veteran naval officers and joined in returning to Hawaii in 1991 to attend the 50th Anniversary remembrance of the attack. There he met a number of

American servicemen who had survived Pearl Harbor, and who had, also, participated in those ceremonies. There is a Pearl Harbor Association in Japan with about 300 members who meet once a year. A fairly large delegation from Takeshi Maeda's group also was in Hawaii for the September 1-4, 1995 ceremonies marking the 50th anniversary of the war's end. They went there to present a friendship plaque to the Punchbowl National Memorial Cemetery of the Pacific looking to a "New Beginning."

I had read in the family register in Fukuoka that Tamotsu had been killed in the war in the eastern part of the Pacific Ocean. With the advance of the war in 1942, the capture and occupation of the strategic Midway Island became crucial to Japan's war effort. By taking Midway, Japan would be able to dominate a large area of the central Pacific even if the United States Navy was able to do rapid repair work in Hawaii.

By the time the Battle of Midway got under way on June 6, 1942, the U.S. had broken the Japanese code and knew Japan's exact plans for Midway. As the Japanese Navy approached Midway for the attack, it was surprised by the presence of the U.S. Navy that took the offensive. The attack by our naval air force was one of the fiercest battles of all time. Since Japan had planned to bomb the island of Midway prior to invading and occupying it, their planes were loaded with bombs. Facing the aerial onslaught of the U.S. Navy, the crew on the carrier *Kaga* tried in haste to unload the bombs manually and reload each fighter plane with torpedoes, which were to be used to attack the U.S. Navy ships. While they struggled to make that change, several bombs hit the *Kaga* and my uncle Tamotsu and hundreds of others trapped in it were killed.

The *Kaga* had been crippled, but not torpedoed below the water line, so it did not sink. Rather than have it fall into American hands, the Japanese Navy torpedoed and sank it to avoid being captured by the enemy. It lies to this day at the bottom of the Pacific, close to Midway, the underwater grave of so many, including my Uncle Tamotsu.

CHAPTER SIX

Back to Civilian Life

I stayed overnight with my mother's family in Yamaguma, Fukuoka Pre-fecture before returning to CIC Headquarters in Sapporo. By visiting my relatives, I had thus satisfied one of the purposes I had in signing up for another year and going to Japan. It was now time to start thinking seriously about resuming my civilian career and returning to college. My military work was interesting, though, and life was pleasant, with a great deal of freedom and camaraderie among fellow officers at headquarters. The war had been over for some two years, and we were not involved in combat duty, so we were able to make some positive contributions to the rebuild-ing and democratization of Japan. As a mess officer, I was in control of ice cream that we received from the 11th Airborne Division in Sapporo, and one December, I arranged a Christmas party for an orphanage there operated by Catholic missionaries. After saving the weekly ration of candies and cig-arettes, I sold them to buy suitable toys and gifts. We were able to sell the cigarettes at a substantial profit, which we also used to buy information from various sources for our investigative work. After a short Christmas program with ice cream, candies, cookies, and the distribution of toys, we showed a movie that I had borrowed from the 11th Airborne unit, sight unseen. It was *Scarface*, shown primarily to rugged military personnel, not suitable at all for 8 to 10-year olds and it had a lot of scary scenes. The kids were horrified. Later, I learned that some of the children had had night-mares that night. I wonder if any of them still remember that traumatic event of their childhood? This is the kind of unofficial activity that many

Japanese Americans in MIS were engaged in during the Occupation of Japan. It made our presence less traumatic and unpleasant since we were able to communicate with them freely while easily understanding their culture and customs.

Many MIS members throughout Japan, in addition to their official duties, helped the Japanese in many ways. One of such example was the planting of cherry trees in a community by Waimo Takaki and his group. There are many other similar stories and the National Japanese American Veterans Council is gathering such stories to complete the MIS Story that will be published by Dr. James MacNaughton, Command Historian of the Army. These stories of MIS during the occupation of Japan will be published eventually on the web site of the Japanese American National Museum. What the MIS did in Japan can be a good example of how the United States should be prepared in occupying any country. We must always know our enemy, as well as our customers in business, in order to succeed.

Several months later, in April of 1947, a few of us began preparations to leave for home. I was called in by my commanding officer, Major George Gargette, and his Executive Officer Captain Shigeru Tsubota, also from Hawaii, to talk about my future. They wanted to have me extend my service for several more years because of a number of important investigations going on at our CIC unit in Sapporo, Hokkaido, including the two teams of espionage agents from Russian-occupied Sakhalin that we had compromised and were using to send misleading information to the Soviets. I was promised immediate promotion to First Lieutenant and, as soon as military regulations permitted, to Captain. I was 24 years old then and I had already served three-and-one-half years in the Army. It was long enough. Not that life was unpleasant, but the work was not challenging and Army life during peacetime seemed unfulfilling for me. It was a tempting offer, but I opted for education and the career that I had laid out for myself some time ago.

In May 1947, I sailed for home and then registered for summer session

Sogi Family in Hawaii, 1947. Back row, left to right: Chiyoko, Harold I.,
Paul H., and Francis Y. Sogi. Front row: Yoshiemon and Nami Sogi

at the University of Hawaii, by which time a large proportion of the student body was composed of veterans. Military equipment of all kinds were being sold by the U.S. Army, including old Jeeps for $25 and up to $100, depending on the condition of the vehicle. I purchased one from a military base in Honolulu for $25, sight unseen, because it was the cheapest one available. It was a gamble I lost: the pistons were frozen and it required a major overhaul and refurbishing. My brother, Harold, being a mechanic, helped me greatly in making it operative. It became usable as a means of transportation and to chauffeur around my dates during the next two years at the University.

Despite minor pains of readjusting to civilian life, I soon found myself coasting along in a new flow of study and social life. I have always been optimistic in life and believed things would always fall into place or work out for the good of the whole, even if only out of sheer luck. Although my life had taken different turns, this could be attributed to the decisions I had made or the effort I put into whatever I had decided to do.

So the first major chapter of my life came to an end on May 27, 1947, when I was discharged formally from active service in the U.S. Army. I remained in the active reserve for many years thereafter, first in the Hawaii Territorial National Guard then in the U. S. Army Reserve Corps in New York, until my retirement from it as a Captain

There was neither much time nor opportunity for dissipation of any kind and no predilection towards it, at least, not until well into my career as a lawyer, a result of association with clients in Japan and New York. This I saw as a necessary evil for the development of my career and clientele. But in the simpler, agricultural community in Kona in which I grew up, things were different. Most farmers in Kona were slim and had physical stamina because of the healthy, lean diet rich in protein (all kinds of conceivable amino acids), vegetables, fruits, an abundance of fresh fish of all kinds, much chicken meat and a little beef or pork. I recall reading somewhere that lack of proper diet in any age bracket will catch up with the individual after two decades or so. For example, lack of proper food in the teens will affect the individual's health in the 30s, much junk food in the 20s will show its bad effects in that person's 40s, and so on. The one staple that we could not raise or acquire off the land was rice. This, along with other things not native to Hawaii, such as dried codfish, shrimp, or dried minnows, we purchased from the Komo Store or American Factors. In later years, I counted the number of vegetables and fruits we raised and that were available naturally in the woods of Kona. I was amazed that there were more than 30 varieties that we consumed almost daily.

Plans for my career began with my high school ambition to study law though I had not the slightest idea as to how I would finance it or even where I would study. (There was no law school in Hawaii during the late 1940s and early 1950s.) A law career seemed to have a polar attraction, for gradually I was pulled towards it as by a force of nature. It was almost as if it were a part of evolution in my small world. My mother often mentioned the "Great Book" she said existed in the Buddhist religion. According to this idea, everyone had a predestined life as set forth in this book. She could not explain whether the course ever changed with exercise of individual will or by means of happenings in the world beyond the control of the individual. This book took into account all such happenings and occurrences, and predestination forged ahead unhampered. This was my mother, formally uneducated, but a fine human, a practical psychologist and a philosopher.

GI BILL OF RIGHTS

Military service had opened windows of opportunities for further education to many veterans. Having served more than three years on active duty, I was entitled to five academic years of education, which meant the two remaining years at the University of Hawaii and three years of law school for me. This eliminated the economic uncertainty that faced me and many other veterans. In addition to the payment of tuition, there was a monthly stipend of $90 for bachelors and $125 a month for married veterans attending school. I was able to use almost all of my benefits to fund not only my two years at the University of Hawaii and three years of law school at Fordham University in New York City, but also to obtain my license to practice law in New York after I passed the bar examination. However, I could not legitimately find use for the last $25, alas, no matter how hard I tried.

Since I had to become an officer in the U, S. Army Reserve, I attended training sessions every Wednesday in New York City for two hours, for which I received $75 a week, and spent two summer weeks at training camp for which I received a couple of hundred dollars. While working in Japan from 1953 to 1955, I attended summer camp there, which gave me commissary privileges. This meant I was able to purchase food, clothing, appliances, liquor, and other things at considerably reduced prices.

Another benefit that came from military service was the opportunity to study Japanese at Camp Savage and Fort Snelling for nine months. I taught the language for about two years, giving me considerable language capability that I would not have acquired otherwise. My service in the Occupation Forces enabled me to polish my conversational Japanese, as our studies had been concerned primarily with reading, writing, and translating. When I completed law school, I was hired immediately by one of the largest and most reputable firms dealing with Japanese clients from pre-war days in New York City because of this language training. It gave me a tremendous boost in my career as an international lawyer.

The discipline of military service also served me well throughout life. We learned early that life should be orderly and structured. Everything requires planning and knowing. As plans are merely guidelines, many changes might be necessary. Flexibility and alternative plans must be built in to meet contingencies. This is done to avoid surprises and to avoid frustration and anxiety when plans cannot be accomplished or must be changed. Improvisation was an important element in all of this. The universe appears chaotic but it is completely harmonious, with every planet or body moving in a fixed course and in its place for the scheme of the whole universe. Occasional collisions may occur but this is not an indication of disharmony or chaos of any kind. When there is order in our lives, there is an inner security that gives confidence and optimism. Life in Kona was like this and I floated with the Kona wind riding to wherever it took me with confidence.

BACK TO SCHOOL

After my return from military service, I immediately registered for summer session at the University of Hawaii (UH) to expedite my undergraduate work with law school in mind. I continued at UH for the next two years, graduating in 1949 and then headed for New York to attend law school. The students were serious in their studies, as many had battlefield experience and hard military training, and were several years older than the regular students. Those who volunteered with me returned en masse, such as Richard Kosaki, Kazuo Nishikawa, the late Ralph Miwa, Wallace Amioka, Theodore Wakai, the late Sohei Yamate, Sidney Kan, Shiro Amioka, Sam

Isokane, Andrew Sato, Gilbert Hayashi, Yoshiaki Fujitani and many others. The late Ralph Miwa and Richard Kosaki and I talked often about all three of us going to law school but they became scholars after getting their doctorates from the University of Minnesota and Johns Hopkins University, respectively. Ralph Miwa and I were very close in the MIS, spending many furloughs and weekends together to visit Chicago and the Wylies and Nelsons in Racine and La Crosse, Wisconsin. He was a prolific writer and active in school publications. Richard Kosaki was a Phi Beta Kappa and had been student-body president of the University of Hawaii. Unfortunately, Ralph passed away while fairly young, but his wife, Hilda, and their three children carry on Ralph's legacy: their son Colin is today a partner in one of the prestigious law firms in Honolulu. Another Army buddy, Kazuo Nishikawa, seemed destined to go to medical school all throughout our Army life, but he got married in Japan and then finally settled in Washington, DC, where he worked for the CIA (Central Intelligence Agency) although no one would say or intimate this was so.

MOVE TO NEW YORK AND MARRIAGE

Upon my return from service, Sarah and I continued where we had left off in 1944 when I volunteered for the military. She had already graduated from the University of Hawaii in 1945 and was working at St. Andrews Episcopal Church but decided to go to Columbia Presbyterian Medical School on a scholarship for the School of Occupational Therapy. This was in 1948, and she left in late summer after we were engaged. My proposal to her was marked by a humorous incident. Sarah was living in an apartment with her sister, Emi, and her mother, so one evening I visited there to ask her mother if she would agree to our marriage (Sarah's father had died in 1944). I remember the radio was on when I got there. Typical of the anxious suitor, I harnessed significant courage to ask her mother if she had any objections and, informing her that we would be married in New York where I was planning to attend school. Just then, on the radio, we heard the voice of a young man asking the father of his girl friend for permission to marry his

Wedding of Francis Y. Sogi and Sarah M. Sogi, June 17, 1949

daughter. The father said, "Young man, are you asking for my daughter's hand?" and the suitor, being nervous and flustered, said, "Yes, if that is what you are serving." It must have been dinner time. Happily, both Sarah and her mother agreed to my proposal.

When I arrived in New York in 1949, LaGuardia was the only major airport in the city. Sarah was living in a cold-water flat at 120 Thompson Street with her brother Sam and his wife, Marietta, who were attending Columbia Teacher's College for their advanced degrees. As I got off the plane, a four-engine propeller plane, I saw Sarah in the observation area waiting for me, my wife-to-be for life. We took a cab into the city and had lunch at the newly opened Trattoria Restaurant facing Times Square at 44th Street and Broadway. The cab driver took the long route across the Triboro Bridge and not the Midtown Tunnel, and the total fare was three dollars plus, quite a bit for someone on a very tight budget who was just about to be married. I had a savings account that was quite special because my sister Chiyoko had started it for me when I was in high school, giving me the first $100 in the account. I kept on saving from my work with the National Youth Administration at $4 per month, the pay at Kona Inn, the tips there, and the yard work I did for the executives of American Factors who lived across from Kona Inn. By the time I came to New York I had a comfortable amount of savings.

The apartment at 120 Thompson Street, at the corner of Prince Street, was a five-floor cold-water walk-up flat with no heating and no bathroom as such except a room with the basic necessities. There was a small bedroom with a small living room and a kitchen/dining room combination. We moved in after Sam and Marietta had gone to Europe on a work/study tour for the summer. The rent was $18 a month, and it was adequate for students going to school. Later, after we moved uptown, the rent was raised to $20 and everyone was up in arms because of the exorbitant increase, but the landlord was relentless.

Sarah had made all the arrangements for the wedding at the little chapel at the Riverside Church through the Rev. Galen Weaver, who had been our minister at the Church of the Crossroads in Honolulu. She ordered a wedding cake from Schraffts, well known at that time for food and pastries. The Rev. Masao and Ai Yamada, Sarah's brother-in-law and older sister, who were in the orchid culture business as a hobby, sent the flowers for our wedding from Hawaii. They later became internationally famous as orchidologists and attended orchid conferences in different parts of the world. They even had their own creation named after Masao. Masao had been chaplain of the 442nd Regimental Combat Team during World War II. He was the first Asian American chaplain in the U.S. Army. For his role as a chaplain, Masao was one of those included at the Smithsonian exhibition on the 442nd, in a display that was provided by Ai Yamada. A collection of his letters from European battle fronts is on display at the Library of Congress.

For our wedding, my best man was Arthur Mori, whom I knew at Fort Snelling and in Tokyo while I was with ATIS, CIC, and later at the University of Hawaii. The maid of honor was Haruko Nakamatsu, one of Sarah's best friends and our classmate from Konawaena, who was working as a nurse in New Jersey. The day before the wedding, the promised flowers did not arrive and we were quite anxious about them but they arrived the next morning, generally in good condition. There was *maile* (vine with aroma) and many decorative greens and a variety of orchids for us and the maid of honor and best man. The night before, Osamu Shimizu and Arthur Mori took me out for a bachelor's party at McSorley's in the East Village at 7th Street, where we had ale. That was their specialty and it was all they served. It was a hangout for college men, as no women were allowed. Even the owner, who inherited the place from her father, could not go in. At midnight, a gong sounded. Customers were required to leave if they had had enough, and if they did not have enough by then, they had to go anyway and this was their policy.

Osamu Shimizu was a Canadian Nisei who was working for his Ph.D. and teaching at the Asian Studies Department at Columbia, specializing in Japanese history and language. He volunteered for the Military Intelligence Service from New York. He was much older than most of us since he had already graduated from a Canadian college and from Keio University. Osamu was an Olympic-quality diver and had a chance to participate in the Olympic tryouts from Japan but turned it down and returned to Canada. He had a car in the Army, and whenever the girls in town invited us to dinner or to social functions, we always invited him, especially during the cold winter, so that we were assured of a mode of transportation. Once, fellow instructor Iwao Suzuki's girl friend was having a group of girls at her apartment and Suzuki asked Mike Okusa, another instructor, and me to join them. With design aforethought, we invited Osamu, or Shim as he was called. It was at that function that he met his future wife.

Sarah invited her O. T. classmates from Columbia to our wedding on June 17, 1949. Those who came were Alice Brown from Connecticut, Millie

Finkel of New Jersey, Vera Resonovitch of New York City and her brother Sam's friends and neighbors Bob Ikari and Larry Kim, who were also from Hawaii. Harry Oshima, also studying for his degree at Columbia, was there with his wife, Chiye. He later earned his doctorate in economics, became an internationally renowned economist on national incomes, and eventually moved to the Philippines. Other guests included Sanford Yanagi and Chic Chikasuye, both architects working in the city. A surprise unexpected guest was Margaret Killam, a childhood friend whom Sarah had known as a girl in Kona. Jim Hicks and Mildred Barbarite were also present at our wedding. Jim was our most liberal leftist New York friend with whom we used to spend many a happy weekend with his other friends at the "Nutshell," an old cottage in Huntington, Long Island, New York.

When I visited New York in 1944 and 1946 while I was still in the Army, I met Otho J. Hicks, formerly with Lord & Taylor's industrial relations department. That meeting had been arranged through my brother, Paul, who had met Jim in Hawaii during the war. Jim, originally from Minnesota, was head of the United Seamen's Service, which was established by oil and shipping companies to operate special service clubs in various ports of the world wherever U.S. ships called. They served the same function as the military USOs. Jim traveled extensively in his position as the executive director. His friends were also our friends: Mildred Barbarite, (who worked at Lord & Taylor in the mail department and retired after more than 60 years of service); Grace and Bill Marvin, fellow Minnesotans; and Jack Kamaiko and Bob and Jo Andrews from the Midwest. Others who came to the wedding included Ed Settee of USS, Jackie and Lloyd Kershaw and a few others. All of these people were liberals and supporters of Vice President Wallace. Some were quite far to the left and some of them as "far left as quarter to nine" and they always challenged the government. On the other hand, they were all intellectuals who were well read. We were not particularly in the same stream politically but it just so happened that we associated with them. We seldom talked politics, however.

At the wedding, Sarah had arranged for music that included a Hawaiian wedding song *Ke Kali Ne Au.* There were about 60 to 65 people, including one or two of whom we did not recognize but welcomed as friends of those who were invited. Sam gave Sarah away. Sam was a professional photographer before he came to New York, and he took pictures of the occasion. Waichi Takemoto and his wife, Chiyono Kuwaye, who were attending Columbia for their masters in teaching, were our guests, as were Richard Furuno and a few others. We got together with them during weekends and often played bridge at our apartment. One member of Sarah's class at Columbia who was not able to attend was Jirina Pospicholova from Czechoslovakia, whom we fondly called "Pepsi Cola." She visited our apartment often and we saw a great deal of her. She was a scholarship student sponsored by the World Health Organization and returned to her country soon after graduation from Occupational Therapy School at Columbia Presbyterian Medical School.

Our wedding ceremony at the chapel of Riverside Church was simple and short and went as we had rehearsed it a week before at Galen Weaver's residence in Scarsdale, New York. Afterwards, there was a reception in an apartment on 23rd Street that Alice Brown and her friend were renting but vacated temporarily because she and her boyfriend (and future husband), Herbert Bainton, had gone to Europe on a bicycle trip. Herbert was the son of a renowned scholar of religion at Yale. Alice was tall and well bred, a graduate of Smith College, with the gentlest of personalities and always gracious and very considerate. She always called Sarah "Little Sarah." They were good friends and we continue to see them even after their six children had all grown up. They still live in Woodbridge, Connecticut, in the home Alice knew as a child. We got to know many of the children of Herb and Alice through the years, especially Cynthia, a sensitive and artistic woman, who developed and launched a successful card designing business. She became known for her whimsical, unique and characteristic "hokey birds" and animals. She is married and happily ensconced now in Florida. Valerie married and moved to Colorado. The oldest son Arthur we did not get to know very well. Neal went to Russia and became quite knowledgeable about that country. Another daughter married and runs an optical business with her husband. The sixth and last child of the family lives in California with her Japanese American husband.

The reception was simple and we had the usual wine, champagne, beer, and other drinks. The wedding cake turned out to be a fruitcake that was so hard we could barely cut it, causing some laughter. After some struggle and more laughs, I managed to cut it through. The next day we took the bus to the Poconos in Pennsylvania for our honeymoon without any plan or reservation anywhere but we managed to find a small summer cottage with a lake where we stayed for about a week of bliss before returning back to city life by bus to New York. By then, Sam and Marietta had left for Europe and so we moved into their apartment at 120 Thompson Street in colorful Greenwich Village in Manhattan, returning the 23rd Street apartment to Alice and her friend, who returned from Europe at about that time.

Sarah began her training at different hospitals, including Mt. Sinai, Bedford Hills, Hospital for Special Surgery, and New York Psychiatric. Jirina Pospicholova of the then Czechoslovakia with whom Sarah became good friends, left for home and we had no contact for many years. We learned later that she was married with two children. The country was then under the control of the Communist Party and she became a Party member though her husband and children did not become members. Like Hungary and Poland, the country had improved economically although it was not at all a free market. Still, the people were able to purchase many things but were not free to travel abroad. Many years later we visited Jirina in Brno. We traveled on the Orient Express, on the way home from Vienna, where we had attended the International Bar Association's International Peace Through Law Conference.

LIFE IN THE "ASPHALT JUNGLE"

During the summer of 1949, while Sam and Marietta were away, we stayed in their fifth floor apartment while looking for our own. There was no air conditioning at 120 Thompson Street so it was necessary to open the windows to let the wind blow through the corner apartment. This meant we could hear the traffic, sirens, and the conversations of the patrons from the bar on the first floor of the building, who often sat outside on the sidewalk, talking well into the night and often into the wee hours of the morning. At other times, we would see a man with a monkey and a music box performing shows on the street below. We had to walk down five floors every morning and back up again at night. In these old unheated buildings, the kitchen was the warmest place in the apartment and served as the social center. You entered the apartment through the kitchen, so if you were invited in, you usually stayed in the kitchen to chat. On the way up in the evening, Sarah was often invited in for tea by an Italian lady who lived on the third-floor apartment with her husband and a son. Being a very curious soul, she always looked through a crack in the door to see who was going up or down. She was a very good cook, though, and often gave us Italian cookies or pieces of cake. By stopping to visit with her often, Sarah learned how to cook Italian spaghetti sauce with hot sausages. For hours, she would cook the tomato paste and tomatoes from cans with Italian sausages, both sweet and hot, and with onions, garlic, and other vegetables. Of course, the olives or olive oil that we added gave a special flavor and made the sauce stick to the spaghetti or to the linguini that we used.

While waiting to start law school in the fall, I worked that summer as a counterman at a chain of coffee shops. The pay was not bad and the hours were decent. I had to learn the lingo, such as "draw" for coffee, "O.J." for orange juice, "to travel" for take-out orders, and so on. This gave me my first insight into the humanity of New York City. All kinds of people came into these places. Early in the morning were the laborers, the hardhats, janitors, and others, then the clerks and those with shirts and ties, and still others with suits and ties. All behaved differently, ordered differently, and ate and tipped differently. Many were regulars for breakfast or lunch. One Chinese man who came in for lunch always ate the same ham omelet, toast and hash browns, and coffee with no milk or cream. He would sit down, I would nod, he would nod and the food came out. He ate, he paid, never tipped, and left. I could almost tell what time it was by his arrival.

FORDHAM UNIVERSITY SCHOOL OF LAW

By the middle of summer, to my great relief, notice of acceptance came from Fordham University Law School, which at the time was located at 302 Broadway at Duane Street, just west of the federal, state and city courts, two blocks north of Chambers Street, City Hall, Brooklyn Bridge, and the Hall of Records where the Surrogates Court was located. It was also six blocks from Chinatown. When school started, I found myself in the morning session with about 60 in my class. There was a fairly good diversity of students, with a Chinese American, a Spanish American, an African American, and a woman in my class. The rest were Jews from New York and Catholics from the various Catholic colleges. One classmate, Thomas Sullivan, later became the District Attorney of Staten Island. There was also Jack Lynch, who was a Bronx Democratic leader and who formed his own firm in New York, as did George D'Amato. Raphael Murphy, whose father was a judge in The Bronx, became general counsel at Union Carbide, a long-term client of Hunt, Hill & Betts. John Mazzola from Bayonne, New Jersey, worked for Millbank Tweed and then for the Rockefeller family before becoming president of Lincoln Center. I got along very well and was friendly with James LeFebre, who was older than most of us. After graduation, he got married and settled down in Torrington, Connecticut. After graduation, we had a few get-togethers at reunions and alumni luncheons, but our paths have not crossed for many years.

On the first day at school, I went up to the library, where the librarian Jim Kennedy asked me if I was a first-year student. I told him my name. He said it was a short name but a difficult one, and announced that my name would be "Monaghan." For three years in the library, I was "Frank Monaghan." I also worked there as his part-time helper. This was valuable to me because he had special textbooks that were not generally available. Suddenly, they would be available for my use. Dean Wilkinson, who taught one of the second-year courses, always reminded us that he was the thirteenth *summa cum laude* at the law school, so he was always hopeful and optimistic that there would be a fourteenth. Godfrey Schmidt taught us Natural Law, Labor Law, and Constitutional Law. He was a labor specialist and the personal counsel to Cardinal Spellman. He was a good teacher, and I admired him for his eloquence and knowledge of the law. Schmidt was also on the Atomic Energy Commission and often made trips to Seattle where the Commission met regularly. He was a Jesuit-school product and a devout Catholic. He told a story about one of his return trips from Seattle, sitting next to a sailor who was very absorbed in a book he was reading. Our professor, who was reading a book on St. Thomas Aquinas, happened to see the title of the sailor's book, *The Private Life of a Harlot,* which may have been that day's *Mayflower Madam.* As the years passed, I was very surprised to learn and read in the paper that Godfrey Schmidt had been indicted and prosecuted for tax evasion. Then, later, I came across his name when he served papers on one of our clients on a small claim of some kind and wanted an extension of time. His office location was not much, and he appeared to be practicing alone. I was surprised by the turn of events for this once-powerful man.

Korean War

The Korean War broke out in June of 1950. Later that year, we received word at reserve training that Hector Dowd, another lawyer and reservist, and two others, including myself, must report to active duty the following Monday to go overseas to Korea. We were all attached to the First Army and were ordered to Governors Island for induction procedure. This was devastating news, as I had just served my time in the Army and I was set on a legal career. I was doing very well at school and was enjoying it. I was spending many hours after school doing research at the school library or at the New York Public Library. Sarah, who had completed her school and training, was about to start at Kings County Hospital in Brooklyn. She was very unhappy, too. During the days until that fateful Monday, I felt as if the whole building was coming down upon me. I have never had a real tragedy or death in the family, except Masaru in the war, and the news of my call-up was devastating. I was ready to resign my commission. I no longer felt the need to serve my country any more, at least not now in the midst of my professional education. Finally, Monday came and we reported to the First Army Headquarters on Governors Island. It was one of the most unpleasant trips I have ever made in New York. When we met the officer in charge at headquarters, we were told that the call was a mistake, since the Army was looking for those who were not actively training in reserve status. You cannot imagine my relief. We took off from Governors Island so fast that we forgot to inform the Army officials of our decision that we wanted to resign from the active reserve and our commissioned status. We were later informed that for the duration of the Korean War, no one was permitted to change his status.

Taking the ferry from Governors Island back to Manhattan was a short few minutes, not at all like the overnight trip to Honolulu from Kona more than 10 years earlier. But both these voyages confirmed my growing sense that I had accomplished much and was flowing ahead still riding the Kona wind. From Kona schools through college, and through the MIS School and the Occupation in Japan, I began to have the feeling that it was entirely up to me as to what I wanted to be and where I wanted to go in life. I began to realize even more the vast possibilities of riding the Kona wind as far, or as high as, I wanted to go. My memory of life in Kona was then still very fresh in my mind and comes back to me in many different situations in different ways. This refreshing feeling stems from my roots in Kona. It may be an atypical community of the United States, but the experience and the story of the people of Kona are archetypal.

CHAPTER SEVEN

Early Days in New York

AFTER LEAVING THE temporary fifth-floor walkup on Thompson Street, Sarah and I moved to an apartment at 107 West 109th Street in Manhattan, next to the famous Women's Hospital. Our first-floor studio apartment there cost us $45 a month with linen service. We succeeded the Roy Kuriharas, who had lived there previously. His wife was a Takami from the famous family of doctors in Brooklyn. We later moved upstairs to the fifth floor. This one-bedroom apartment had the same amenities but was without the noise of the garbage trucks coming in at 5 a.m. clankety-clanging the trashcans outside our first-floor apartment. In the building also were Haru and Frank Okazaki who had a private accounting practice and with whom I socialized and worked together professionally for many years, referring many Japanese clients to him until he retired at age 60, a requirement of the firm he merged with, Peat Marwick Mitchell & Company. Frank started this firm's Japanese practice after the merger, contributing greatly to their growth and development. He and his current wife, Fran, were happily retired in Banning, California; unfortunately, he passed away at a fairly young age. His first wife, Haru had predeceased him earlier.

Another neighbor at 107 West 109th Street was Tami Ogata, a nutritionist, who retired to California, and who remains a very long-time friend. Sarah used to listen to her radio broadcasts in which she gave learned talks on nutrition. She was an active participant in demonstrations and in walks dealing with civil rights and peace, as well as Japanese American causes demanding justice and redress for abrogation of constitutional rights and redress of wrongs committed during World War II. Tami was one of those 120,000 Japanese Americans imprisoned in America's concentration camps. During the cold winter when days were short and nights were long, we usually had tea on weekends in the afternoon. Her apartment was immediately below ours, and an uncovered hot water pipe passed through our two flats. At the appropriate time, we would tap several times on the pipe as a signal for tea time.

On an upper floor was Cissy Suyat, a Filipino student from Hawaii, who later married Thurgood Marshall, the first African American Associate Justice of the Supreme Court of the United States. She still lives in Washington, D.C. with her family, her husband having died several years ago. Our neighbors next door were the Kagawas from Hawaii, Shoso and Kay, who were going to school in New York. They returned to Hawaii where Shoso settled and became a successful architect.

Another couple that Sarah and I associated with in New York during our school days was Tadashi and Kiyoko Sato. Tadashi has been an artist as well as a student of art for a number of years. He was true to his calling and would not compromise his situation and do commercial art that would have brought him immediate income. He made only one exception, telling us how he took advantage of an opportunity to paint a portrait of Charles Laughton, the famous Hollywood actor of the time.

Tadashi later went to Japan and did wood block prints as well as *sumi-e*, black ink art and calligraphy, although it does not seem as though he pursued this line of art insofar as I am aware. In later years we noticed only his paintings of a particular style that is readily recognizable with his very special touch. For example, while we were dining at Halekulani Hotel one evening, years after our retirement and return to Hawaii, a large painting in the lobby area attracted our attention. By the style of the painting, we felt certain that it was by Tadashi Sato and it was. He is now a renowned, a well established artist in Hawaii, with many paintings and artworks in many museums and prominent locations throughout the islands. Sarah and I also saw a retrospective of his work at the Museum of Contemporary Art of

Honolulu, and we were astounded and amazed at the tremendous number of works of art that he has produced, and with his very own distinctive style.

The McCarthy Era

A part of the early 1950s was known as the McCarthy Era in the United States. Many famous people, both in and outside of government, were called in before Congressional committees to have their names tainted with trumped-up charges of being left-wingers. These people were castigated by Senator Joseph McCarthy and his cohort, Roy Cohn, who served as counsel in the Senator's committee hearings. Robert Morgenthau, the Manhattan District Attorney, spent many years going after Cohn, and finally indicted him on many counts but couldn't convict him. The rumor is that Cohn mistreated or maligned Morgenthau's father, who was FDR's Secretary of the Treasury, and that this was his vendetta. Cohn finally died of AIDS in the 1980s. Another man crucified by McCarthy was Owen Lattimore, under whom the late Ralph Miwa, a classmate and close friend of mine, studied at Johns Hopkins University and whom he admired greatly, in the early 1950s. *Ordeal by Slander* was Lattimore's version of this witch hunt.

I attended many court trials while at Fordham Law School because the courts in Foley Square were only several blocks away. When judges saw law students in the audience, they would take pains to explain their rulings in court for our benefit. It was a live class in action, especially on procedural matters.

None of our liberal friends and progressive Wallace-ites were called in or questioned by the McCarthy hearings. They included Harry and Chiye Oshima and Sam and Marietta Mukaida, graduate students at Columbia, who received their doctorates. Liberalism was the trend of the time, an "in" ideology with intellectuals and academics. Wealth was not a criterion, for Corliss Lamont, a person of considerable wealth in his own right, was one of the most liberal of many others similarly situated. They all participated in liberal causes and, of course, were stigmatized with all kinds of labels by the conservatives, especially after Eisenhower became president in 1952, riding the tide of the military victory in Europe.

Otho J. Hicks, executive director of the United Seaman's Service (USS) was as liberal as they came. He hailed from Minnesota and worked in industrial relations at Lord & Taylor, where he met Mildred Barbarite, who had been working in the shipping department since she was 15. He spent some time as a newspaper reporter before taking on the position with United Seamen's Service (USS), which was formed by oil and shipping companies to take care of sailors and others sent overseas, where they could enjoy American cooking and atmosphere while away from home. He would say, "I would rather make several left turns to go in the direction than that which a right turn would take me."

I was somewhat naive and apolitical when I arrived in New York, concentrating primarily on my legal studies, which fascinated me. My studies brought me unlimited challenges and the belief that any cause can be won with imagination and creativity if supported with the right arguments and legal precedents. Or, if there were no precedents, a judge or jury could be convinced of the righteousness of your cause if you appealed to their sense of social justice and psychology. A lawyer is truly a conservative of the past, a liberal of the present, and a radical of the future. I discovered how the great legal minds, such as Oliver Wendell Holmes, Benjamin Cardozo, and Louis Brandeis, made the law a living thing. They kept up with the times and interpreted the law and established precedents to fit changing times.

One of the most memorable trials I attended in New York during my law school days was that of Alger Hiss, who was being tried for perjury, with Whittaker Chambers as the Government's principal witness. Both had been in Communist cells in the 1930s when it was fashionable for intellectuals to join them. Hiss denied this and was found guilty of perjury, but until his death he was not able to redeem himself. Hiss had been one of the top aides to Franklin D. Roosevelt and accompanied him to the Yalta Conference where the Allied leaders met with Stalin. Another memorable trial involved the Rosenbergs, who were being tried on a charge that they passed on atomic-bomb secrets to the Russians. The trial judge was Irving Kaufman, a Fordham Law School graduate. He sentenced them to death upon being found guilty as charged, and they were executed. A former KGB official revealed later that the information passed on to the Russians by the Rosenbergs was not at all valuable to them. Judge Harold Medina tried another group of reported communists in the federal court in Herald Square. He was famous for the Medina bar-exam cram course. In the early 1950s, there was any number of these high-profile trials going on at Foley Square.

This was a period when the right wing was in the ascendancy, and the scars of this period still remain in the minds of many people. The country should never allow such a thing to happen again to its citizens, any more than its citizens should be incarcerated in concentration camps merely for reasons of color, race, national origin, or beliefs. It was a time of name-calling, when any liberal was called a radical or a commie who could not be trusted, since it was believed they were involved in a conspiracy to topple the government. However, now that the Soviet Union has collapsed and the Communist International, or COMINTERN, is no longer a threat to our national security, liberals are no longer tainted in this way.

Early Days in a Law Firm

In my third year at law school, there was a call for part-time work by a number of law firms in the city. Fordham was rated very highly in New York, and its students were in great demand by the larger firms. A law firm with 50 lawyers was then considered large, although the number today would be any number over 400. But as a student I was attracted to Hunt, Hill & Betts that represented many Japanese clients, near Wall Street in lower Manhattan.

I went down to the firm's offices at 120 Broadway, on the 31st floor of the Equitable Building, just across from Trinity Church, with the grave of Alexander Hamilton in its churchyard. The managing partner who interviewed me told me I was a natural for the firm because of my language ability. George Yamaoka, one of the partners, was a Japanese American from Seattle who had a substantial number of Japanese companies as his clients from pre-war days. After participating in the war-crimes trial in Tokyo as head of the defense team, he and his partner, Bill Logan, who represented Marquis Kido, decided to open an office in Tokyo, in room 886 of the old Marunouchi Building, which had survived the earthquake of 1923 only to be torn down and replaced by a new and taller modern building in the 1990s. Although the firm was traditionally an admiralty firm, its Japanese practice was growing because of its Tokyo office and because of George Yamaoka's reputation from pre-war days in New York. He had also served as counsel to the Japanese Government and was involved in the Naval Conference of 1929 that limited the tonnage of the Japanese Navy. With this connection, Hunt, Hill & Betts grew rapidly as the premier firm handling many major Japanese banks, shipping companies, trading houses, and manufacturers, all interested in learning from the United States, importing American goods, exporting products here, and obtaining licenses for the technology that the United States had developed so rapidly because of the accelerated war effort. It was the leading admiralty firm, having handled major ship collisions and representing many Japanese, European, and Chinese shipowners.

Hunt, Hill & Betts agreed that my Japanese language ability, though really quite rusty by then, would serve their Japanese clients well. I was hired on the spot to work afternoons for four hours at $50 a week. It was big money, but I was really excited by the chance to finally learn and observe experienced lawyers in practice. My future plans were completely unformed at the time. I did not know whether I wanted to practice in New York, or go back to Hawaii, or to where all of this would lead. It was an impulsive decision to go with Hunt, Hill & Betts, but I remembered Taro Suyenaga, who was with me in Fort Snelling, suggesting that I should not return to Hawaii. To this day, I do not regret the decision in accepting this part-time work. If anything else, I was full of optimism and was interested in absorbing as much as I could.

The firm was small, with about 10 partners, including the three named partners, every one of whom was close to 90 years of age, but who still came to the office every day. George Whittefield Betts, Jr., was the youngest of the three and was still practicing law. The firm never grew very large because many of the young promising lawyers attracted to the firm by its reputation would leave when they saw that the named partners were, even at an advanced age, siphoning off income from the younger partners. Only a few loyal ones remained.

Finally, in the summer of 1952, I graduated from law school and participated in an elaborate graduation ceremony at the main campus of Fordham University in the Bronx. I now started to work full time at Hunt, Hill & Betts. The next major step for me was to pass the bar examination, so I enrolled in the Practicing Law Institute's six-week cram course at the Stuyvesant High School auditorium at 15th Street and Second Avenue. I went there mostly at night and had a few sessions on Saturdays. For the bar exams I took on July 1 and 2, 1952, I was fortunate to have been assigned to the New York University Law School auditorium, which was new and was air-conditioned. All others, and all previous exams, had been in locations with no air conditioning like the City Center. July in New York can be unbearably hot and humid. Our location was, as a matter of fact, somewhat chilly, for I was not at the time used to the luxury of air conditioning. The exam was tough and required great concentration, with time allotted to deal with many essay questions. A very good grasp of the law was needed, as well as knowledge of concepts. If the analysis was correct, and you gave good arguments for the answer, credit was given even though it might not have been the answer expected by the examiner. There were, as I learned later, at least 10 legal points involved in each question and we were required to identify and answer at least six correctly in order to pass this portion of the exam.

The first day covered substantive law and the second covered procedures. The second day was much easier. There was not much reasoning involved. After six weeks of studying day and night for the two-day exam, I reported to work and everyone said, of course, they expected me to pass with flying colors. The pressure was excruciating, but I was personally satisfied that, at least, I had recognized and covered, or at least tried to answer, six of the ten points that were involved in each essay question. The multiple choice and the yes-and-no questions were relatively simple, and I was confident that I had passed this part of the exam.

During this time, it was a relief to be able to spend many weekends in Huntington, Long Island, where Otho (Jim) Hicks had custody of a Massachusetts friend's old house, called the "Nutshell" after a reference in Shakespeare. As I recall it, an individual came into this world and found it so cruel and harsh that he wanted to go into a nutshell and call it a kingdom of his own. Sarah and I would join the weekend crowd that would congregate there every Friday night and work in the yard for two days with much drinking, eating, and relaxing. Jim's friends were many liberal intellectuals from past associations and we learned many things by associating with them. There was a teacher, a psychologist, a naval architect, a close ally of Nelson Rockefeller, a writer, and a number of others who were regulars at the Nutshell. This form of weekend socializing and relaxation went on for a number of years until we left for Japan to join our Tokyo office in 1953. Some of the regulars we saw from time to time after returning from Japan were Mildred Barbarite, who lived in Brooklyn once she retired from Lord & Taylor after 60 years; the late Bob and Jo Andrews and their daughter, Tina; Elizabeth Hicks, Jim's niece from Minnesota, and a few others.

At about the end of the summer of 1952, about three months after I took the bar exam, word got around that the results were coming out soon and would be published, as usual, in *The New York Times*. Those who had contacts with the Clerk of the Appellate Division, First Department, which had jurisdiction over lawyers in the city, would know in advance when this was going to happen. They would go to Times Square at about 11 p.m. the night before to pick up the *Times* early edition being delivered to the vendors there. I watched the paper every day but nothing was published. One Monday morning, after a weekend at the Nutshell, I came into the office and some of the associates congratulated me on passing the difficult New York State bar exam. Deep inside I was suspicious because there was too much horsing around, and it could have been a joke. At lunch break, I went to the *Times* office on 43rd Street, west of Times Square, to check the previous Saturday's issue. I finally found the listing. Out of more than two thousand who took the exam, fewer than fifty percent had passed, which was the usual rate. I quickly went through the alphabet to the "S" section, then I looked for the "O" after the "S" and I finally saw my name! What a relief it was.

I had done it. Now it will be Easy Street, I thought. I walked out proudly and went back to the office, facing more congratulations. The next step was the bar-admission and the procedure was cumbersome and time-consuming, as it called for work records from high-school days, any debts, character references, and detailed information from my past.

The firm was also happy that I had passed the bar exam on the first attempt. G. W. Betts, one of the named partners, wrote a letter of recommendation and was a character reference for me. He also obtained a letter from an attorney in the building, whom he knew well, and who had been a former law partner of Franklin D. Roosevelt. When all of the papers were in, we received a call from the Clerk of the Appellate Division for an interview by the Character Committee of the Court. I arrived at the appointed time and waited nearly an hour. When my turn came, a senior judge asked me two questions and the interview was over in about three minutes. He asked me, "First, why did you leave a place like Hawaii and why do you want to become a lawyer?" Little did I realize that the bar admission on December 1, 1952 was to be merely the beginning of a rough and bumpy ride ahead.

On December 1, 1952, I was formally sworn in and admitted to the New York Bar, just five months after I took the bar examination. As if the excitement of my swearing-in were not enough, Sarah chose December 1 to tell me that she was pregnant. Suddenly, in a flash, I saw myself crossing two major milestones: one professional and another personal. In a single moment, it seemed as if that whole, complex wartime era had finally been put behind me. Was it already 11 years since Pearl Harbor had changed my life forever, and the lives of hundreds of millions of people around the globe? Was life finally achieving a kind of normalcy? American life in the 1950s has often been criticized for its banality, conformity, and its acceptance of "Eisenhower" values. But after 20 years of depression and war, the country needed a period of rest and recreation. In Japan, things were very different and far more overwhelming. Some of its major cities had been devastated, its economy was in ruins, and its social organization had to be rebuilt from the bottom up.

THREE LAW FIRMS IN WHICH I SERVED

Hunt, Hill & Betts I faced the prospect, too, of building my own legal practice with my own clients. How it was to go, again, all seemed to fall into place as it always did. Somehow years of long hours of hard work became my way of life but I enjoyed it. In my entire legal career, there were three law firms in which I was involved in my career as a lawyer in New York. The first was Hunt, Hill & Betts, an admiralty firm, which was located in the Equitable Building. It later moved to 26 Broadway, which was the Socony-Vacuum Company headquarters until John D. Rockefeller was charged with massive anti-trust law violations and the company was broken up into its smaller parts. This was located close to the old Custom House, which is known as Hanover Square, at the southern end of Manhattan.

After my admission to the New York State Bar, I worked at these two locations until I was sent to the Tokyo Office in 1953. I practiced law in Japan for about two and one-half years, which I will describe in greater detail later. The partners with whom I worked most in the firm were George Yamaoka from Seattle, Washington, and William Logan, Jr. from New Jersey, who headed the litigation department. They both represented Japanese war criminals at the International War Crimes trials in Japan. When I resumed my practice in New York with Hunt, Hill & Betts in 1955, a young secretary was assigned to me who had considerable skill in producing legal documents and handling a large volume of correspondence. She was Joellen Leone who started with me in this firm and, when I moved to Miller, Montgomery, Spalding & Sogi, continued to assist me at the new law firm. Her skill in communicating with my clients greatly facilitated my practice, especially when I was traveling extensively, managing the matters that I was handling and any new matters that might come in to me in our office. Later, she was so knowledgeable about my practice that she was effectively a paralegal in the office. When we merged with Kelley Drye & Warren, she joined the firm with me and remained with the firm until about the time of my retirement, when she transferred to do other work in New Jersey. I was then assigned another capable assistant by the name of Patricia Glaviano. She has been helping me since my retirement, and with e-mail in vogue she sends me messages, almost daily, concerning my personal matters, including mail that still seems to come into my office from former clients, as well as mail regarding our Tokyo office. She arranges my schedule and appointments efficiently during my frequent visits to New York, Los Angeles and Washington, D. C., as well as to our office in Tokyo.

Miller, Montgomery, Spalding & Sogi After becoming a partner of Hunt, Hill & Betts in 1958, I remained with the firm until 1967, during which time my practice started to grow rapidly. The firm was primarily an admiralty firm with not much corporate expertise or practice and it was necessary for me to have more partners and associates with expertise in the areas of my practice. One day, I came across Dudley Miller, a partner of Miller, Montgomery & Spalding at One Wall Street, at the corner of Broadway and Wall Street and across from Trinity Church, which is reputed to be one of the richest churches in the world. There was no significance to the fact that the address was One Wall Street, but it coincided with the fact that we lived at One Payne Road, I had one wife and one child.

Dudley Miller was a graduate of Hotchkiss Preparatory Academy in Lakeville, Connecticut, Yale College, and Yale Law School. He said that he wanted to become a medical doctor and started out as a medical student, but he realized that medicine followed established and fixed procedures and required no analysis or reasoning as it was all prescribed in a formula. He, therefore, transferred over to the law school. Dudley and I got along very well since the time we first met. He was gregarious, sociable, and very sharp, bright and an intellectual and, at the same time, a very good human being. Unquestionably, he was meticulous about social graces. I recall one occasion when we decided to hire a lawyer to join our firm and interviewed a prospect at the office and then went off to lunch. After lunch, we evaluated the potential partner for our firm and Dudley rejected him summarily since the candidate wore short socks and not sup-hose and his ankles showed, and, also, he did not follow the simple etiquette of passing the bread tray at lunch As young as Dudley was, sadly, he was diabetic and we lost him very early. There were 20 or more lawyers in the firm and we did very well, building our practice gradually and well enough that we were able to move uptown to the Pan Am Building at 200 Park Avenue in 1974, just when our lease at One Wall expired. By then, we had added many more lawyers to the firm to serve the large number of clients we had attracted.

All of the partners, including George Marchese, Jeffrey Cook, Alton Peters, James Stanton, Susan Onuma, Alan Epstein and other lawyers were deeply involved in corporate practice, including mergers and acquisitions. We learned later that Alton Peters was well connected with the Lincoln Center, Metropolitan Opera, New York Philharmonic, and others. He was married to the daughter of Irving Berlin, the composer who died at age 101. Also, from a paralegal school in Philadelphia came Molly McEneny, who managed the firm's administration for us. She was quite an asset to our firm. I brought in the international practice that fit in very well with the partners and lawyers and their practice. Boardman Spalding was the nephew of the founder of A.G. Spalding Company, famous in the sporting goods business for many years. When I joined the firm, he was about to retire from the practice of law, and the name of the firm was changed to Miller, Montgomery & Sogi.

By then, we had expanded nationally and internationally with many affiliations and operations throughout the country and in Tokyo. We thrived at the new location and continued to add partners and associates. We had capability in just about all areas of law practice by Richard W. Brady joining us and adding his specialty in defined benefits to our firm. The firm name was then changed to Miller, Montgomery, Sogi & Brady. My 10-hour days stretched into 12 and 16 hours a day, six days a week, more or less, and, at times, seven days a week. It also meant traveling all over the globe regularly. On one matter, I still remember working for 24 hours or more to meet the demands of our client.

Kelley Drye & Warren Having grown considerably, after nearly 10 years in the Pan Am Building, we reached a level of growth where we had to decide whether to grow from within or merge with another firm with a larger number of lawyers who could represent our growing clientele and perform the work for our clients. Coincidentally, not too far away, there was another old-line firm in a similar situation. It was organized in 1836, and had about 50 lawyers, considered a large firm in New York City at that time. To discuss the matter of a possible merger, I had lunch with Bud Holman, the senior partner of Kelley Drye & Warren, at the Sky Club in the Pan Am Building. He impressed me since he was open in discussing his firm's situation. It definitely sounded like a very good mix. After one or two social events to get to know each other, our partners were in favor of the merger. It looked like a good fit and it has been so. We learned that Kelley Drye represented Walter Chrysler and incorporated the Chrysler Company, and for many years did the Company's legal work and still represents some of the heirs and descendants of that company's founder.

We were a smaller firm with about 25 lawyers, but I was invited to join the Executive Committee, which managed the firm, and I served on it for 10 years until my mandatory retirement age of 70 when I became a Life Partner with secretarial help and an office. I had brought into the firm many Japanese financial, industrial, shipping, trading and other companies. The merger was very timely for my firm since we were handling many compli-

Gang of five: Executive committee Chauncey Walker (from left), Bud Holman, Francis Sogi, Terrance Schwab and John Callagy.

Law firm makes its case
Old-line Kelley Drye branches out via mergers

Kelley Drye & Warren, Executive Committee, 1986. Left to right: Chauncey Walker, Bud Holman, Francis Y. Sogi, Terrance Schwab, John Callagy

cated and major transactions, as well as litigation. Japan was becoming a major industrial power of the world, second only to the United States. With all of the technology they imported after the war, Japan was now manufacturing and exporting to all parts of the world, including many consumer goods at very reasonable prices. Japan prospered and established companies throughout the world, and began to buy major properties in the United States, including the likes of Rockefeller Center. This continued for ten or more years beginning in the early 1980s. We benefited greatly by this growth and expansion in our legal practice, coinciding with the last ten years before my retirement in 1993. Following my retirement and through the 1990s, the Japanese economy suffered and declined unfortunately, but it will no doubt bounce back like the *daruma*. I still maintain an office at Kelley Drye & Warren with clerical assistance and visit New York regularly during the year and promote the firm at every opportunity that I have with a number of boards on which I still serve. I have been visiting our Tokyo office that is in my name as I am the qualified Japanese lawyer, admitted under the Japanese Foreign Lawyers Law, in the firm. I may be one of the last of two foreign lawyers still active in Japan in my 51st year.

At about this time, our collaboration with Mori & Ota in Los Angeles had become quite close and we mutually referred clients to each other. They were also growing very quickly with the Japan practice in Los Angeles and were also looking to merge with a larger firm. They had tentatively come to an agreement with the Pepper Hamilton firm in Philadelphia, but they found our situation with Kelley Drye & Warren more appealing and merged with our firm in 1984, increasing our Japan practice. Jun Mori is one of the few Japanese Americans who is completely bilingual and bicultural, having graduated from Waseda University in Japan, UCLA, and the law school of the University of Southern California.

To further expand our Japan practice, we invited Glen Fukushima to join our firm when he left the U.S. Trade Representative's Office in Washington, D.C. He has an impressive educational background that would have fit in well with our practice. He opted to be a business executive in Japan. I saw Glen as definitely more equal than others, to use George Orwell's expression.

After our merger with Kelley Drye, it gradually grew to over 400 lawyers during the ten years I was active with them, with offices in New Jersey, Connecticut, Washington, D.C., Virginia, Chicago and Los Angeles, and internationally in Brussels, Tokyo, and Hong Kong. It continues to grow and expand under the able leadership of John Callagy. With my license in Japan, I maintain an office of the firm in Tokyo and I continue to write Japanese law opinions for our clients in collaboration with John Lynagh of the firm.

CHAPTER EIGHT

Practice of Law in Japan

L ITTLE DID I IMAGINE, as I took my oath as a New York attorney, and overjoyed at the prospect of starting a family, that during the 1950s I would be fated to experience life on both sides of the Pacific. We lived in Tokyo from 1953 to 1955, and during this time, many major American companies were coming to Japan to license technology to the Japanese. Of course, I was no stranger to all this, having spent time with the Japanese in Hokkaido for about a year. However, on this assignment to Japan, it was a matter of choice as I was no longer acting under orders from my military superiors.

Our son, Jim, was born just about the time we were making the move for the Tokyo assignment. We named him Jun James Sogi, after Dr. Jun Arima of Hokkaido, a medical doctor. His name is very appropriate for it signifies purity when written in a Chinese character, like a pearl, for the month of June. We expected Jim to be born in June of 1953 and he arrived on the very last day of the month.

Hunt, Hill & Betts had opened its Tokyo office immediately after the Peace Treaty with Japan was signed in 1952 and overseas lawyers were admitted to practice law there under the Foreign Lawyers Law. I arrived there just several months after my swearing-in ceremony in New York. The office was located in the Marunouchi Building, in a sublet of about 30 tsubo (118.62 square yards), divided into four rooms. The partners occupied two of them, and I shared another room with two senior Japanese lawyers and two associates. The fourth room served as a general area staffed by a receptionist, a messenger, a filing clerk, and the managing partner's chauffeur.

It was a meager office by modern American and Japanese standards, but it was a real power center where Hunt, Hill & Betts was representing a large number of Fortune 500 companies doing megabuck business in Japan. George Yamaoka and Bill Logan had established the office after the war-crimes trials had ended because they saw the potential of the demand for legal services by businesses being established in that country. It was a great success from the beginning and, for many years, was considered the premier law firm in Japan. Our client list was straight out of the Fortune 500 list: American Cyanamid, Willys-Overland, Motion Picture Export Association of America, Ford Motor Company, Chase Manhattan Bank, IBM, Lockheed Aircraft, Vertol Aircraft, and many others.

Sarah, our baby, Jun, and I moved into a 350-tsubo Western-style house and then to 96 Sakuragaoka in Shibuya. As any home of consequence should, it had a southern exposure. The house was owned by the widow of a former director of Ajinomoto Company that Hunt, Hill & Betts represented from pre-war days. It had a *tatami* (straw mat) room, but rugs and carpets as in any home in America or Europe. We had a live-in cook and maid to help Sarah with meals and housework. There was no central heating, just a pot-bellied stove with a chimney to carry off the fumes from the coal we burned during the winter. In the morning we would fire the stove with coal until it was red-hot, and it would keep the two-story house warm for the entire day. With the sun streaming in through the southern-facing windows all day, it was rather comfortable. Tokyo's climate is a little warmer than New York's and certainly far warmer than the wintry weather to which I was accustomed in Hokkaido during my days of occupation of Japan.

Tokyo, then as now, was extremely crowded, so our house did not have much of a yard, but there was a good-sized pine tree that was tended meticulously by a gardener who came by once a year in the spring. It required an entire day of methodical work to take care of that single tree. He would start by erecting a scaffolding of bamboo tied together with straw ropes. Then he climbed up and plucked each dried needle one-by-one, placing it meticulously into his bamboo basket. We quickly learned that patience was one of the most important Japanese virtues, even in those difficult days of postwar reconstruction.

We soon became used to the unfamiliar sounds that heralded our daily life in Tokyo. All the temples had cast-iron bells, including the one across the way from our house, which sounded precisely at six a.m. and again at seven. This was followed by the tofu and *natto* (fermented soy beans) vendors sounding their unique horns or bells. Evenings were marked by the click clack of the *geta*, or wooden clogs, that everyone wore on their way to the public bathhouse. Many homes still did not have the luxury of a private bath, as ours did. At nine o'clock, a clack-clack sound would herald the onset of nighttime as the *hino yoojin*, or fire warden, would strike together his two rectangular pieces of solid wood. For two years, our lives moved to these familiar sounds and rhythms, so unlike the clangorous sounds of cities today, with their automobile horns, sirens of emergency vehicles, or loud music from radios or CD players. In some respects, we were living a fortunate life in Tokyo. In addition to our comfortable house, we had an American car, imported duty-free, which I drove to the office each day and parked on the street outside my office building.

Tokyo, in spite of its size and energy, was still just beginning to rise above the rubble of the World War II era. New buildings were springing up everywhere. Though the Tokyo and Yokohoma districts had been highly industrialized, whole areas of it had been decimated by American incendiary bombs of our Air Force. Only the smokestacks survived because they were made from bricks that did not burn like many of the wooden houses and buildings around them.

Although a part of the Imperial Palace had been damaged by the air raids, all of the buildings around the moat circling the palace remained intact. These included the Imperial Hotel, the Marunouchi Building and Marunouchi Hotel, the NYK Building, Tokyo Station, and the Dai-Ichi

Insurance Building, where General MacArthur's headquarters was located. How ironic that Frank Lloyd Wright's impressive Imperial Hotel, which had so readily survived both the Great Kanto Earthquake of 1923 and the wartime bombings, was finally torn down in 1968 to make way for progress, a new high-rise modern hotel.

In the 1950s, there was still much rebuilding to do. While Americans, myself included, drove around in sleek and powerful cars, there were still many Jeeps all around the country that were remnants of the Occupation. There was still, of course, a large contingent of U.S. military personnel. The exchange rate was favorable to Americans, about 360 yen to the U.S. dollar. Taxis existed but were not plentiful and the fare was less than 70 yen (about 20 cents a ride), which was still the fare in 1962. There was as yet no *Shinkansen*, the bullet train, which would be the envy of the world that came on the scene in the 1970s. There were no McDonald's outlets in Tokyo as they were just getting started in the United States in the middle 1950s, nor Burberry Fashions nor Kentucky Fried Chicken. Johnny Walker Black Label, which was the favored drink, cost 10,000 yen (or about $33) for a bottle that could be purchased in the U.S. for $5. Goods were not plentiful and their quality was shoddy; those were the days when a "made in Japan" label signified that styles were poor imitations of Western fashions. Very few Japanese traveled abroad, even to Guam or Hawaii. Schoolboys were required to wear black school uniforms with black caps, and the girls wore black skirts and white blouses. Even factory and office workers, especially the women, were provided with company uniforms all of the same color, a practice that generally continues to this day.

As new businesses emerged during this period, some of them tried to cater to the foreigners who began arriving in Tokyo in droves to develop new connections. One of the more interesting of these new arrivals was a furrier that occupied a two-story building. I still chuckle when I think of the large sign he placed in front of the building. It read, in English: "We make fur coats with your skin or our skin and ladies will have fits upstairs."

Recalling this humorous vignette about the perils of translation, I ponder about how the two cultures of Japan and the United States differ in other, more fundamental ways. Western societies are far more individualistic than those of Asia, particularly Japan. Perhaps because I have been steeped in both cultures, I am more aware of the nuances that sometimes baffle people the first time they experience such a situation. Although I had grown up in a Japanese family based on custom and tradition imported directly from Meiji-era Japan by my parents, the influence of American values was strong. While I understood these things, I could not easily appreciate them and conform to them. Many of the customs and traditions I learned at home did not withstand critical analysis or follow the logical standards that we are accustomed to in the United States. Still, many things I learned as a youngster in Hawaii I found good and meaningful to human relationships when I encountered them later in Japan.

The Japanese, for example, are not an ostentatious people. Characteristically, they do not want to attract attention to themselves or boast about their accomplishments. On the other hand, they do not want to be criticized and feel badly hurt when they are. Instead, the Japanese strive for a much sought-after quality called *wa,* or harmony. Americans usually find such harmony and order when things are moving in a parallel course. To the Japanese, this is the worst possible situation, for they find disorder or disharmony in a situation where there is a gap between two elements. Many Americans have heard the familiar refrain that, to the Japanese, a nail that sticks out gets pounded down. In Japan, a maverick that strays from the group is ostracized. Conformity and groupism are prized. The group and its interest are paramount, and the individual's interest must always be secondary. In unity there is strength, order, and harmony. Despite my allegiance to my parents and their values, I found it difficult to adhere to these traditional norms of conformity. In a sense, I tried to have it both ways by working for the good of the group while at the same time maintaining individualism and complete freedom of movement and thought. I especially had a great deal of difficulty in traveling in a group, unwilling to be held captive to the group's schedule and movements. I traveled in a group only

once, with the Young Presidents' Organization in 1959 for its YPO conference at the University of Hawaii. I was a lecturer at the University for about
a week and then accompanied the group as a resource person to Japan,
where we met with the local YPO chapters.

Issues involving family and marriage often differ in the two cultures as
well. I remember that my mother had come to Hawaii to get married, earn
money, and eventually return to Japan. All of this changed, obviously, and
she adopted the United States as her country, along with my father. She suffered very badly when her mother died and her father remarried. In Japan,
it is quite a common practice for men to remarry soon after their wives
have died, often arranged, probably so they will have someone to take care
of them. My mother often mentioned the hard times she experienced living
with her stepmother. As a result, she resolved that she would do all in her
power to prevent her own children from being raised in this fashion.
Though her options were limited, she kept her resolve and struggled to
raise her five children. All of this was rewarded, for she lived to a happy old
age and saw all her children grow to be successful and have many grandchildren.

My bilingualism in English and Japanese offered many opportunities
for my legal career during my two-year stay in Japan. It was an excellent
opportunity for me to polish up my spoken language ability. Colloquial
Japanese is simple once you become accustomed to it, but it is really necessary to associate with the Japanese, preferably in Japan, on a daily basis to
achieve any degree of fluency. I made many mistakes but forged ahead
whether people were laughing at me or with me. Years earlier, as a grade-
school pupil back in Kona, I attended one hour of Japanese school somewhat similar to the *Hoshuko* (supplementary education) that Japanese
children today are required to attend in the New York area where such privately operated schools exist. It was not difficult; it was a simple matter of
memorizing words and learning to write kanji (Chinese characters). My
stints at the Military Intelligence School at Camp Savage and Fort Snelling
and my two years of teaching experience gave me a fairly good foundation

in the language, as did the additional two years of study at the University of Hawaii.

We did not have television during my stay in Japan, so I had more time to devote both to my legal reading and my language study. As I progressed, I found myself in the role of talking to my clients primarily in Japanese since, in the middle of 1950s, there were very few Japanese who could speak plausible English. They really struggled at trying to express themselves while discussing technical legal matters. This gave me an excellent opportunity to practice my Japanese and learn both how business was done in Japan and how international business was carried out. Today, some fifty years after having been admitted to the Tokyo Bar, and with many hours of bilingual negotiations under my belt, I can truly say that these opportunities have served me well.

Some of my colleagues at Hunt, Hill & Betts were very active in the business community in postwar Tokyo. Bill Logan was the first president of the Tokyo American Club, which was organized in 1928, and the American Chamber of Commerce of Tokyo and many of our clients belonged to both. One of the first assignments I received in the Tokyo Office was to file a claim against the Japanese Government on behalf of the Tokyo American Club, for compensation for the prewar property that the Government had confiscated during World War II. The Club received compensation of 15 million yen, enabling the club to purchase the property that is situated behind the Russian Embassy and that had formerly been owned by the Manchurian Railway, in liquidation. Financed by a bond issue, a new clubhouse was built, which was eventually replaced by the current building erected in 1975. Bill Logan served as its first president. Because of my role in obtaining compensation for the Club, I was made a Life Member, paying no annual dues or fees. I visit Japan once or twice a year, now in retirement, and enjoy its facilities for entertainment because of its high quality of food and service and reasonable prices as compared to those at hotels or restaurants in Tokyo.

The other partners of our Tokyo office included Masao Migita, who with George Yamaoka and Bill Logan had been one of the defense counselors for Marquis Kido during the war crimes trials. Marquis Kido was one of the lower-ranking officials in the Peerage class, which had been completely eliminated by General MacArthur as a step toward the democratization of Japan.

Masao Migita was the senior Japanese attorney in the office. His many connections with Japanese officials helped facilitate our work there. It was through him that I was able to gain admission to the Tokyo Bar. I was admitted based solely on my New York license, waiving the examination requirements. Thanks to his support, I became a *jun kaiin* (a quasi-member) of the First Tokyo Bar Association, which was a prerequisite to the practice of law in Japan. My *jun kaiin* status was regulated by the Foreign Lawyers Law, and I was almost equal to a Japanese lawyer who had gone through the two-year Legal Institute. My license served me well, as it enabled me to carry on a full practice of representing foreign and Japanese clients. As a qualified foreign lawyer, I was able to write opinions on Japanese law, which I still do, and do everything that a full-fledged Japanese lawyer was authorized to do except perhaps represent a Japanese client in a Japanese court, which I would not do in any case. This qualification enables me still to maintain and manage our Tokyo office. In the early 1950s there were 76 lawyers admitted as foreign lawyers from abroad working in Japan, including one barrister from London. We were called *gaiben*, the short form for *gaikoku bengoshi* (foreign lawyers). There are now only one or two who are still as active as I am.

Mr. Migita, who lectured at Chuo University Law School, also arranged for me to matriculate there as an auditor in the evening class. This enabled me to study the *Roppo Zensho*, the six basic major civil and criminal codes of law without which I could not truly practice law in Japan. Because of these powerful codes, scores of rules and regulations (and sub-rules and sub-regulations) are issued, all of which require the interpretations of the bureaucrats. As the laws were not always very clear, it was necessary to read commentaries of scholars and confer with the appropriate Ministry having jurisdiction over the subject matter for interpretation of the provisions. Of course, this was without ever revealing the name of the client. The government officials were therefore free to give their opinions, interpretations, and advice, and many practitioners relied on them.

My daily grind in the office was punctuated by its own sounds and noises. Today, thanks to computers and telephones that beep instead of ring, our large offices are much quieter than they were half a century ago. I worked every day from nine a.m. to six p.m. in a cacophonous small office that had nearly fifteen people crammed together. By the end of the day, everyone needed a respite, and our senior attorney encouraged us to follow the good Japanese custom of relaxing with colleagues after hours to dispel the pressures of the day. I quickly learned that not too many males of consequence went straight home from the office after work. If he did, his family and neighbors would get the impression that he was either ill or had no standing in the business world, something that might also cause him to lose face with his colleagues. This is quite different from the practice in the United States. Since I had a car, I drove my coworkers home as they all lived in the same area in Setagaya at first, and then later, in Shibuya, where 96 Sakuragaoka was situated.

I was not averse to the idea of relaxing after work in this way, enjoying a bit of aperitif and refreshments in the hour or so before dinner, which was served at 7:30 p.m. at our house. Masao Migita was from the old school, and so, on our way home, we would first stop at a street stall that served a variety of warm snacks, such as skewers of broiled chicken cooked over charcoal. Depending on the weather, we also quaffed some hot or cold sake or beer. During my first few months on the job, I enjoyed this little routine that got me home in time for dinner, maintaining a semblance of calm and harmony in my family.

However, as time went on, the hour at the street stall expanded into another hour in a more substantial establishment with hostesses, then gradually into two or three hours drinking in clubs where Migita was well-known by the owner, the so-called Mama-san. In Tokyo, the trains stopped operating at 1 a.m., and taxis would double the fare after midnight, so the entertainment world would close at 11 p.m., unlike in New York, where the bars stayed open (as they still do) until 4 a.m.

Sarah became quite upset at this lifestyle and demanded to return to New York with our son, Jimmy. "Your lifestyle is not for me," she complained. This was a real dilemma for me, because if I left Japan at that crucial time, it would have ruined my career with the firm. I was devastated by this turn of events and sought to be more attentive to Sarah's feelings. In a way, she was able to enjoy many perks not available to Japanese women during this period. She had nothing to do at home, since our maid and cook took care of the house and also our infant son. And every week she had herself coiffed and manicured. I felt that she needed to express her artistic and her activist side. I thought giving her a little more mobility would help, so I bought her a car, a Hillman Minx made in Japan.

With her car, Sarah was able to travel all around Tokyo. She was always interested in flowers and soon began to take a course in ikebana (flower arranging). She received a certificate from the Sogetsu School, taught by Mariko Kanai from Hokkaido, the daughter of Hideji (Chinese characters could also be read as Eiji) Arima, who was married to a Dr. Susumu Kanai, a medical doctor in the Health and Welfare Ministry until his retirement, after which he went into private practice. The Kanais had five wonderful children: Yooko, Koichi, Harumi, Naoko, and Shinji. I had met all of them in Hokkaido when I served with CIC during the occupation of Japan from 1946 to 1947.

After a month or so of her new artistic lifestyle, Sarah did not complain any further. I had started spending Saturdays playing golf, which was another useful lubricant for doing business in Tokyo. Happily, this arrangement continued for the rest of the time we were in Tokyo, as Sarah became quite absorbed in all of the art forms she was trying. Her repertoire grew to include *hanga* (wood-block printing), *nanga* (Chinese brush painting), and *sumi-e* (ink brush painting). Her skills in flower arranging enabled her to do many things after we returned to New York, including being asked to do

Kanai Family. Back row, left to right: Mrs. Mariko Kanai, Harumi, Dr. S. Kanai, Koichi. Front row, left to right: Mrs. H. Arima, Shinji, Naoko.

the arrangements for the visits of Emperor Hirohito and Empress Nagako at Nelson Rockefeller's estate. She also became an accomplished amateur sculptor as evidenced by the many pieces in wood, stone, marble, cement, and bronze she has created, all of which are now crowded into our home in Hawaii. There's even a bust of me she had cast in bronze in addition to the gymnastic and *karate* figures of our grandchildren, Kimberly and Kenneth.

In addition to all of these social pastimes, Sarah arranged for college students to come to our house over weekends to learn English conversation as well as American manners. She would speak only in English. Though the students would struggle, they managed to express their ideas and carry on a conversation by the time we left Japan. During the course of her lessons, she would serve American dishes and explain how the plates, spoons, forks, and knives should be arranged, how the napkins should be placed, and how guests should be served. Finally, she emphasized how American manners did not look favorably on slurping soup and noodles out of a bowl as it is done in Japan. Like the Japanese, I agree that the soup and noodles do indeed taste better when they are slurped into the mouth. As her final examination, Sarah asked the students to plan a luncheon party. They worked very hard to set the table and made all the required arrangements. At the end of lunch, a student served coffee and asked how each one wanted it: "black or white?"

Many of the students we mentored later became successful professionals and bureaucrats. Sarah's students included Koichi Kanai, Kozo Okabe, and Ken Nakayama, all from Hokkaido, who were attending Tokyo University. There were also Ken Migita, Masao Migita's son, who attended International Christian University, and Yooko Kanai, who attended Tokyo Women's University. Koichi Kanai and Nakayama became medical doctors, and Okabe became a bureaucrat at the Ministry of Labor. Ken Migita went into international business. Yooko Kanai married Seiichi Takahashi, an architect, and they have a son and daughter. We visit them often in Tokyo and they have visited us in New York. The son is married and has two children. Koichi became a medical doctor, but sadly died early in his 40s. Yooko remains our closest and dearest friend from the Arima family in Tokyo and we visit each other in our respective countries. Having known five generations of the Arima family, they remain our dear friends in Japan.

Sarah never attended Japanese school when she was young, unlike many of us who were required by our parents to attend one hour of Japanese classes after our regular English school. The Japanese she knew was a mixture of farm-worker verbiage plus local and Hawaiian words mixed with Yamaguchi dialect from her parent's prefecture in southern Japan. Her Japanese friends tried to teach her, but too often they were shy and too polite to correct her. Still she managed to forge ahead and be understood.

But not all of my after-hours time was spent relaxing. I enrolled at the Chuo University Law School. One of my fellow students was Arthur Mori, another so-called gaiben, who had been best man at our wedding in 1949.

As one of the old-line admiralty law firms, Hunt, Hill, & Betts had represented Japanese companies in New York since before the war through connections established by George Yamaoka. Our firm represented the U.S. Maritime Commission in their dealings in Japan as well as many Japanese shipping companies engaged in international commerce. During the

Korean War in the early 1950s the marine traffic in the Inland Sea passing through Shimonoseki between Kyushu and Honshu on to Korea was very heavy. There were many marine accidents and collisions. All of this meant much more business for us as an admiralty law firm. I regularly attended hearings equivalent to our Coast Guard hearings on behalf of our American shipping clients.

As Japanese industry recovered after the war and started exporting their products, we began representing many clients who ordered ships from Japan because of their expertise in delivery of high quality cargo vessels and large oil tankers, in some cases exceeding 250,000 tons, at reasonable prices. At first, many of the foreign ship owners were largely Greeks. However, most of the ships being exported by Japan at this time were sold on credit with a small down payment and the balance being paid by installments over a stipulated period. As security for the installment payments, our firm developed one of the earliest forms of a first preferred ship mortgage, subsequently given the imprimatur of the Japanese government. Typically, the ship would be leased or chartered out to an operator, and the charter hire would be assigned as security for the installment payments. If everything went well, after a term of years, the ship owner would finally own the vessel outright by making a mere 10 percent or so of down payment. The ships we were dealing with were iron-ore and oil tankers of various sizes. Many of them were registered in a third country, such as the Republic of Liberia or Panama, where ownership requirements were liberal and tax-free. At one time, I was responsible for 75 or more of these offshore companies, each with all the necessary corporate documents, officers, and directors. I am greatly indebted to the management team of many of the companies within the Kawasaki group for being able to represent them for so many years in very complex financial transactions and ventures. These included Kawasaki Heavy Industries, Kawasaki Steamship Company, Kawasaki Steel, Kawasaki Aircraft Company, and others. Gradually, the rate of Japanese ship exports declined as the cost of shipbuilding in Japan became expensive and as competition appeared in other Asian countries.

The Kawasaki group was founded in Kobe by Kojiro Matsukata, the third son of Masayoshi Matsukata, one of the nine councilors of Emperor Meiji. One day, Emperor Meiji inquired of Masayoshi Matsukata as to the number of children he had, and he is supposed to have replied that he wanted to respond the following day. Emperor Meiji thought this strange, but waited until the next day when Masayoshi responded that he had 15 sons and nine daughters. One of the descendants of the Matsukata family was married to U.S. Ambassador Reischauer, another to a Morimura who started the silk trade in New York through the Morimura Brothers business enterprise. A more complete description and information on Kojiro Matsukata can be found in "Karin No Umi," published by Kobe News.

Another matter that occupied my time almost from the beginning of my arrival in the Tokyo Office of Hunt, Hill & Betts was the claim of Ford Motor Company against the Japanese Government for the confiscation of their Tsurumi property in Yokohama at the outbreak of World War II. As I mentioned earlier, Ford Motor Company was our client from the very beginning of our Tokyo office. Ford got interested in Japan very early after the war, for prior to World War II it had a large assembly plant in Tsurumi, close to Yokohama, along the waterfront. This site consisted of about 100 acres, the size of Battery Park City that was built in lower Manhattan in New York City with the excavation from the World Trade Center. Ford retained our firm to lodge a claim against the Japanese Government for the return of the property that had been confiscated during the war, and for compensation covering the cost of repair of the property to restore it to the condition it was when it was confiscated.

Having done the Tokyo American Club claim successfully and having gotten to know many government officials who handled this type of claim, I was assigned Ford's claim against the Government. It was quite a monumental task putting together a formal claim with supporting documents from pre-1941 days of successful operation to the current condition of disrepair and destruction by the war. There were many meetings to talk about minute details with the Government. The officials asked for documentary proof for just about every item of financial claim to satisfy them that a compensation payment was justified. The easiest part was the fact that Ford owned the property and assembly plant, as they were recorded in the land registry in Japan.

From our client, we received cables and telephone calls regularly to be sure the facts and documents were presented to the Government accurately and in a timely fashion. The laws, regulations, administrative guidance and detailed regulations were clear that the property must be returned and compensation paid by the Government. There was no problem on the question; it was only a question of how soon and how much compensation would be paid.

I had come to know the government official responsible for the claim fairly well and we spent some time chitchatting about the United States and Japan and my role during World War II and the fact that my parents came from Fukuoka. He was very interested in the situation at the outbreak of the War at Pearl Harbor and our wartime experience as Japanese Americans. My service in the Military Intelligence Service and Counter Intelligence Corps in Hokkaido indicated to him how close I had been to Japan, both during and after the war. I explained the fact that my uncle was a fighter pilot who flew a zero plane off the carrier Kaga and participated in the attack on Pearl Harbor, but died in the battle of Midway, by which time our Navy had already broken the Japanese naval code and we knew, more or less, Japanese naval intentions at Midway. For this reason, Japan was defeated in that battle. Through these informal conversations, I may have developed some feeling of trust and credibility with the official although we were on opposite sides.

After nearly two years of negotiations with the Government, we were getting close to the return of the property and to the determination of the amount of compensation that the Government would pay Ford Motor Company. In a casual conversation, the official said that I must have quite an important standing in my law firm (I was only an associate out of law school for a couple of years) to be handling such an important claim for a major U.S. company as Ford Motor Company. He also intimated that the firm would be paid a very high fee for this work. It made me very uncomfortable since I was quite inexperienced in Japan and did not know the ways of the bureaucrats. Was there a hidden meaning to all this? Was he suggesting that the amount of compensation might be different depending on how we responded to his comments? Very fortunately, there was nothing to it and the claims were satisfactorily resolved by the return of the Tsurumi property and payment of an adequate compensation to Ford Motor Company. Then, I returned to the New York Office.

PRACTICE OF LAW IN NEW YORK

My two years in Japan as a Foreign Lawyer passed quickly. It was a grueling schedule: long hours at the office and an unending round of schmoozing with clients after work or on the golf course. In 1955, I returned to the life of a New York lawyer. In the early 1950s, all the major law firms that had their offices downtown in the Financial District were called Wall Street firms. The designation is still used today, giving these large firms a degree of respect and prestige, though they might not be located on Wall Street itself.

Before we departed for New York, Samuel Mukaida, Sarah's recently widowed older brother came to stay with us in Tokyo with his three sons, Allen Kamuela, Donald Take, and Nathan Charles. Samuel, who had received his Ph.D. in education from Columbia in the early 1950s, had lost Marietta during the birth of their third son, Nathan, in the South Pacific where he had been working. Sam continued to occupy our house and he later moved to Okinawa with his three sons and worked for the U.S. Government in education and cultural affairs and became quite renowned in Okinawa for his contributions to education. There, he married Yoshiko Taira from Okinawa and had two sons, William and Frank. Frank later became a medical doctor. He married his classmate who also became a doctor at the medical school and they have two sons and are living and practicing medicine in Oregon.

Upon my return, I quickly discovered that the practice of law in New

York was, and still is, quite different from that in Tokyo. In Japan, case law was practically non-existent, and no one spent too much time on it. When I got back to the United States, I joined the International Bar Association, American Bar Association, the New York State Bar Association, the Association of the Bar of the City of New York, and the New York County Bar Association, the largest local bar association in the country. I also joined the District of Columbia Bar Association after I was qualified and opened an office there. There were also the World Peace Through Law International Bar Association and the Maritime Law Association. I wanted to get to know, and get to be known by, many lawyers in international practice. I joined the Committee on International Law at the City Bar, which included many excellent lawyers from the major firms, such as Sullivan and Cromwell, Davis Polk, Shearman & Sterling, Wilkie Farr Gallagher, Milbank Tweed Hadley & McCloy, Breed Abbott, and many others.

Equipped with the tools to serve Japanese clients in New York, my firm represented many who were coming to the United States, especially in New York, to re-establish businesses after the war, as well as others who were coming here for the first time. We represented some of the leading firms in Japan, some from pre-war days, with a client list that included Mitsubishi International, C. Itoh & Company, Marubeni-Iida, Nissho-Iwai, Toyoda Tsusho and Toyota Motors, Kawasaki Heavy Industries, Kawasaki Steel, Kawasaki Shipping Company and many others. We also represented some of the major city banks such as Bank of Tokyo, Mitsubishi Bank, Mitsui Bank, Tokai Bank, Daiwa Bank, Fuji Bank, and others. We also represented a number of U.S. companies who were investing in Japan such as Ford Motor Company, American Cyanamid, Lederle Laboratories, Chase Manhattan Bank, IBM, Readers Digest, Union Carbide, Lockheed Aircraft, AIU, and many other Fortune 500 companies.

In the early 1950s, as George Yamaoka and I were the only lawyers able to speak both English and Japanese and were the only ones who were qualified to practice in both jurisdictions, we attracted a lot of business from American companies eager to do business in Japan.

LIFE AS AN EXURBANITE

Sarah and I were now living at 360 Riverside Drive, quite a step up from our earlier digs downtown, but after a year on Riverside Drive, we finally decided that apartment living was not for us. Our son, Jimmy, was three years old now, almost ready for nursery school, so we decided to follow the tracks of so many others during this period and moved to the suburbs. We found a house in the Town of Greenburgh, in Westchester County, about 25 miles north of New York City. It was a 35-minute commute by train, but bearable except in the oppressive summer heat, especially in the subway from Grand Central Station to Wall Street, which was not air conditioned at the time.

The property we bought included a two-story clapboard house on over an acre of wooded land with tall trees of all kinds, such as dogwood, oak, hickory, maple, tulip, and cherry. It was far more prolific than the single pine tree we enjoyed in our garden in Tokyo. With its interesting partly sloping terrain, the location of the corner property on Payne Road and Knollwood Road appealed to us immediately. The neighbors lived at a distance and could not be seen except through the woods during the winter after the trees were bare. Even then, they were visible only from a distance, because each house had to be set back 40 feet, away from the street in an acre zoned area. There were four distinct seasons during the year and the best were spring and autumn. The spring flowers were a delightfully welcomed sight after a long, cold and dreary winter. The first flowers were crocuses (popping out through the snow in the early spring), forsythia, then the dogwood and the cherry blossoms. After a hot and humid summer came the colorful autumn foliage with the splendor of all of the warm colors of the rainbow.

It was a convenient commute on the Harlem Line, since all of the trains stopped at the nearby White Plains or North White Plains station, which was only eight minutes away on the expressway (Route 278) by car. The trains ran all day and all night in 1956 when we moved there, although the schedule was more limited in later years. The last train now leaves Grand

Central Station at 1:30 a.m. The longest ride on a local train is 52 minutes, as it stopped at every station, and there are limited trains that take 42 minutes and express trains that take only 38. Over the years, the fare increased six-fold: from $20 or so a month to the present $128, which offers unlimited rides to and from North White Plains to Grand Central Station, located at 42nd Street and Park Avenue, directly below the law office of Miller, Montgomery & Sogi in the Pan Am Building and, later, only two blocks from the office of Kelley Drye & Warren.

At first, I drove to the station and parked the car there, as did my neighbor Gordon Bickert. The meter then cost only 25 cents for 12 hours. Commuting was most unpleasant in the rain or during snowy winter. On days like these, I wondered why we had not stayed in the city. But the morning train ride was not unpleasant, allowing just enough time to keep up with current events and the stock market in *The New York Times* or, if it was sold out, *The Wall Street Journal*. Reading these two newspapers was an education in itself, as they gave national and international coverage as well as most of the major happenings in the city. I looked forward to reading the editorials and Op-Ed articles of *The New York Times* every day. There'd be enough time for a catnap, too, especially after a heavy night with the grapes. After a while, my commute turned into a regular pattern. After a hard day's work, like many of the other commuters, I would have a drink at the station bar or from the vendor on the platform, then settle into a comfortable seat for a short nap.

After moving out of New York City, one of the first things I did was to buy a book on suburban living. I had lived in different parts of the world, such as in Hawaii, in Tokyo, and in Greenwich Village and yet I never had to read a book to tell me how to get around until now. The suburbs were truly a new experience for me and many other Americans in the 1950s.

I found a very enlightening book by A. C. Spectorsky called *The Exurbanites* that purported to be a field guide to the new species that was building its nest in a more bucolic environment. Spectorsky was full of amusing insights into the eccentric migration patterns of the exurbanite, which required a car just to get to the train station. One incident that he related seemed very similar to my experience. Spectorsky, who had only a Jeep and a sedan, had moved to a prestigious residential area of Connecticut, one where chauffeured, luxury cars were the norm. He decided to take his Jeep to the station so his fellow commuters would assume he probably had a Mercedes or Cadillac at home. After all, no one knows what kind of cars you may be hiding on your wooded lots. If you have to park your luxury car in the very public parking lot at the station, people would think that's the only one you have. Parking a simple Jeep there, however, would be the ultimate in snobbish one-upmanship. The author related another incident about the vicissitudes of commuting. The first few days, he stood with a group of fellow passengers as the train pulled in. Each time, the door opened and whisked them off, so he thought he'd gotten himself into a routine. The next day, he stood at exactly the same place on the platform, even though the other commuters were now standing a few yards away. This time, the doors opened at a new location and he had to trot down the platform to avoid missing the train. It turned out that, on Thursdays, a different engineer would stop the train at a new location. Such is the life of a commuter.

POCANTICO HILLS, WESTCHESTER, NEW YORK

During my years in the town of Greenburgh, I heard and read a lot about Nelson Rockefeller, who served as Governor of New York from the late 1960s to the early 1970s. He was appointed Vice President under President Ford after the resignation of Richard Nixon. After his marriage to Happy Murphy who had four children, Rockefeller built a new modern house on the Pocantico Hills estate and also a typical Japanese house that was designed by an architect from Kyoto. All of the materials in the Japanese house were made in Japan with the exception of the kitchen and bath hardware. It was assembled in Japan with 11 layers of wooden shingles on the roof, then taken apart piece by piece and reassembled on the Rockefeller estate by seven Japanese artisans, each of them a specialist in a specific craft, such as roofing and flooring. Sarah and I invited all of the Japanese workmen over to our house for a typical American Thanksgiving dinner. Though a turkey dinner was, for them, strange and totally unheard of, they consumed almost the entire 15-pound turkey, all of the stuffing, and topped with pumpkin pie a la mode.

The team of artisans had arrived from Japan in the summer and had originally planned to finish the Japanese house in six months. Each of these specialists worked on a particular phase of the construction, but the whole team worked as a unified group on the flooring, roofing, interiors and other parts, regardless of specialization, under the guidance of that particular craftsperson. It was their idea to seal the perimeter with a tent covering the whole house and concentrate on the interior by November or December, when cold weather set in. It took twice as long, in fact: a full twelve months. The foundation had to be laid by local union laborers, the plumbing installed by another team, and as is customary, none of the local laborers would lift a finger to help another worker from a different trade. Besides that, there was delay after delay and the job ended up taking twice as long as originally estimated. When it was finally finished and Nelson Rockefeller did his final inspection, he noticed that the electric light switches were too visible, something that obviously violated the Japanese esthetics in his mind and had to be replaced. The bathroom also had to be redone by replacing the marble tub with a very expensive and difficult to find pale white wooden Japanese tub, the kind used only by one of high status in Japan, causing yet another delay.

Once it was completed, the Japanese house was truly a work of art, with a Japanese garden with stones and gravel, as well as an imitation of the Ryoanji garden in Kyoto. The gardens were designed by an American named Jensen, a famous landscape artist, who has published a book on Japanese gardens. The new modern Japanese house is on two levels, divided by a 3,000-gallon pool and a waterfall cascading from a huge slab of rock twenty feet tall.

The main new residence, where Nelson and Happy lived, close to the

Japanese house on the Rockefeller estate, was modern and furnished with a complete set of dining room and other pieces of furniture designed by the famous furniture designer George Nakashima of New Hope, Pennsylvania, who was originally from Seattle, Washington.

The Rockefeller family used the Japanese house as a guesthouse, and it is where the Beatles were once guests. The modern Western-styled house with Japanese influences had to be graced with ikebana, or Japanese flower arrangements. Lester Sleinkoffer, the Superintendent of the Rockefeller Estate, knew that Sarah had earned a certificate in flower arranging when we were in Japan in the mid-1950s. Sarah was introduced to the house-keeper, a woman from Seattle named Helen Seo, by the first Mrs. Nelson Rockefeller who used to attend Union Church of Pocantico Hills where Sarah attended regularly. And so it was that Sarah went over to the house on Fridays to do the Japanese style flower arrangements, a situation that continued for several years until Nelson Rockefeller died in 1979.

A MATTER OF TWO EMPERORS

Two of the first guests the Rockefellers entertained at their new western style house were Emperor Hirohito and Empress Nagako, who were invited there during their U.S. tour in 1975 and were the first to sign on the first page of the new guest book of the new house. There was a huge entourage of Japanese Imperial Household staff, newsmen, and photographers and journalists surrounding the perimeter of the room with the Imperial couple. All wore dark and formal suits. Nelson Rockefeller, however, main-tained his American informal image by wearing a sports jacket and a sporty necktie. He enjoyed himself by snapping many pictures of the first guests in his new house, without embarrassment or hesitation or restraint. We still have pictures taken on that occasion and kindly given to us by Governor Rockefeller. For the Imperial visit, Sarah and Misao Furuta, whose hus-band, Soichi Furuta, is a poet and writer, did a special floral arrangement for the tokonoma on this occasion. Attired in kimono, Sarah also served tea to the Imperial guests. We have a picture with the rear-end view of Sarah serving tea to the Imperial couple. We also have pictures showing them signing the guest book. In preparation for the event, the kitchen staff was wondering, half-jokingly, what kind of tea should be served to someone considered to be a god in Japan. They finally settled on Lipton's Orange Pekoe, which could be found on any grocery store shelf in America. The Governor decided to use a black tea set of western style that had belonged to his mother. Helen Seo had found some special Japanese mochi teacakes of pastel colored floral shapes, filled with sweet bean paste, and they were served to the Imperial guests.

Memories of the Imperial visit to the Rockefeller estate brought back to me memories of 1990, when I had the singular honor of being invited by the Japanese government to represent the East Coast Japanese Americans at the

Sarah M. Sogi serving tea to Emperor Hirohito and Empress Nagako at the Rockefeller estate, 1975. At top left, the Imperial couple flanked by Happy and Nelson A. Rockefeller

Ikebana floral arrangement by
Sarah M. Sogi

Ikebana floral arrangement by
Sarah M. Sogi

THE VICE PRESIDENT
WASHINGTON

November 24, 1975

Dear Mrs. Sogi:

It occurred to me you might like to have
the attached photographs as mementos of a
great occasion.

I would like to take this opportunity to
again tell you how wonderful your help was and
how much Mrs. Rockefeller and I admired the
flower arrangements, as I know did the Emperor
and Empress.

Sincerely,

Nelson A. Rockefeller

Mrs. Francis Sogi
1 Payne Road
Elmsford, New York
10523

Letter from Vice President
Nelson Rockefeller

enthronement ceremonies for Emperor Akihito, who succeeded his father to the Chrysanthemum Throne when Hirohito died in 1989 after a 63-year reign. Only 28 Nikkei from the Western Hemisphere were invited as official representatives. I wrote in 1990, "The opportunity to carry a simple message from the Japanese Americans in the United States to Japan was gratifying. Hopefully, this experience will enable me to be truly international and global in my thinking and continue to exert my efforts in building a better country in which to live for all of us." The full text of my observations of this ceremony is found as an appendix at the end of this book.

FAMILY MATTERS

Many families moved to the suburbs as their numbers increased, and we were no exception. Our son, Jim, was three years old when we made the move to Westchester County. Sarah immediately registered him for preschool, then nursery school and kindergarten at Pocantico Hills School, about five miles west of where we lived. The school district adjoined the Rockefeller estate of about 4,500 acres. Sarah was actively involved in his schooling from kindergarten through eighth grade, and I served on the Pocantico Hills School District Board for eight years. When Jim attended grade school, we introduced him to skiing by taking a family vacation at a nearby resort during the year-end holidays. It was only a small hill with rope tows and crude equipment, but we enjoyed relaxing together and watching Jim try to navigate the tiny slope. This was in the early 1960s, when Chubby Checker and the Twist were all the rage. Having skied through high school, he became an accomplished competitive skier.

As a family, we enjoyed many quick getaways, plus driving two hours each way to Vermont for many weekends of skiing. We skied just about every major ski slope on the east coast, up to New Hampshire, west and the Rockies since Jim was involved in competitive skiing. Occasionally, we would go to places like Snow Bird in Alta, Utah, or Jackson Hole, Wyoming and all of the major slopes from Seattle down to New Mexico. With sheer vertical drops of 4,000 feet, these places offered the most challenging con-

Wedding of J. James Sogi and Sarah J. Smith, December 20, 1980

ditions in the whole United States. These slopes required serious and skill-ful skiing. We found the snow in the Rockies to be more powdery than back east. At Jackson Hole resort, there was a gondola that took 10 minutes to reach the top of the peak of the mountain. Jim raced the gondola coming down and he beat it.

Our ski trips must have had a good effect on Jim because he became quite a skillful skier and competed with many students his age from throughout the country. He was never injured, even when the temperature at Jackson Hole was down to 40 below zero and the ears could freeze within five minutes unless one moved down the slope immediately. My left earlobe got frostbitten once at Jackson Hole Ski Resort and I had to sleep as motionless as I could until it defrosted.

Jim also manifested his love for music while in grade school and started to play the guitar. He encouraged a group of classmates from the neighborhood to form a rock band with him as the lead guitar.

Although I believed implicitly in public schools, we sent Jim, our only child, to Hackley, a private school in nearby Tarrytown, which had been founded during the Civil War. Hackley was a sectarian school and there was obligatory chapel service every Friday. When he was a senior, Jim's rebellious nature emerged and he and a few other students demonstrated against this requirement, but lost out. The headmaster was adamant and he wouldn't tolerate any type of protesting. Jim was told point-blank: "Chapel on Friday or out you go." Fortunately, he went back to chapel.

During his four years at Hackley, Jim was not an ambitious student though his instructors told us that he was bright and would do better if he only applied himself. He participated readily in sports, especially diving, soccer and lacrosse, a Native American sport played with a basket on a long handle.

After four years at Hackley, Jim set his sights on a college as far west as possible. His advisor recommended Reed College in Oregon as ideal for a student with his temperament, and he was accepted. Chief Justice Rehnquist had spent his freshman year at Reed but thought it too liberal and transferred to Stanford. Jim went off to Reed when he was 18, on his own in every way except for financial support from his parents. He was happy to leave the East Coast for a warmer climate, but once he settled in out there, he wrote how good it had been at home. I guess there will always be a generation gap. I am reminded of teenagers at 15 who whine, "I just can't understand how uninformed my parents are," only to admit 10 years later, "It's amazing how much my parents have learned during the past 10 years." It was at Reed that he met and married a fellow classmate, Sarah J. Smith, of Scottish and English descent.

Jim majored in philosophy and minored in psychology, so it's not surprising that few employers were clamoring to give him a job after graduation. He opted for a year of rest and recuperation at his mother's simple old family home in Kona, Hawaii. After a year, I paid him a visit and informed him that it was time for him to face the hard realities of life because his stipend and welfare payments from his parents were about to terminate. I made it clear, however, that I would continue to support him if he wanted to continue his education. He jumped at this opportunity and decided to go to law school. Sarah J. Smith, a California girl, a bright, intelligent and a

Sogi Family. Back row, left to right: Francis Y. Sogi, Sarah M Sogi, J. James Sogi, Sarah J. Smith; Front row: Kimberly M. Sogi, Kenneth T. Sogi

truly fine and sophisticated person who became his bride, attended Northwestern Law School. Jim also went to Northwestern Law School and both are now practicing in Kona, sharing an office in Kailua.

Jim and Sarah live in a large home they built on a two-acre lot in Holualoa, with their children Kimberly Makiko and Kenneth Tadashi. Both of them attended private schools at Hawaii Preparatory Academy in Waimea, Hawaii, from kindergarten on through high school on the Big Island of Hawaii. Kim is a junior at Columbia-Barnard University in New York City, traveled to France with her mother, and worked at Keck Observatory at Mauna Kea during the summer of 2003. She worked with me in my New York office in 2001, during the summer when I chaired the XII COPANI (the Twelfth Conference of PanAmerican Nikkei) as President of the PanAmerican Nikkei Association USA East. She was intent on going to school in New York. Though she was accepted by Mt. Holyoke and Smith College, she opted for Barnard College of Columbia University. She received a summer internship at Wyeth Pharmaceutical Company in Princeton, New Jersey, and she worked there for the summer of 2004.

Kenneth, our grandson, who is 17, is a senior at Hawaii Preparatory Academy in Waimea, Hawaii, where Parker Ranch is located. He was awarded a number of prizes in his junior class for leadership and community services and top grades. He had been elected to the Senate for two years. He is ambitious and looking forward to serving as the president of his student body in his senior year, and wants to attend Stanford in California. The probability of his realizing his plans is fairly good, since he achieved a very high academic performance, and was the top student of his junior class.

As I watch my grandchildren move into adulthood just as Jim did 30 years ago, I realize that, ultimately, it all comes back to the individual household, which is the building block of all society. The emotional ties and responsible behavior nurtured in these loving communities wherever they are found is what truly makes the world go round. I am proud to be able to look back on a long heritage that stretches back to Japan, and to be able to look forward to a heritage that is still in the making on the mainland United States as well as in Hawaii.

For the benefit of those of my relatives in the United States, it would be meaningful to mention some of our immediate relatives in Fukuoka and in Tokyo. The family chart shows their names and relationships. It goes back to my father, Yoshiemon Sogi, who was the oldest son; he would have succeeded to the family farm had he remained in Japan, but he immigrated to Hawaii. His younger brother, Kaemon Sonogi (the name the family used in Japan), succeeded to the family farm and became the head of the household of the Sonogi family.

Kaemon and his wife, Sayo Kiyotake, had four sons and a daughter: Seigen, Yoshikazu, Kumeji, Hideto, and Ayako. The oldest, Seigen, married Yoshiko and had a son Yoshihiro (the seventh generation). He and his wife Chizuko have two children, Takahiro and Yukari, who is my contact in Japan.

Seigen passed away in 1945 and his wife, Yoshiko, married Yoshikazu, the second oldest son to succeed to the family farm. Yoshikazu and Yoshiko

Hidemi Shibata, his two sons, and their families in Fukuoka

had three children; two are married, with two children in each family. The third child Kimio passed away in 1949. The oldest son Hiromasa and Nobuko, are parents of Seigou and Asuka, while the younger brother Toshiaki and Chikako are parents of Yasutomo and Takafumi. A number of the seventh and eighth generation Sonogis are residing and working in Tokyo and Chiba Prefecture.

Kenneth is very fortunate in going to Japan to study conversational Japanese and will stay with Toshiaki and Chikako with their children Yasutomo and Takafumi.

Jamie, Wayne, Laverne, and Ren Kinoshita

On my trip to Tokyo, in August 2003, I was privileged to meet some of my relatives from Fukuoka in Tokyo and, at that time, I met Seigen's grandchildren, Takahisa and Yukari. Yoshikazu was living with his oldest son, Yoshihiro, and his family, who have taken over the family farm. His children represent the eighth generation of the family line. Through the convenience of e-mail, I maintain a regular channel of communication with Yukari in Tokyo who is employed by PRG-Schultz Japan.

My cousin on my mother's side, Hidemi Shibata, passed away several years ago. His younger sister, Yasue, lives with her family in Tokyo with their two sons, and the other brothers and sisters live with their families in Fukuoka. Hidemi's two sons lived with him, both of whom have families tending the Yamaguma farm. My paternal uncle, who was adopted by the Nakaderas, lived in Tokyo and was a judge of the Tokyo District court prior to the war. His daughter, Chikako, now married to Ito, lives in Tokyo with their only son. When I see them, my emotional attitude toward them is certainly affected by the fact that they are blood relatives. They live in a completely different world but we have a common interest in having the younger generation maintain contact with each other, or at least, know of their existence. Through this book or family trees that Yukari and I are trying to develop, everyone in the family that started from the Sonogi and Shibata families in Soneda and Yamaguma, Fukuoka Prefecture, will be aware of the others.

It has been said that East is East and West is West, and ne'er the twain shall met, but I take the liberty of changing the refrain to say: the 'twain will meet.

My sister Chiyoko, the oldest of the American family, lives in Manoa on the island of Oahu, after having raised four sons: Paul, Jr., Wayne, Ronald and Glen. All of them are married with children, except Ronald. We occasionally have a reunion including all the children and grandchildren just to see how they've grown and changed. I always try to encourage the younger generation to be interested in education so that, over the generations, there will be an improvement in their lives and standards of living. For an immigrant family like ours, this is a real sign of achievement. After the second or third generation, it may not really matter, but the Asian's dream of education and property ownership can indeed be achieved. Educational opportunities might be there, but the interest in seeking higher education must be developed in children from a young age. When I was in high school back in Kona many years ago, it was almost taken for granted that we would go on to college. Education, however, is the foremost tool that will enable us to advance in life, since many parents may not be able to leave an estate sufficient to give them a life of more comfort and ease.

My nephew Wayne was one of my sister Chiyoko's four sons who went to college as did his brother, Paul, Jr. Wayne came to New York to live with us in his junior year, and attended Sleepy Hollow High School in Tarrytown, New York. This school was on contract with our K-8 Pocantico Hills Elementary School, adjoining the Rockefeller estate and built on property given by the Rockefeller family many years ago. Wayne then went on to Macmurray College in Illinois for a couple of years, finishing his college education at the University of Hawaii. He has two lovely children, Jamie and Ren, living in a multi-family complex with a commanding view of Manoa and Waikiki. Jamie has finished college and is working. Ren is married and in medical school to become a medical doctor, his long-time ambition. Wayne's brother, Paul, Jr., the oldest, attended college and has been working for many years in a salaried position in Los Angeles. His two other brothers, Ronald and Glen, are doing well carrying on the family construction business that their father, Paul Kinoshita, had developed until he passed away. Paul was not a large contractor but a very successful one.

I still see my brother, Harold, and his wife Ethel, from time to time. Their children Sterna and Kenneth both have families and live in Honolulu, the former with two sons and a daughter and the latter with two daughters. Sterna is in a supervisory position with a local company. Kenneth went to college and became an engineer and is now working for the U.S. Navy at Pearl Harbor.

My older brother Paul passed away in 2002, leaving a daughter and two

Kenneth Sogi with his wife Janet and their two daughters Jennifer and Melanie Sogi

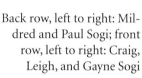

Back row, left to right: Mildred and Paul Sogi; front row, left to right: Craig, Leigh, and Gayne Sogi

Glen Makoto, Sasha Ihilani Leon, and Raynette Leon Kinoshita

CHAPTER NINE

Mid-Career: 1960s-1980s

N. Kinoshita, Jr., front row left to right:
...noshita, Sr., and Glen Kinoshita

...noshita

The first half of my life was truly eventful. Schooling interrupted by World War II, then back to civilian life, marriage and family, starting a career and a move to the suburbs. Millions of other Americans were going through the same routine, but my experience was quite different as I was moving constantly between two different cultures, and that has made all the difference.

After returning from practice of law in Japan, I resettled in New York and resumed the active practice of law here in 1955. My network of contacts with Japanese organizations and clients began developing rapidly. Many clients started to come to see me directly and not through someone else in the office, such as George Yamaoka, who headed the law firm and who was quite well known in these circles. Just as I had done in Tokyo, I cultivated clients by being willing to drink, entertain and dine with them. Many of our Japanese clients in New York were men who were living here only by themselves in the 1960s. In those days, families did not usually accompany them abroad because Japanese companies were short of foreign exchange or hard currency necessary to support their families. Whatever foreign exchange was available was used for business purposes only. As a result, many of our clients had substantial business allowances and were free to entertain even their lawyers. Sometimes our evening sessions flowed over into nightclubs and piano bars and, on the weekends, into golf. I was a fairly good golfer and tennis player, too, so I would often invite clients to lob a few balls over the net on Friday evenings at a tennis club in Grand

Kenneth Sogi with his wife Janet and their two daughters Jennifer and Melanie Sogi

Back row, left to right: Mildred and Paul Sogi; front row, left to right: Craig, Leigh, and Gayne Sogi

Glen Makoto, Sasha Ihilani Leon, and Raynette Leon Kinoshita

Back row, left to right: Wayne and Paul N. Kinoshita, Jr., front row left to right: Ron Kinoshita, Chiyoko and Paul N. Kinoshita, Sr., and Glen Kinoshita

Kristy, Paul N., Jr., Cindy, and Daren Kinoshita

Mid-Career: 1960s-1980s

The first half of my life was truly eventful. Schooling interrupted by World War II, then back to civilian life, marriage and family, starting a career and a move to the suburbs. Millions of other Americans were going through the same routine, but my experience was quite different as I was moving constantly between two different cultures, and that has made all the difference.

After returning from practice of law in Japan, I resettled in New York and resumed the active practice of law here in 1955. My network of contacts with Japanese organizations and clients began developing rapidly. Many clients started to come to see me directly and not through someone else in the office, such as George Yamaoka, who headed the law firm and who was quite well known in these circles. Just as I had done in Tokyo, I cultivated clients by being willing to drink, entertain and dine with them. Many of our Japanese clients in New York were men who were living here only by themselves in the 1960s. In those days, families did not usually accompany them abroad because Japanese companies were short of foreign exchange or hard currency necessary to support their families. Whatever foreign exchange was available was used for business purposes only. As a result, many of our clients had substantial business allowances and were free to entertain even their lawyers. Sometimes our evening sessions flowed over into nightclubs and piano bars and, on the weekends, into golf. I was a fairly good golfer and tennis player, too, so I would often invite clients to lob a few balls over the net on Friday evenings at a tennis club in Grand sons, Leigh, Gayne, and Craig. They all have families with children attending college or having graduated. Leigh is the manager of Gucci in Waikiki and her son Brandon is a professional baseball pitcher for the Toronto Blue Jays. Gayne and Craig are employed in Honolulu and Kauai. Gayne carries on his father's business in electric signs and Craig works for the electric company in Kauai.

As I watch the newest generation of Sogis come of age at the beginning of the twenty-first century, easily linked by e-mail and the new global economy, I realize what a different world we are all entering into compared to the one that my parents encountered a century ago as they took their long sea voyage to Hawaii, when such things as jet travel, television, and the Internet were unimaginable. Today, our family chart is expanding beyond the wildest imaginings of Yoshikazu Sogi, who succeeded to the Sogi family farm in Soneda, and beyond those of Hidemi Shibata, who succeeded to the Shibata family farm in Yamaguma, and their children, brothers and sisters. The Kona wind has taken all of us a long, long way. Who knows where the humble beginnings in Kona will take us all as the winds of change ever shift hither and yon in the midst of life's vicissitudes.

Central Station on 42nd Street in Manhattan. Many fine personal relationships developed over the years on the golf course and the tennis courts. Quite a number of the lower echelon clients I met in this way later became senior executive officers of their corporations and I still keep in touch with them when I visit Japan or when they come to New York. We still have lunch, dinner, or play golf together. It is a pleasure to deal with Japanese companies as they appreciated our work since we rendered reliable and preferential service, and they always paid their fees without question.

Early in my career, as every lawyer aspired, I determined that my immediate goal was to become a partner in a law firm. At the time, Hunt, Hill & Betts was not considered one of the largest in New York City. We had only about 25 lawyers. To be considered a true "Wall Street" firm, there must be at, least, 50 lawyers. Today, there are law firms with more than a thousand lawyers, and quite a number with more than 500. Eight years in active practice is considered the standard length of time it takes for a lawyer to become a partner. After eight years, a lawyer is considered capable of doing independent work and being responsible for a client. In 1960, I was made a partner and was assigned points enabling me to share in the profits and losses of the firm. This entitled me to an expense account based on the number of points I was assigned. I was also entitled to one luncheon-club membership.

In addition to my many work commitments, I got involved in voluntary and public service work in community affairs and non-profit organizations. As noted earlier, we had returned from Tokyo in 1955 and lived for about a year at 360 Riverside Drive (at 108th Street) in Manhattan. In September of 1956 we moved to a house with over an acre of wooded land at One Payne Road in Elmsford, New York. Our property was located in the K-8 Pocantico Hills School District.

Since her childhood days, Sarah was always involved in church activities, and so we joined the Union Church of Pocantico Hills, just next to the school and the Rockefeller estate, with its nearly 200 acres of manicured lawns and landscaping and 4,000 plus acres of pasture and forest land around the main mansion of KyKuit, now a national museum. In the area, there are some buildings that go back to the Revolutionary War period, including George Washington's headquarters during the Battle of White Plains. The Rockefeller family members attended services at the Union Church of Pocantico Hills, as did their Superintendent of Grounds, Lester Sleinkoffer and his wife.

Lester was on the school board of the Pocantico Hills Elementary School and, when a vacancy occurred, he asked me if I would serve as an appointee. It was an elective position, and I was later re-elected twice for two five-year terms from 1964 to 1972 and served as president of the board for two years. The Union Church of Pocantico Hills was often referred to as the "Rockefeller Church." It is well known for the world famous Chagall stained-glass window which was installed by the Rockefellers. Another memorial window in front of the chapel was designed by Matisse for Mrs. John D. Rockefeller. Another memorial Chagall window was also installed for Michael when he was killed in the South Pacific. All this happened during the period when our son James was attending Pocantico Hills School. We did not have a high school and so we were under contract with Sleepy Hollow High School, the school named after the fictional setting for the "Headless Horseman" story by Washington Irving, in North Tarrytown. The Pocantico Hills School had only 450 students but we paid for their tuition and busing throughout their public high school years. We also paid for transportation to private schools, but not tuition.

There were monthly school board meetings, except during the time when the budget process was in progress. In New York State, many school districts, large and small, were operated like ours. We would prepare a budget for the year and obtain the approval of the community residents. Then the local town would assess taxes on the properties situated within the school district. Being on the school board was a real eye-opener for me, because I realized what a great difference there could be between affluent and poorer school districts. Depending on the affluence of the district (i.e., property values), the school district could be very good and be able to offer top-quality education with the best teachers and facilities. For example, Scarsdale High School is a public school, but it sent 96 percent of its graduates on to four-year colleges and universities, one of the highest proportions of any public school. This is attributed to the fact that many of the residents are living in a district with high real-estate values. Many of the students receive after-school private tutoring, too. We were fortunate to be in a similar situation. Pocantico School has never had any problem with its school tax because the Rockefeller estate paid close to 45% of the tax each year. Part of the estate was operated as a ranch so the family could have fresh milk and it was not entirely underdeveloped land. The Rockefeller Brothers were quite generous in many ways; for example, when the school district needed a recreation center, they contributed land for a picnic area and built a swimming pool and tennis courts. When the nearby highway had to be rerouted and the facilities were condemned, the brothers again donated land next to our school and built another recreation center.

Serving on the Pocantico Hills School Board was my first experience with a nonprofit institution, and the first of many to come in later years. It has always been gratifying to be able to render service and devote time although without compensation. The Rockefeller family had great wealth but also devoted a lot of time to philanthropic interests. They were quite interested in Japan, and generously lent their support to such institutions as the Japan Society and others interested in promoting good relations between the United States and Japan.

While attending the Union Church regularly, Sarah met the first Mrs. Nelson Rockefeller, and she wanted Sarah to meet Helen Seo, the then head housekeeper at KyKuit, from Seattle. Through this connection Sarah became much involved with the Rockefeller Estate and the happenings there.

My visit to Tokyo for the Imperial Enthronement in 1989 was certainly a high point of my life. Neither my parents imagined—nor did I as a youngster in Kona—that I would some day be present at such an event. It never crossed my mind when I was in the Military Intelligence Service in Hokkaido during the Occupation of Japan, or when Sarah and I were living in Tokyo during the early 1950s, that I would witness such a ceremony at the Imperial Palace. None of my legal work over the years brought me in close contact with any member of the Imperial family, except when I was Chairman of the Japanese American National Museum from 1992-1996. During this time, the Emperor Akihito and Empress Michiko of Japan visited the museum in Los Angeles and it was my responsibility to greet them and guide them through the facility. In many ways, my legal practice was pretty routine business, working with contracts, licensing agreements, patents and trademarks, shipbuilding documents and a multitude of complicated international transactions. These were hardly the ingredients of solemn Imperial pageantry. But I suppose the little things in life do eventually add up to something more substantial.

Doing business in Japan during this time was far more serious and difficult, however. It was not uncommon for Americans and Japanese to misinterpret cultural signals and expressions. We were representing Lockheed Aircraft whose T-94 Trainers were being used by the U.S. Air Force in Japan for training purposes and the craft required periodic overhaul. As the major industrial companies started to prepare their bids, the Air Force permitted them to visit its Tachikawa Air Force Base for further discussions. At one of these meetings, the Japanese agents were complimented for their approach to the overhaul project and were told to "sharpen their pencils." Elated, they rushed home to their home office to inform senior management that they had been told to sign a contract. The Americans, on the other hand, had merely meant that they should fine-tune their proposals and reduce the cost.

TECHNOLOGY EXCHANGE BETWEEN THE UNTED STATES AND JAPAN

In addition to the scores of shipbuilding contracts and ship mortgages I drafted and recorded in various countries, I prepared many license and technological agreements. I handled two transactions of interest early in my career, when I practiced law in Japan. They are described below. I might add that with advanced technology and low cost of production,

Japan was able to sell and export millions of ship tonnage to foreign countries.

Link Aviation Simulator Technology licensing occupied much of my time as a lawyer during my mid-career years. My work in this specialty actually began soon after my return to New York from Tokyo in 1955. As an American, I might have appeared to be quite a conformist in the eyes of the Japanese, but I was obviously considered sufficiently Japanese by my law firm to be entrusted with many business and legal negotiations involving Japanese firms during the 1950s and later. This was during a period when Japan was quickly trying to modernize and rebuild from the devastation of World War II. One of Japan's top priorities during this period was to develop an aviation infrastructure, an area in which I was to become rather heavily involved in the 1960s through 1980s.

My law firm, Hunt, Hill & Betts, represented Link Aviation in Binghamton, New York. Link developed and produced a pilot-training simulator to help Japan create both its domestic and international airlines. Japan Airlines came into being soon after the war, but all of its pilots were either Americans or on leave from other airlines. When they started their training in the 1950s, the Japanese were only copilots or assistant pilots. Link's pilot-training simulator helped Japan develop a ready reserve of pilots for its emerging domestic airline industry. I was assigned the task of negotiating a license agreement in behalf of Link, and as a result, a Japanese manufacturer obtained a license to produce the simulator. The U.S. Air Force was not directly connected with the license agreement, but it was in a position to assist in the training of pilots because of its ongoing training program for American military pilots stationed in Japan. The technical aspects of the equipment posed no difficulties, so the license agreement was negotiated, signed, and approved by the Japanese government.

One incident involving these negotiations stands out in my mind. It so happened that the president of Link Aviation and the Commanding General for Procurement of the Air Force were good friends, so to celebrate the signing of the agreement, Link hosted a party at a Japanese *ryotei,* or geisha house, that was situated along the famous Sumidagawa (Sumida River). Having been in the Army for three-and-a-half years, I experienced first hand how stuffy military general officers could be. However, I was delighted to see the general loosened up after a considerable amount of sake had been served by the geisha. He was all over the place, dancing to Japanese songs such as *Tanko Bushi* (coal miners dance), *Tora, Tora* (Tiger, Tiger), and *Yakyu* (baseball)—typical singing and dancing games.

Willys-Overland, Detroit, Michigan Another of my productive and interesting clients was Willys-Overland, manufacturer of the famous Jeep that was such a prominent military vehicle in World War II and afterwards. I handled Willys-Overland's 10-year license agreement with Mitsubishi Heavy Industries Co., Ltd. (MHI). This had all started early in 1954 when Toyota Motor Company had developed a car similar to the American Jeep. When they called it by the trademarked "Jeep" name, I sent to Toyota a claim letter that they were using a registered trademark. They discontinued further use of the term.

I got involved in this whole situation because Japan's Self-Defense Force was strongly urging the Japanese government to buy the technology for the Willys Jeep. Up to this point, the Self-Defense Force was using Toyota vehicles like the one described above, but was dismayed to learn that it didn't perform well at speeds in excess of 45 miles per hour. The Toyota vehicles rattled, shook, and were generally unsteady at excessive speeds. Thanks to a special "know-how" technology in the carburetor of the Willys Jeep, these problems were eliminated and the Jeeps were able to withstand considerable wear and tear. For these reasons, MHI approached our client for a license to manufacture the Jeep in Japan. After about three months of continuous meetings, we worked out the terms of agreement after many long negotiating sessions in Tokyo. MHI, like most Japanese companies, did not initially bring a lawyer to these sessions. Only later, because of our presence, did Mitsubishi hire a lawyer, Fumio Uchida, who had been a former ambassador to West Germany. Mr. Uchida was a practicing lawyer, but he had started his career at the Ministry of Foreign Affairs after graduating from the former Tokyo Imperial University. Although he was present at the meetings, he was not openly consulted and did not say much during the proceedings. His role was to review the license agreement to see to it that it complied with Japanese law.

After the parties had reached an agreement on basic terms, the negotiations stalled for months over a single point, which we later learned had been at the insistence of the Japanese Government. Government approval was necessary because all deals involving the payment of foreign exchange had to have its blessing. In the United States, it was standard practice for the licensor of "know-how" technology to include a prohibition on the part of the licensee to use the know-how technology in any manner or form for a period of 10 years after the termination of the license agreement. The Government would not accept this stipulation, even though MHI was anxious to conclude the agreement and get the Jeep into production. All the while, the Self-Defense Force was urging the Government to get moving.

During this impasse, we learned that all other licensing agreements, such as for the manufacture of the Hillman Minx and Renault, which had been approved by the Japanese Government, did not have a similar restrictive clause. We learned that the Government wanted a uniform treatment of this type of restriction, even though the typical car was quite different from the Jeep transaction and no secret know-how was involved. Needless to say, our client was exasperated. It was a very hot summer, too. As much as Willys-Overland wanted to conclude the agreement, the vice president and chief negotiator finally informed MHI that he would remain in Japan for only one more week. If a deal could not be reached, he would return to Michigan and there would be no agreement. After a considerable number of phone calls, meetings, and behind-the-scene negotiations, the Government finally relented. The agreement lasted for ten years and was renewed for another ten. This whole experience was an eye-opener for me. I learned that in any international contract, the Government of Japan had to be a necessary partner. Immediately after the signing of the Peace Treaty after World War II, the laws of Japan were very general and brief. There was a blanket prohibition against any international transactions unless the business arrangement involving foreign exchange was approved by the appropriate Government Ministry. Without the Government's approval, no deal could be made that involved foreign exchange. Sometimes, Japanese companies shrewdly used this as a ploy to leverage a better arrangement: they would quickly come to terms and sign a contract knowing that the Government would insist on changing any unfavorable conditions for them while going through the approval process. When we represented the Japanese, we were also prone to consider this strategy, but did not use it to its fullest extent.

Bureaucratic control has always been strong in Japan, as is the case in Belgium and some other countries. Bureaucrats are selected by highly competitive examinations each year. Pay was low and the hours were long, but these officials wield considerable power through their interpretation of regulations, orders, and other provisions under the law. Their bonus payments are considerable, however, and there is always a good future for them in Japan's lockstep hierarchical system. After rising to a certain position, many of these bureaucrats would consider running for the Diet or other political office, or would join private enterprise at a fairly high level. There are substantial cash pensions upon retirement from the Government; if the official is also on the payroll of a private enterprise, he can then draw another cash pension on retirement.

Thanks to an accident of history, my mid-career years witnessed a period of tremendous activity in which Japan rose from the ashes of World War II to a point of significant business and technological activity. Some Americans subscribe to the idea that it was only the generosity of the United States that helped Japan and Europe recover from the war. There is no question that Japan was supported and assisted by the United States in many ways, including technological assistance through licensing and service agreements. Because of such infusion of technology and foreign exchange, the devastated nation was able to develop its industries very rapidly after the war. The entrenched system, called "Japan, Inc." by some American critics in later years, fused two important elements: the business clout of a manufacturing economy and the government's power in granting tax and other benefits. Only individual benefits and comforts were sacrificed. Financial institutions favored business loans over private ones to individuals, and many of these owned a small interest or shares in their customers, uncommon in the United States.

International geopolitics also contributed to Japan's success during this period. The Korean War broke out in 1950, just two years before the signing of the final peace treaty with Japan. The outbreak of hostilities on the Korean peninsula prompted General MacArthur to strongly recommend the formation of a police force in Japan, now called the Self-Defense Force. Though it was short, the Korean conflict benefited the Japanese economy to some extent. In the 1960s, the Vietnam War definitely benefited Japan without straining any of its resources. As a result of all of these conflicts, it was clear that the United States definitely needed to have Japan on its side because of its sometimes paranoid fear of Communism, something that was not a factor in Great Britain, Canada, or Japan itself. All three of these countries did business with and carried on trade with the Communist countries, while the United States did not.

Now that Gulf War II is over, Japan will again be one of the beneficiaries in the reconstruction of Afghanistan and Iraq since it has been one of the staunchest supporters of the United States, right or wrong, and seldom, if ever, criticizes the United States openly. With heavy reliance on imported oil from the Middle East, Japan must work together with others in assuring themselves of the supply of oil. Also, Japan has advanced technology and equipment that can be useful to the reconstruction of Iraq. It is said that in Gulf War I (Desert Storm), Japan contributed much technology that helped the United States greatly. If the work in Iraq is based on an international open bid system, Japan will be an important player because of its efficiency and ability to perform the work effectively at a relatively low cost. Finally, Japan's experience after World War II can be a valuable resource to the United States in the rebuilding of Iraq although the human problems are poles apart between the Japanese and Iraqis.

There was a time when technology flowed only into Japan. However, in the 1980s, the process changed somewhat and Japan began exporting its own technology to the United States, again through licensing and service agreements. Japan also exported its technology to other countries, especially in Asia, and is now in a position to export and give direct assistance to almost any country. For Japan, trade and ideology are mutually exclusive and they are able to do business with almost any country.

YKK AND "CYCLE OF GOODNESS"

It is fascinating that a simple, everyday device like a zipper helped me hone my expertise in dealing with Japanese business clients during this early period in my legal career. It was in 1958, through the introduction of T. Shinohara on the West Coast, that I was asked to meet with Tadao Yoshida, the founder of Yoshida Kogyo KK (YKK) of Kurobe, Japan. Kurobe is on the island of Honshu, facing the Japan Sea. Mr. Yoshida arrived in New York with Harry Isaka, an assistant who served as his interpreter. I met them at the Statler Hotel in midtown Manhattan prior to escorting them to dinner in a nearby restaurant. After introducing ourselves and chatting for a while, we started to leave the room and head out when Tadao Yoshida said, "Excuse me, the lights are on and I should turn them off. We should not be wasteful of valuable electricity."

That experience remains with me nearly half a century later. I was most impressed with a man who was mindful of waste even in a hotel where the room charges included all utilities.

"This man will succeed," I said to myself.

During the course of our dinner, Mr. Yoshida talked about his philosophy of life and business. He said that he was convinced he could succeed if he had a location, a piece of machinery, and a roof over it. His mechanical skills and creativity were beyond limits and he was way ahead of his time. His philosophy, the "Cycle of Goodness" *(Zen No Jyunkan),* was based on principles advocated by Andrew Carnegie of U.S. Steel, whom he admired. According to this philosophy, by serving the people and society, an enterprise will prosper as it will cycle back returns to the entrepreneur, similar to a Mobius strip. This is a surface with only one side, formed by giving a half twist to a narrow, rectangular strip of paper and then pasting its ends together. Goodness flows continuously as there is no end to the strip after the ends are pasted together. The "Cycle of Goodness" works generally in this manner: YKK must produce quality products at a reasonable cost. For example, a piece of product that costs 100 yen to produce initially will be produced for 50 yen, resulting in a profit of 50 yen. This profit is divided among the ultimate customer, the dealer, and YKK. With this profit, YKK could invest in research, development, purchase materials in large quantities, thus lowering the cost, paying dividends, and increasing the wages and salaries of its employees.

Based on this philosophy, Tadao Yoshida led YKK to become one of the largest privately owned companies in the world. It now operates in 66 countries with 132 companies in its group. YKK is reputed to be the Fastener King of the world and its market share is the largest in the world. I was privileged to have been part of this expansion over the years. YKK started as a manufacturer of metal zippers and later developed "slide fasteners" out of other material never imagined possible by old-time zipper makers. Through its founder's forward-looking creativity and charisma the company grew and there is every indication that its scope of operation and expansion will continue. When Mr. Yoshida started in the business, he said his goal was to produce enough fasteners to reach the moon, but he has in reality gone to the moon and back many times over. When he started using aluminum in YKK's fasteners, he mentioned to me the possibility that his firm could manufacture automobiles or refrigerators, but he saw a greater potential in the building materials field. YKK has since developed its own unique designs for building homes and office buildings. In expanding its operations worldwide, YKK also acquired smaller specialty-products companies in the fashion industry and related fields and expanded its opera-

S. Nishizaki, K. Yoshida, Tadao Yoshida, Frank Sogi, and Harry Isaka at factory in Toyama

tions worldwide. In addition, YKK produces its own machinery and tools. Also, Tadao Yoshida's management style was to train his employees in such a way that everyone would become an entrepreneur like him. After his death, his son, Tadahiro Yoshida, succeeded him and is the president of the YKK group.

My association with the Yoshidas goes back to that first meeting in 1958. The reason he came to New York in 1958 was to seek a solution to a problem with a $300,000 shipment of aluminum zippers that customers complained were defective. After agreeing that the zippers were indeed not operating properly, he summarily decided to return the total price he had received and recalled the entire shipment to Japan. Since that time, I have never heard of the company experiencing any endemic defects in its products again.

United States Operation After settling this first problem, Mr. Yoshida decided to deal with his customers directly rather than through intermediaries or trading companies, as had been the custom in Japan for many centuries. To accomplish this, he asked me to organize a New York corporation so that he could start an operation in the United States. It was incorporated as Yoshida International, Inc. in 1960 and it established a warehouse operation on the second floor of a building at Canal Street and Broadway, close to the garment district. Mr. Tamura was the head of the operation, and with two assistants he imported and distributed zippers manufactured in Japan. I was the Secretary of the company, a position I held until I retired a couple of years ago, after more than 40 years with the company, and I will continue for a second term of two years as a special advisor until 2004.

Kurobe, Toyama Prefecture, Japan In Japan, YKK has a substantial manufacturing operation in Kurobe, with machine shops, weaving plants with more spindles than an ordinary textile company, and other wholly integrated manufacturing facilities. Tadao Yoshida always wanted to replicate this Kurobe operation, first in the United States and then elsewhere, to avoid the hassles that restrictive export-import policies might bring.

Mr. And Mrs. Tadahiro (Tad) Yoshida with Francis Y. Sogi

During the times that I made frequent trips to Japan, Tadao Yoshida would invite me to visit the Kurobe operation. The trip started at 10 p.m. and the train left for Kurobe from Ueno Station and arrived there at about 8 a.m. We were up in our sleeper cabins at 6 a.m. and I would listen to his dreams of the future and his philosophy of business ethics. After arriving in Kurobe, we would go to a *ryokan* bath and have a bottle of beer with breakfast. On one trip, he showed me a piece of equipment he had imported from the United States. He placed a bolt of aluminum that was about 10 inches in diameter and about 18 inches long into this new machine, and when he pressed a couple of buttons, the machine smoothly spewed out hundreds of feet of flat aluminum which could be used to press out elements of zippers. In this way, I got to know this client much better than any other client. I appreciated this, as he was the soul of the company and he was determined to succeed, having started it in 1934.

Varick Street, Manhattan, New York City In order to realize his dream to get into the U.S. market in a big way, Tadao Yoshida started his modest manufacturing operations on Varick Street in downtown Manhattan, close to the Holland Tunnel. Business began improving and YKK was soon able to reduce the import of a major part of its products from Japan as it had established a factory operation that could produce them in the United States. Afterwards, he moved to a slightly larger manufacturing operation on Long Island, later buying land and erecting a building to house his own machinery.

Lyndhurst, New Jersey Seeing how successful the Varick Street and Long Island operations had been, I embarked on acquiring a parcel of land in Lyndhurst, New Jersey, whose owners I had dealt with earlier, in the area of the Meadowlands where the major baseball and football stadiums would later be built. Toyota Motor Sales, another firm I was representing at the time, had already established a large East Coast sales office nearby. To run the Lyndhurst factory, Tadao Yoshida sent his niece's husband, Mr. Kita, accompanied by his family to be president of the New Jersey operation. A large factory was built there, and the entire machinery for zipper manufacture was imported from Japan, having been built by YKK in its own machine shops. By this time, YKK had gone into the manufacture of zippers made of nylon and other plastics, under the Ziplon and other YKK trademarks. This was the first real estate that YKK owned in the United States for its operations and it was successful from the start. Under the aggressive leadership of Mr. Kita, the company thrived and its customer base expanded, so much so that YKK's rivals, such as Talon and others, started a campaign to stop its fast-growing competitor. Even so it was one of many trade and industry problems that came up as part of its growing pains.

Macon, Georgia When the Lyndhurst operation was underway, Ken Kitano, an engineer, arrived as part of its management team. Mr. Kitano later became one of the most senior executives in the YKK organization in Japan. Like Tadao Yoshida, Mr. Kitano was a mechanically minded manager with a keen sense of numbers and one who could "sharpen the pencil" to a fine point when necessary. Not long after his arrival, I was asked to accompany Tadao Yoshida to find a suitable location in the South where a new and bigger operation could be started. It was YKK's strategy to reduce the number of imported products and make more of them domestically. Since I knew some officials in Atlanta and Macon, Georgia, we decided to concentrate on land in that state. We even flew over in a small plane to view some potential sites from the air. Tadao Yoshida finally decided on some 50-plus acres in Macon. We dealt with local officials led by Buckner F. Melton, a lawyer and politician of the first order with a warm southern heart who performed as he promised he would. From the first meeting, there was good chemistry between YKK and the Macon officials, and negotiations proceeded smoothly. The people and the city of Macon were true to their word and welcomed YKK warmly. Former President Jimmy Carter was Governor of Georgia during this period, whose support encouraged YKK to expand its operations in Macon, where about 50 acres became available. Ken Kitano designed the factory for the first area and also for the second

Former President Jimmy Carter is seated in front of Francis Y. Sogi at 50th anniversary celebration of YKK, Kurobe Japan, 1994.

expansion of about 250 acres. Afterwards, Eric Watanabe, Tom Sakata and many others carried on the operation successfully in Macon, which expanded once more to Dublin, east of Macon, about an hour away. After the Macon and Dublin factories came on stream, the headquarters office was gradually moved from Lyndhurst to Atlanta as it should have been, because of the substantial investments made by YKK in the State of Georgia. Since then YKK has acquired other related businesses, such as notions and fasteners, and has incorporated new companies to take care of new products, such as Alumerica, Inc., YKK AP America, Inc., Tape Craft Corporation, and YKK Universal Fasteners, Inc.

Tadao Yoshida was a great supporter of Jimmy Carter as Governor and later as President of the United States, and was the only civilian from Japan invited to Carter's inauguration in Washington in 1977. In 1984, when YKK celebrated its 50th Anniversary in Kurobe, Japan, President Jimmy and Rosalyn Carter were present for the celebrations and I was present for that event as a member of YKK and one of the speakers for the occasion. When the Carter Center was established in the Atlanta area after the President's retirement, Tadao Yoshida contributed the Japanese Garden at the Center. It is my understanding that YKK provides for the care and maintenance of the Garden by Japanese caretakers. The current president of YKK, Tadahiro (Tad) Yoshida, and his family continue a warm relationship with former President Carter and his family.

Many products being manufactured by DuPont were also used by YKK, such as nylon, and when Tadao Yoshida was experimenting with the Ziplon product, the big American chemical company was not too happy about supplying materials to the Japanese upstart. DuPont was afraid that YKK might use it to manufacture kitchenware and other competitive products. Assured by Tadao Yoshida that it would be used for zippers only, DuPont was delighted to supply raw materials in substantial quantities for this new and novel application it had never anticipated.

I have represented many major industrial, financial, aircraft, show business, food and steel manufacturers and shipping companies since beginning my legal career in 1952, such as Ajinomoto, Shimadzu Seisakusho, Kawasaki Heavy Industries, Kawasaki Shipping, Kawasaki Steel and many others in Japan's industrial complex. YKK has been one of the most exciting, though, because I was involved with such an entrepreneur as Tadao Yoshida, who made all of this possible with such a wonderful philosophy that has universal application in the business world.

Quite a few old timers have retired from the Board of Directors, as well as its officers. Even though I've retired from YKK's board of directors and as its general counsel, I still maintain a good relationship with the Yoshida family. I call on them on my annual trips to Japan to visit our Tokyo office that I still manage. For many years, I stayed in touch with Tadao Yoshida, his brothers and their respective children.

I also continue to stay in touch with Buckner F. Melton and his wife, Tammie. Buckner Melton was Mayor of Macon when YKK was involved in its early negotiations to relocate there. He was even mentioned as a potential candidate for the governorship of the State of Georgia. Truly a fine Southern gentleman of the highest order, he was a pleasure to know and work with. He and Charles Jones visited us in Lyndhurst when YKK was interested in purchasing its first 50 acres of property in Macon.

Buckner was also a fine golfer with a low handicap and belonged to a well-known local club. He, Mr. Kita, and I also enjoyed playing gin rummy after a round of golf, with a little wagering on the side to make it interesting.

Over the years, I've had the pleasure of working with a number of YKK executives here and abroad. I met Seijiro Nishizaki, who became vice chairman of YKK Corporation of America. I visited him when I was in Oslo, Norway in connection with the sale of YS-11 aircraft to MayAir. Mr. Nishizaki at the time was manager of YKK's assembly operation in Sneek, Holland and since then he has occupied many other important positions with the company. He has also developed his skills as a golfer, though he didn't take much time out for leisure activities when the late Tadao Yoshida was still around.

In the Lyndhurst operation, David Schwartz joined YKK early on, and he has been a devoted leader of the local staff, also occupying important positions in several companies. G. Edward Reck, a more recent arrival, has gotten involved in the financial side of the business and now occupies responsible positions in a number of YKK companies in the United States. In Georgia, Bernard J. Rubin, William T. Wiley, Jr., and E. Alex Gregory, Jr. joined the Macon operation. Sometime later, when the YKK operation had grown substantially and the company required in-house counsel, John C. Castellano joined as corporate counsel and was later promoted to be corporate Secretary. Eric Watanabe, who was a super golfer, remained in Macon for many years until he returned to Japan. Shinichi Kawamoto and Masahiro Ujihara were also some YKK old-timers in the U.S., though they moved around quite a bit.

Early on, I spotted E. Alex Gregory as being one of the future leaders of YKK operations. His demeanor and charisma in work and social settings seemed to put him one notch above the others. I must have been right, for he was later tapped to be president of YKK's entire operation in the United States. Alex's predecessors, such as Nick Tsubokawa and Jay Takahashi, also performed well and developed and led the U.S. operations for some time out of Atlanta. All of this resulted from the foundation laid by Ken Kitano, who is now one of the top officers in YKK Japan as well as being an avid golfer, like Mr. Nishizaki.

Globalization The expansion of YKK into the state of Georgia was only the beginning. Today, through its network of assembly plants and sales offices throughout the hemisphere, YKK is meeting the global needs of its customers. This is all part of YKK's "Cycle of Goodness" philosophy of giving good service and quality products to its customers at reasonable prices. Also, YKK follows the adage: "know your customers." Since its humble beginnings in the 1950s, YKK has continued to spring forward from Japan to the United States, Canada, South America, Europe, Africa, Asia, and other parts of the world. I had the privilege of visiting many of their operations in Holland, Belgium, London, South America, Canada, Hong Kong, Taiwan, and other locations, at every one of which the YKK management was extremely courteous and hospitable in receiving me.

YKK is a very unusual company in that, unlike other Japanese companies that sent personnel to the United States only for two or three years and then rotated them back to Japan, it sent its personnel to the U.S. with their families, where they remained for long periods, sometimes as long as 10 years or more. As a result, many of its Japanese staff became quite fluent in English. Tadao Yoshida believed in having all its leaders become acquainted with the company's operations in other parts of the country and around the world. For this purpose, periodic and annual national and global meetings took place in Japan. There are many others with whom I have met and worked with during my association with YKK, but with limited space, regrettably, I cannot write about them all..

Tongass National Park Project, Alaska

One of the significant projects I worked on in the 1960s put me literally at loggerheads with the Sierra Club. Two of our clients, the Kanzaki Paper Company in Japan and the Champion Paper Company, formed a joint venture to harvest 840 billion board feet of lumber from the Tongass National Park in Alaska, which covers millions of acres. The plan was to export this lumber from federal land to Japan over a 15-year period, involving more than $600 million. The exported lumber would be used to make 4x4 lumber for building homes there, unlike the situation in the U.S., where 2x4 lumber is standard. At the time, U.S. law did not permit exporting logs to Japan from a national forest. To comply with American export regulations, the logs were to be canted–that is, the four sides of the log were to be sliced off so they would be qualified as lumber and not be classified as logs. A mere technicality, but it worked.

Tongass National Park is a vast area of land with glaciers, streams, ponds, animal and bird-nesting habitats and shorelines. It was a virgin forest that had not been logged before. Our proposal involved only a small portion of this vast area of forest. More than a dozen permits were obtained and plans for logging were drawn up, including the establishment of a water-purification plant to protect salmon life that might be adversely affected. A lot of technologies that would preserve much of the natural habitat of the forest were considered and included. Cost calculations showed that the operation could be feasible if it proceeded on a timely basis as planned.

When the Tongass National Park project came up for a hearing for per-mitting in Juneau, the Sierra Club appeared to file objections and legal actions. Though their objections were not insurmountable, it might have added to the cost of the project. We met objections to the water-purifica-tion plant by building a second plant that would come into operation should the first plant for any reason fail to operate. When Sierra claimed that our proposed operation would destroy the scenic drives that ran through the forest, we agreed to provide a two-mile buffer zone along the highways. We even proposed a "balloon logging" operation in which the trees would be cut and lifted out of the forest by balloons so that roads into the logging area would not be necessary.

All of this happened immediately after the Sierra Club campaigned against Disneyland and succeeded in stopping its proposed Storm King Project on the East Coast, where Disney had planned to create a major ski resort and recreation area. As much as Sarah and I enjoyed skiing, we were overjoyed with the news that the Sierra Club had stopped this project. The

Storm King Project would have cleared vast forested areas in the mountains, eliminating the pristine natural habitat for the bald eagle and other birds, as well as other wild animals.

However, I thought our Tongass logging project was good for Alaska and good for the rebuilding of Japan. It was my function to get the Tongass Project approved for our client, which was relying heavily on American wood for its manufacture of paper products. The Sierra Club did not succeed on environmental grounds because our client was able to meet all the environmental objections that were being raised. Even the Sierra Club itself was violating the environment by massacring the grizzly bears in the Tongass National Park. The forest was a popular hunting ground for many, including members of the Sierra Club, which maintained hunting lodges there. At the trial in Juneau the Sierra Club was represented by a single lawyer, and we had a battery of four attorneys representing our group. We introduced a colored picture of a grizzly bear that had just been killed by members of the Sierra Club in the forest. They never mentioned the grizzly bear again while making their case. One of their last objections was that our plan might have led to the possible extinction of the bald eagle in the forest.

In this situation, and not because it was my client that was involved, the Sierra Club was not doing the public a service in stopping this project that made very good economic sense. Also, it would have served Alaska well and it would have been a great benefit to our client, which was forced to look at other sources of wood supply, perhaps in another country. It was an entirely different situation from the Storm King development of a ski resort. The project failed because of the long delay resulting in an escalation of cost and making it economically unfeasible.

NATIONAL FEDERATION OF FARMERS COOPERATIVE ASSOCIATIONS (ZEN-NOH)

In the late 1960s, I moved to One Wall Street to join and help form the law firm of Miller, Montgomery, Spalding & Sogi with about 35 lawyers. For the first time, my own name was in the name of a law firm. It seemed like I had crossed another threshold in my career. Soon afterwards, I began representing ZEN-NOH, a farmers' cooperative with a membership of four million farmers throughout Japan. The cooperative imported all the materials necessary for the farmers, including raw materials for fertilizer and animal feed. It also handled all exports of farm products from Japan in collaboration with trading companies. ZEN-NOH maintained an office on Wall Street and was scheduled to move into the new World Trade Center that was then under construction.

The site of the World Trade Center was a rundown section of meat and vegetable markets whose products were brought in by boat or barge plowing the Hudson River. The meat market was a huge area with every conceivable type of meat product, including buffalo and whale meat. When the Trade Center was being built, I could see the huge hole from which the excavated materials were deposited into the Hudson River to build a 100-acre landfill that eventually became the office and residential complexes of Battery Park City. To prevent the water from the Hudson River leaking into the dugout, a watertight barrier was erected, the so-called "bathtub," that figured so prominently in the discussions of Ground Zero after September 11, 2001.

When the foundations of the Twin Towers were laid, I could look out from my office window on the 31st floor of the Irving Trust Building, at One Wall Street, facing the Hudson River, at the corner of Broadway, across from Trinity Church, to see the steel beams being erected like Tinker Toys, one piece at a time until it eventually reached its maximum height of 107 floors. New York skyscrapers have traditionally employed Native Americans at these high levels, because their sure-footedness is crucial for buildings that swayed slightly at these altitudes. As wind velocity reached a high enough level, even the Native Americans stopped working. When the Twin Towers were finally completed in the early 1970s, the first offices were rented for something like $4.25 a square foot. Tenants who took an entire floor of 30,000 square feet received even a better rate from their landlord, the Port Authority of New York and New Jersey.

It seems almost inconceivable that such huge structures, deemed the tallest buildings in the world at one time and with the largest number of tenants, could disappear from this earth in a matter of minutes and cause such disruption and havoc around the downtown areas of Manhattan and indeed the whole world. Only great evil can do what happened on September 11, 2001. I can still remember the problems that Minoru Yamasaki, the architect, encountered as the structures were being built when he asked the Port Authority, the owners, for an additional fee of six million dollars. There was a sculpture by Nagare of Japan, who did his piece by having his stone sculpture done in three parts: one in Japan, one in Spain, and the other in Italy, then put together in New York and placed in front of One World Trade Center. The restaurant on the 107th floor by the name of Windows of the World was quite an attraction and I was a frequent customer with clients who deserved special service as the tab was not modest.

ZEN-NOH moved into the Trade Center and started to engage itself with large projects. One of the first was with a Chicago company called Estech, part of a large conglomerate that owned over 10,000 acres of land in and around Sarasota, Florida. This land had a proven reserve of phosphate rock for fertilizer, which the farmers in Japan were then importing from Israel and other parts of the world. Because Japan was also importing substantial quantities of oil from the Arabian countries, the supply of phosphate from Israel could have been threatened, so it was necessary to locate alternative sources and one was found in Florida.

This proposed joint venture involved an investment in excess of $300 million for a startup operation that would require a dragline for digging the phosphate and a plant for processing the shipment to Japan. We formed the Zen-Noh Phosphate Corporation in Florida for this venture. Many wealthy Northerners had retirement homes in the area and were quite vocal about potential environmental issues. The whole situation was quite sensitive, and it was crucial to do some preliminary public relations work while approaching the regulatory officials in Sarasota. Estech took responsibility for handling the permitting of the venture. They announced the project and informed local officials that they were going to apply for all of the necessary permits. When the public became aware of the project, they became very vocal against it. In due time, all but one of the permits were obtained after considerable time and expense. This final permit was the one that would allow digging into the soil. Without it, the entire project would fail. Things dragged on for more than a year, and finally Estech decided not to continue. Estech sold the land, though we considered the advisability of claiming that this was, in effect, a taking without compensation, since the land was not usable for any purpose other than phosphate rock mining. And there was fear of radiation if it were used for residential purposes.

In another entirely different project in Louisiana, ZEN-NOH incorporated Zen-Noh Grain Corporation to explore the feasibility of building a grain elevator upstream on the Mississippi River. There was a strong demand for American grain in Japan and the proposed facility would be used to export grain from the mid-western states to assure a steady supply. After much study and research for a suitable site, an area was proposed in Saint James Parish, about an hour and a half upstream from New Orleans. It was to be a state-of-the-art grain elevator, one designed to be immune from the explosions that sometimes resulted from the volatility of the dust in the elevator bins.

As with the phosphate mining operation, it was necessary to obtain a dozen or more permits from local, state, and federal agencies, since the proposed elevator was to be located in navigable waters. To assure ourselves of the success of this project, we did not announce it through public media during the early stages. Instead, we arranged for the president of Zen-Noh Grain to visit the local regulatory officials and neighboring property owners to make sure that all parties understood our project and its benefits to Louisiana and were in accord with us. We emphasized the benefits that would flow from the investment well in excess of $100 million, and we highlighted the safety factors that would be in place. State and Federal officials were concerned about any adverse environmental impacts and whether the facility would tax the traffic of the navigable waters of the Mississippi River.

The elevator was built on schedule and without any major incidents. It became operable after several years of construction, and has since operated without any mishap of any kind. Much grain has been exported to Japan and other parts of the world through this facility. This was an exemplary case study of a successful venture, one in which the community being impacted was kept informed from the early stages so there would be no surprises or opposition. The investment was a substantial one, and a minor local official could have opposed it and rallied the community against the project. It was a good example of the need of good public relations spadework, or *nemawashi,* from the beginning.

WOLOGISI IRON ORE MINE, REPUBLIC OF LIBERIA, AFRICA

In 1965, while a partner at Hunt, Hill & Betts, I heard that some of the other partners were going to the Republic of Liberia, which was founded in 1847, concerning the development of an iron ore mine in that country. Someone knew President Tubman of Liberia and was able to obtain a concession for the rights to commercially mine iron ore until the year 2040 for export to the world. The iron-ore content was low, but it could be raised by a proper sintering process. As a result, the potential of the mine was substantial, with possible yields from 500 million to a billion tons. Our firm represented Kinoshita Shoten, which was assigned to put together a Japanese group to raise funds and technical support for the operation by 1985. Kinoshita shortly pulled out, to be replaced by the Nichimen Company. Gradually, a group of Japanese companies was formed. The consortium was known as the Japanese Group. It was composed of several major trading companies and Kawasaki Steel Company as the prime mover of the Japanese Group. The trading companies included Marubeni Co., Ltd., Nissho-Iwai Co., Ltd., C. Itoh & Co., Ltd. (Itochu), and Toyo Menka Kaisha, Ltd.

It should be noted that Liberia and Japan had an interesting though indirect and obscure connection in the nineteenth century through Commodore Matthew Perry. Commodore Perry is best known as the man who "opened" Japan to the West by sailing into Yokohoma harbor in 1853, 150 years ago. It's a little known fact that Commodore Perry had earlier stopped ships on the high seas that were bringing African slaves to America and settled them in Liberia. The Republic of Liberia was a country where slaves were settled in 1821 under the auspices of the American Colonization Society. Through the support of President James Monroe, for whom the capital of Monrovia was named, slave ships coming from Africa were stopped by the American Navy ships and taken to Liberia. Liberia has long been an important country to the United States although it has not been its colony. It is English-speaking, uses U.S. currency, and had a democratic form of government. Many of the Liberians in Monrovia are called Americo-Liberians and have relatives in the United States. Many of them attended American universities. Liberia is thus Africa's oldest independent black republic. It has a population of about 1.9 million, and is bounded on the north by Sierra Leone and Guinea, on the east by Cote d'Ivoire, and on the south and west by the Atlantic Ocean. Liberia has substantial rice, palm oil, coffee, and rubber plantations. Firestone Rubber operated a 20,000-acre rubber plantation there. Liberia also exports teak, mahogany, walnut, ironwood, and giant makore, a tree that is 200 feet tall and eight feet in diameter.

In 1975, Liberia Iron and Steel Corporation (LISCO), a Liberian corporation, was organized by American interests that had acquired concession rights to the Wologisi Iron Ore Mine. The shares of LISCO were acquired by Liberian International American Corp. (LIAC), a Delaware corporation. In 1974, JG, LIAC, and LISCO, together with AMAX, Inc., which introduced the project to JG, entered into a stock agreement whereby JG became a partner of the venture. The target date for the venture was to begin mining iron ore by the year 1985, depending on the condition of the steel industry at that time. In preparation for this, it was necessary to conduct all types of feasibility studies, including determining the amount of proven and potential reserves of iron ore that was available. Bechtel & Co. was engaged to do these studies. Many experts were assigned to do additional studies and surveys, and periodic reports showed promising signs. JG had budgeted about $20 million for these purposes.

During the negotiations for the iron-ore mine and thereafter, it was necessary for the JG delegation to travel to Liberia at least twice a year, or more in some years, for a total of about 20 trips for the annual meeting of stockholders and board of directors of LIAC and LISCO. The feasibility studies were progressing as expected, and for 15 years I accompanied the JG delegation there, serving both as an interpreter and a lawyer. I always accompanied the JG delegates with Shinsaburo Kato, who headed the project from Kawasaki Steel. We'd leave from Kennedy Airport in New York at 8 p.m. and stop over in Dakar, Senegal, to change to a plane with different insignia. This was because the flight from Senegal to Monrovia continued on to South Africa, and there was then some peculiar requirement that a plane with different insignia be used. We usually arrived in Dakar early in the morning and in Monrovia at about 8 a.m. There was only one decent hotel there, the Ducor Hotel, and that is where we stayed after a ride of about an hour on a more or less paved road from the airport.

During the time we spent in Liberia, I noticed that the Americo-Liberians lived very comfortably, with air-conditioned offices, cars, substantial homes and summer residences in the mountains. One weekend, we were invited to a summer resort of Americo-Liberian Clarence Simpson with whom we were working on the mine. It was located high up in the mountains and had a pool and tennis court. After lunch, I walked outside in the nearly 100-degree heat. I felt that if I had to live in such heat daily, it would take away all my incentive and energy to work and improve my situation. The native Liberians have been doing this not only for a lifetime but for many generations.

There were times when it was necessary to meet Liberian President Tolbert in person. We would arrive at the hotel at 10 a.m. and meet him about an hour later. He made no appointments, and any citizen of Liberia was free to see him by showing up at his office. After waiting a while, he or she would get to see the President, whose formal attire consisted of a swearing-in suit with no tie. I served as the interpreter for Shinsaburo Kato, especially in our talks with President Tolbert. Before the time came for JG to make its final decisions on the mine, an unexpected catastrophe occurred in Monrovia at the Presidential mansion in 1980. One weekend, there was much talk about a Liberian who was to be executed the following week. The Liberian was a relative of Master Sergeant Samuel K. Doe, who with a small contingent of 17 enlisted men stormed the mansion and proclaimed a revolution of the Liberian people against the ruling elite of the True Whig Party. According to reports we received President Tolbert was assassinated, as well as his 13 ministers who faced Sergeant Doe's firing squad, while strapped to telephone poles. Doe proclaimed his own self Head of State, and for the first time the native people, or aborigines, of Liberia took over power. The revolution effectively closed the Wologisi Mine, and the iron-ore reserves will remain in situ indefinitely unless another entity arrives to develop it. Doe's uprising was only the beginning of a long period of turmoil in a Liberia where the Americo-Liberians are no longer in control.

An internal strife of warlords started in 1990, when Samuel Doe was captured, tortured, and deposed as president. Later reports indicate that Charles Taylor became the president of the Republic of Liberia after an election in 1997. But Liberia is far from stable until Charles Taylor leaves the country as he has promised to do and a new government is put in place through a democratic process. In August 2003, Charles Taylor officially resigned as President and took refuge in Nigeria.

Nihon Aeroplane Mfg. Co., Ltd., Tokyo, Japan

In the early 1960s, Japan attempted to enter the commercial aircraft industry with the development of the YS-11 turboprop, a twin-engine, short-takeoff-and-landing (STOL) aircraft with Rolls Royce engines. The aircraft was developed by the Nihon Aeroplane Manufacturing Co., Ltd. (NAMC), a company established by the Japanese government. After many test flights and receiving all regulatory approvals, the YS-11 went into the market in 1966. Its sales in the United States began in 1967. I became involved in this project when I was a partner in Hunt, Hill & Betts because I had worked with Joji Yusa, a director of Sales of NAMC, when he was with Kinoshita Shoten, a Japanese trading company that started after World War II. His offices were in our old building at 26 Broadway in downtown Manhattan. I was retained to represent NAMC in all of their exports of YS-11 to Canada, North and South America, and Europe.

Piedmont Aviation, Winston-Salem, N.C. In New York, Kennosuke Itoh, an employee of NAMC, was stationed in the office of C. Itoh & Co., commonly known as ITOCHU. It was one of the leading trading companies in Japan, which was involved in the sale of YS-11 aircraft. My principal contact in that company was Yoshinobu Sugihara in the legal department.

The first potential sale of the YS-11 was to Piedmont Aviation, a regional airline based in Winston-Salem, North Carolina. Piedmont was started by several executives under the leadership of Thomas Davis, its president. At the time, the airline was operating Martin 404s and other small aircraft to serve the region. Piedmont ordered 20 YS-11's to be delivered over a period of time. The negotiations lasted six months on such matters as price, service, technical support, and spare parts. Since this was the first significant order that NAMC received from abroad, especially from the United States, it would establish the confidence of future buyers if such a large order was concluded by a substantial regional airline. The STOL aircraft was ideal for Piedmont, since the carrier ran many short-haul flights with frequent stops. For these reasons, NAMC was unwilling to cut its price below cost and give extensive technical support for fear of setting a precedent that other airlines would demand. After a number of trips to Japan by Piedmont executives and technical personnel, and after many trips to Winston-Salem for negotiations, we finally came to an agreement. However, to further accommodate Piedmont, 14 of their Martin 404 aircraft were transferred to NAMC. I was asked to register them in my name, as an American citizen, until they could be resold by various brokers at the FAA aircraft registration office in Oklahoma City. For a period before they were sold, I was the proud owner of 14 Martin 404 aircraft.

Transair, Winnipeg, Canada The next transaction I handled for NAMC was with Transair in Winnipeg, Canada, for three aircraft. I retained local counsel in Winnipeg to assist us in preparing the necessary documents and assuring us that we had met all the regulatory requirements of Canada. The Japanese trading company handling this transaction was Marubeni Corporation in Vancouver.

The export sale by Japan, at this time, like nearly all other exports, was handled by a trading company that received a small commission. The Piedmont sale was primarily the responsibility of Mitsui Bussan Co, Ltd., and Mr. Kashiwada was the lead man. Delivery began about six months later. Twenty aircraft were delivered, but one was destroyed as a result of an accident, and Piedmont purchased another YS-11, making a total of 21. After many years of operation, Piedmont became very successful as a regional carrier and expanded its region, making STOL aircraft unnecessary. Finally, the carrier merged with a larger national airline. By this time, NAMC had exported quite a number of YS-11's to Asian, South American, European, Canadian and other carriers and established a niche in the aircraft industry. With all of these activities, Kennosuke Itoh was stationed in New York to represent NAMC in all dealings in the Western Hemisphere. He was quite knowledgeable and a delightful person and is an accomplished tennis player and a golfer as well. We traveled together to many locations, including Oslo, Norway; Buenos Aires, Argentina; Lima, Peru; and Athens, Greece in connection with the sale of YS-11's to airlines in those countries.

MayAir, Oslo, Norway After the Piedmont and Transair transactions, MayAir in Oslo, Norway became interested in the YS-11. Together with NAMC representatives, I visited Otto Mayer, owner of MayAir and also a ship owner of some consequence. Mayer wanted to lease three YS-11 aircraft to start airline service within Norway, mostly short-hauls, so a

STOL aircraft would have been ideal for him. After two visits to Oslo and a meeting in my New York office, we did not consummate the deal because of MayAir's financial weakness. Still, the experience was memorable. It brought back memories of the Scandinavians we associated with in Minnesota during the war. My visit to Oslo was my first to that part of the world, and our host treated us royally. In the evenings after long negotiating sessions, we all enjoyed a boilermaker, aquavit (Aalborg Akvavit) and beer, with boiled crayfish that was served as a chaser. To this day, aquavit is still an attraction and a favored drink for me, although many restaurants outside of New York do not serve it, let alone know about it. It is made out of potato or corn though not as potent as whiskey, vodka, or gin.

ALA-AUSTRAL, Buenos Aires, Argentina I also visited Argentina as part of my involvement with the YS-11 aircraft. Argentina has many large ranches and farms and is a large exporter of agricultural products and animal meat. One of the ranchers with large land holdings was involved in purchasing three YS-11's for a domestic airline he established. The sale of the aircraft was concluded by Nichimen Trading Company. Ken Itoh of NAMC in New York and I visited Buenos Aires to finalize the sale and to record the aircraft mortgage, which was part of the sale. Conferring with local counsel, I arranged to record the mortgages pursuant to their system of establishing a security interest in a chattel, which is somewhat different from a mortgage on land. When the installment payments were completed, I visited Buenos Aires again with Y. Mori of NAMC to record the satisfaction of mortgage.

Nightlife in the Argentine capital was very lively, and everyone seemed to dine late at night, around 9 o'clock. Those looking for relaxation headed out to the nightclubs around midnight. It was in these clubs that I was introduced to the tango, the Argentinean national dance. It was quite a delight to watch professionals gliding through the steps so smoothly and rhythmically. Try as I might, after three trips to Buenos Aires, however, I could not learn the tango.

In Brazil, C. Itoh & Co., Ltd. had already sold eleven YS-11's to CRUZERO DO SUL and VASP. One of the aircraft was named the "Samurai." While I did not have anything to do with the sale of YS-11's to Brazil, I visited there a number of times. Street crimes were rampant, and even in Japan Town, we were warned that we should not go out on the streets alone, especially at night.

When we stopped in Brazil on our way home to New York from Argentina, we were amazed to learn of the number of Japanese living in that country (1.3 million), much larger than the number residing in the United States (850,000). Most of the 1.3 million Japanese Brazilians live in Sao Paulo although there are still many farmers in the northern part of Brazil. I visited South America numerous times on business. A large amount of trade was going on between Japan and South America, and most of the major Japanese trading companies were operating there, importing products from Japan and exporting raw materials in return.

LANSA, Lima, Peru The Japanese have also lived in Peru for many years, many of them fluent in Spanish, and are able to speak as well as the natives. One was reputed to speak Castilian Spanish, the highest level of proficiency by a foreigner.

I traveled to Peru to do legal work for Nihon Aeroplane involving an airline in Lima that had leased three YS-11's. The lease was about to expire and the aircraft was to be returned to Japan, but the local airline operated by the Peruvian government would not deliver them to NAMC. Three of us were assigned to negotiate the return of the aircraft with the Peruvian government: Hiroshi Yajima from NAMC in Tokyo, Kennosuke Itoh from NAMC's office in New York, and myself. As a part of this transaction, NAMC had stationed an employee in Lima, coordinating the leasing agreement while it was in force. He was our point man in our dealings with the government. I might add that Kennosuke Itoh is an independent businessman in New York living in Larchmont. Hiroshi Yajima, after leaving NAMC, joined one of our earliest clients for whom I did legal work in 1953, the Shimadzu Seisakusho. This company has been very much involved in highly technical equipment, and Mr. Yajima was promoted to President. Recently, one of the employees of his company was named a Nobel Laureate in science and gained considerable recognition throughout the world.

It was necessary to make three or four trips to Peru, which required stops in Miami, Panama City, Quito, Ecuador and then to Lima from New York, primarily on Pan American Airlines. It was a military government but we had no problems obtaining visas and in entering or exiting the country. We stayed at the Riviera Hotel, a moderate hotel next to the government offices. General Trudeau was responsible for the leasing and return of the aircraft, and it was usually not necessary to make any appointment with him under their system. We would arrive at the appointed hour, or at our convenience, we would still wait an hour or two.

If we saw him on a Friday (usually about 10 a.m. in the morning), we would exchange pleasantries for a few minutes and then hear his stock answer, "It's too close to the weekend and I would like to review the matter further. Can we meet again, perhaps, on Monday?" If we saw him on Monday, the answer would be somewhat different, but he suggested that we meet again the next day. This went on for three or four months, during which we made three trips to Lima. While waiting for the meetings with General Trudeau, Ken Itoh, Hiroshi Yajima, and I played golf with the local NAMC representative at his private golf course. Each of us would have a caddie and walked the course. While playing, we noticed that the caddies were very supportive of each of us, becoming quite downtrodden whenever one of us did not perform too well. We found out later that the caddies had a wager among themselves in the same way that we players did with each other. This was also the reason the caddies were all barefooted. When we were certain a ball had gone into a very bad rough with tall grass and could not be played very well, we'd walk over to the area only to find the ball out on the course in an easily playable area.

As was the practice in Peru, at the time all of this was happening, we played golf in the morning or had unproductive meetings with General

Trudeau until noon and then ate lunch, usually in a Japanese restaurant. Following the good custom of Peru, we slept in pajamas until mid-afternoon, and then did business again from 4 to 6 p.m., when we met with Marubeni's representative to discuss the events of the day and plan for the next. In the evening, following our usual practice in New York, we would have dinner until about 10 o'clock and then go to a local nightclub for live entertainment until midnight or so. As we left the nightclub, we noticed that many of the locals were just arriving for the evening and that the establishment was only then getting crowded. We learned later that this was the typical lifestyle of Peruvians. The long evenings are not a problem, for they can look forward to the afternoon siesta every day. After our three trips to Lima, the three YS-11's were finally returned to NAMC. A number of years later, I visited Lima again on three occasions: in connection with the Kona Coffee exhibit in Sao Paulo, Brazil, the conference of Pan American Nikkei (X COPANI) in Santiago, Chile, and when we in New York hosted the XI COPANI conference in 2001.

On one of these trips, I also visited Ajinomoto's factory located outside of Lima, where I met their local representatives. I usually visited my client's companies operating in every country I visited. Ajinomoto operated a factory located close to the coast of Peru, producing monosodium glutamate for sale within the country.

I visited Asuncion, Paraguay for the Pan-American Nikkei conference there in 1989 and spent five days meeting many friends that I had gotten to know after attending these conferences since the first one I attended in Sao Paulo in 1985. There were two casinos in the city but there was just no time for it since we were fully occupied day and night, playing golf, having dinners, and just socializing through the late hours.

The same situation occurred in Santiago, Chile. I visited there twice, once for the Pan-American Nikkei conference in 1999 and once thereafter to learn more about their experience in hosting the conference prior to that in New York, which our group, PNA USA EAST, hosted in 2001. Chile elected its presidents for many years under the watchful eyes of General

Pinochet. Chile has one of the most advanced economies in South America. Years ago, Chile sent many of its young economists to the University of Chicago Business School, where they learned the American theory of economics and boldly applied it to the business situation at home. It is reputed to be the most economically advanced country in South America.

Because La Paz, Bolivia might have been the site for the next Pan-American Nikkei conference, I stopped in that country two or three times at the airport on the way to Sao Paulo and Buenos Aires, Argentina. This was also true with Ecuador, where it was necessary to make a refueling stop on my way to Lima, Peru. Uruguay was somewhat different as I never stopped there. My only involvement with it was in connection with the rebate that NAMC paid Aristotle Socrates Onassis's Olympic Airlines when it delivered a YS-11 to the airline. It was paid to Uruguay because his brother-in-law maintained an account in that country, and it was there that the rebate payments had to be deposited.

Olympic Airlines, Athens, Greece During the later phase of my legal career, the last large order with which I was involved came from Olympic Airlines, which operated an international and domestic airline out of Athens, Greece. The carrier, of course, was owned by the shy Greek shipping magnate, Aristotle Onassis, who married Jackie Kennedy. Olympic's domestic routes involved lots of island hopping, and the YS-11 STOL aircraft was perfect for this kind of operation. Initial negotiations took place at the airline's Fifth Avenue office with their attorney, Tryfon Koutalidis, who came from Athens to handle all negotiations. Olympic wanted eight YS-11's and assurances of prompt and regular delivery on schedule. Such a large order was very desirable, so Joji Yusa and the aircraft sales manager of NAMC's trading company, Mr. Kashiwada of Mitsui & Co., came from Japan to work on the deal. With the compliments of Olympic, four of us, including Ken Itoh, were all flown first class to Athens and put up in a luxurious hotel. We did not have much free time, but arranged to visit the Parthenon still shimmering high on the rocky Acropolis. While walking around, I noticed loose rocks, small enough so that they could be put into one's pocket and that is where one piece of rock went. However, on the way out there was a sign in large red letters containing a warning that anyone caught removing any rocks from the premises would be prosecuted to the fullest extent of the law. Seeing the sign, I quickly returned the historic piece of rock and returned home without any memento from the Acropolis.

After several days of meetings on the price and delivery schedule, Olympic committed to the purchase of eight YS-11's and was willing to conclude the deal with NAMC the following day. We were all delighted, and Joji Yusa called Japan to inform his company and the Ministry of International Trade and Industry of the sale. That evening, we returned to the hotel and celebrated the sale in the hotel bar from about 5 p.m. We were all martini drinkers, and at last count, we had 11 martinis each, standing up, not even on the rocks, without dinner. Ken Itoh and I excused ourselves somewhat early, at 11 p.m., had a snack somewhere in the hotel, and went to bed. Joji Yusa and the Mitsui Bussan representative had a few more before retiring.

We had expected that the meeting at 10 a.m. the following morning would be a social courtesy call to exchange pleasantries and to sign a few papers to confirm the transaction subject to signing the formal documents. I met with legal counsel to finalize these papers while Joji Yusa and Ken Itoh went to visit Aristotle Onassis, expecting just to shake hands, wish each other well and express our appreciation for the huge order. The man from Mitsui was not able to attend the meeting and rested at the hotel from the long evening the night before. Much to Joji Yusa's surprise, Onassis told him that there was one last commercial point open, and it was usually worked out after the price and other details had been determined. Following the practice in his shipbuilding contracts, where he received a rebate of three percent for his seamen's welfare fund, he was asking for a rebate of six percent of the price, to be paid at the time of delivery of each aircraft into an account in Uruguay.

Joji Yusa was flabbergasted. Though usually quite verbal, he was speechless for a moment and could not respond or utter a word. He had

had dealings with Onassis's shipping companies while he was with Kinoshita & Co. During this time, Onassis had ordered many millions of tons of ships from the emerging Japanese companies because the price was so attractive and competitive. After many international telephone calls, NAMC agreed to pay the rebate and finalized the sale. Later, upon the delivery of each aircraft, I had the responsibility of sending a check of over $600,000 to Uruguay, where Onassis's brother-in-law maintained an account. The transaction was an installment payment sale, and Olympic Airways paid every installment on time, and usually, a few days in advance.

In the 1980s, the manufacture and sale of YS-11's were being phased out, and the original airlines were converting to jet aircraft, having grown and expanded to become larger national routes, such as Piedmont Airlines. NAMC asked me to purchase USASC since it was the only foreign company it owned, and any assets the company owned would be transferred to me with the ownership. Once all claims were finally recovered, I liquidated the company. Japan was not quite ready for the next generation of aircraft.

Gone With The Wind

As a result of my work with the Motion Picture Export Association of America, (related to the Motion Picture Association of America in Hollywood), in our Tokyo office in the 1950s, I started to do work for Toho Co., Ltd. in New York. Toho is the leading producer of motion pictures and stage performances in Japan. With copyright license from Stephen Mitchell, heir to Margaret Mitchell, the author of the book, it produced, in association with Joe Leyton, the musical *Scarlett*, based on *Gone With the Wind*. In Japan, it was a great success and Toho decided to produce it for foreign consumption with Hollywood actors and actresses. I assisted Toho in handling the legal aspects of such production in the United States under the direction of Kazuo Kikuta. When it opened in London, it was sold out and a great success. Then it opened in Los Angeles and it was equally successful with sold out performances. The plan was to go to Atlanta and then to Broadway for a grand opening, but it was not to be. The reason for the sellouts in London and Los Angeles was that the performances were attended by season ticket holders and not by the general public. The conclusion reached by the backers and Toho was that it would not be successful in Atlanta or on Broadway, so they decided to discontinue performances of *Scarlett* for American audiences.

CHAPTER TEN

Diversity is Strength

D URING THE 1980s and later, Japanese and other Asian peoples became much more visible in the United States. Trade increased considerably during these decades, and Japanese automobiles, appliances, and electronic products became commonplace in this country. During the 1980s, the Japanese American redress movement gained momentum, finally resulting in federal legislation acknowledging the injustice of the Japanese American internment in American concentration camps during World War II. In *1992*, after many years of preparation, the Japanese American National Museum opened in Los Angeles, honoring the legacy of the past and offering resources for the future. I have been privileged in these later years of my career to be part of these and other movements, and to observe how the world has changed tremendously during the postwar period.

Ever since the Japanese attack on Hawaii catapulted us into World War II, the phrase "Remember Pearl Harbor" has echoed over and over again, reminding the nation of this fateful deed. We have heard many veterans still saying, "we can forgive but cannot forget" their war experiences. This is certainly understandable and the concentration camp experience should not only be not forgotten, but the American public should be repeatedly reminded of it. As the inscription on the Archives Building in Washington, D.C. says: "What is Past is Prologue." The past should be recorded for posterity so that it can be understood in the correct context of the time and not in hindsight. Those who were enemies so many years ago are now strong allies in the present-day world. Those who were allies then, like the former

Soviet Union, became archenemies for generations, causing tremendous upheaval and disruption around the world. After the fall of communism, Russia turned around to become a member of the international community and sought aid and assistance to build a better country for its people who had been subjugated for at least two generations. This goes to show the fluidity of politics in this modern world, for example, in Rwanda, fighting erupted out of ethnocentricity all because some were Hutus and the others were Tutsis. The result was strife and the killing of neighbors who had been long-time friends and social partners. Can you imagine that one of your neighbors of so many years would cross over onto your property and cut you up or shoot you because you were of a different ethnicity, race, religion, or color, or because you came from a different village? This is what is happening in some parts of the world today.

After World War I, the then U.S. Secretary of State warned Americans of the dangers of creating too many independent countries. Empires like Austria-Hungary and that of the Ottoman Turks were overthrown, but they had somehow managed to hold together a wide variety of peoples with different languages and traditions. In modern times, the same thing happened after the end of the era of colonization. It may happen again with the Balkanization of Russia. With the downfall of communism, the number of countries has grown considerably and what has been happening in Yugoslavia and Rwanda could occur in other parts of the world. The cause of all of this is deep-rooted hatred, distrust, and ethnocentricity. It is hoped that the world will change for the better, with a deeper understanding and appreciation of the world's ethnic and cultural diversity, so that we can live in relative harmony and consider this, to use Wendell Willkie's words, "One World," as our community. America can be a good example and world leader in this regard.

My impression of America's emotional makeup is that we have less animosity or strong feelings against our former enemies in the European Theater of World War II because so many Americans trace their origins to the various European countries from which they emigrated. There seems to be less of a stigma toward those of European stock, and less suspicion. Not so with Asians, especially the Japanese in Japan, or even Americans of Japanese ancestry, as many people believe the Asians are different and they are reputed to be sinister. Even the Chinese and Koreans, who were not enemies but allies, still do not fare well in this scenario. They are not fully accepted as Americans in America. It is incumbent on us Japanese Americans and other Asian Americans, therefore, that we educate others in any way we can so that there is better understanding and appreciation of our ethnic and cultural diversity. Later in this chapter, I will talk about my involvement with the Japanese American National Museum in Los Angeles, which was designed to play just this kind of educational role.

Some scholars believe in the "melting-pot" model, that is, that there should be one American culture in which people of many backgrounds lose their individual identities and become a single uniform or equable mass. But this is not to be, and should never be. The only way this can probably happen is by way of continuous intermarriage between and among different ethnic and racial groups. This is certainly happening throughout the country, and in good time we may all be so mixed racially and ethnically that we may become one in that sense. But the vestigial remains of the different cultures cannot be erased and eliminated in this country when the mobility of the peoples of the world is only accelerating, not decelerating.

A far better approach to this whole issue would be to emphasize the diversity of Americans as the strength of our country, not a weakness. President Carter acknowledged this, as did the first President Bush later. Demographers predict that in the next 45 years or so, during the course of our next adult generation, people of color may become a part of the majority, or at least that no ethnic group will be able to claim to occupy the mainstream, as is true now. This is already the case in the state of Hawaii. While one ethnic group may be larger in population than another, no single ethnic or racial group occupies a dominant position in this state, which makes its whole social, economic, and political structure one of the case studies of the century. If America understands how the people of Hawaii have been able to live together in a multicultural society as a single community with many racial and ethnic groups, we will be able to eliminate many social problems that seem to be occupying so much of our time and energy. Since 2001, people of color in California have been in the majority of the state's population.

CULTURAL BAGGAGE

In 1996, many of the younger people of Japan began adopting the *chapatsu* fashion. *Chapatsu,* which comes from the Japanese words for "tea-colored" and "hair," refers to the practice of dying their beautiful black hair a brownish or blondish color to look more like Westerners, or at least more like the mannequins in Japanese department stores. Since the end of World War II, with very few exceptions, mannequins in Japan have generally been Western types, with blonde hair and non-Japanese features. This may be understandable. After all, Japan lost the war, and it makes sense that the Japanese would admire the conqueror or follow their example, especially since they have traditionally and characteristically respected the stronger, the more educated, the more senior, and so on. This *chapatsu* trend is a continuation of what happened after the war. American fashion, music, and language became a fad because Japan has always followed us in many ways. This marks quite a difference from the prewar days when Europe and Great Britain were the respected trendsetters for the Japanese people.

Japan has traditionally been an importer of different things. For example, in the Japanese language, the Chinese characters were obviously imported from China. Historically, Japan has been an importer of many things that make up modern Japan. It began in 1853 after the arrival of Commodore Perry. But it has always improved the imported products

From the Meiji Period up until the beginning of World War II, prescriptions were written in German, many books contained French and German words, and many Japanese children were sent to Europe to study, primarily to Great Britain. But today, many students go to the U.S. to study at college and at graduate and professional schools. While the Japanese may be six months behind in this respect, there is a real secondary market for American cultural trends. Many of the advertisements that I see in Japan in magazines, newspapers, posters, and on television contain many English words written in *katakana*. If the word is in *katakana* it is usually a foreign word, but occasionally it is not and this can be embarrassing for the unwary foreigners who are good in Japanese but who have not been to Japan for some time and are therefore not familiar with the most recent Japanese English For example, *karaoke*, a popular songfest is a mixture of a Japanese word and an abbreviated English word. *Kara* means empty, or without, and *oke* means orchestra although *karaoke* is now in the English dictionary.

This predominance of American influence in recent Japanese modern culture has created a sort of idolatry for things American in Japan. I see a trend that may affect us Japanese Americans indirectly because of the inherent Japanese subservience to someone or something that they regard as superior in some way. As the Japanese expression goes, *hakujin ni yowai,* meaning weak to the white man. This attitude may manifest itself in Western mannequins or in *chapatsu* hairstyles, even though there are so many beautiful people in Japan whose image or beautiful black hair can be used as the standard bearer. To my mind, I believe this has created a mindset that Westerners are superior and the Japanese are one notch below Westerners. This may be the reason why so many Japanese constantly bow and smile at Westerners, seeming almost obsequious and not equal to them. Prime Minister Nakasone is reported to have said when he visited Washington and met with President Reagan: "United States, you be the pitcher and we, Japan, will always be the catcher." This is unlike the case with the Chinese, who seem to do much better in relating to Westerners as equals. This has caused many Westerners to view the Japanese as obedient and subservient even while respecting their technical abilities and their achievements in the business world. When they come across Japanese Americans in the United States, Westerners probably look at them as Japanese, not being able to distinguish them even from among other Asians. Naturally,

Westerners expect the Japanese Americans to act accordingly and speak like the Japanese in Japan. When they are seen acting and speaking like other Americans, Japanese Americans can appear as interlopers and a threat.

This assumption that Westerners are somehow superior explains why the Japanese would prefer to deal with Westerners directly rather than to hire a Japanese American to represent them or serve in high positions. For example, I have seen many newspaper ads in *The Japan Times* specifying that a teacher of English must be a Westerner, a rank discrimination but not illegal in Japan. In many other situations, a Westerner will be employed over a very qualified Japanese American when both are considered for a position. The Japanese are not interested in the deep insight that we Japanese Americans can give them in many situations they might face while doing business in the United States. Many Japanese companies have made mistakes as a result of this bias, and they have paid very dearly for it. Because of this image of the Westerner, the Japanese have difficulty in being accepted as true internationalists. In Japan, they act as typical Japanese heavily burdened with tradition, custom, bureaucracy, and the vestigial remains of feudalism, all of which affect their lives and human relationships. This is all well and good, but it can also make the Japanese appear inscrutable in the eyes of Westerners. To make themselves acceptable and appreciated, the Japanese frequently put on an international mask to make them compatible to the West. Many of us Japanese Americans can easily see through the facade and the mask. This is why Japanese often feel uncomfortable with us, if we are with them in the company of Westerners. Since we seem to straddle both cultures, being facile in English and in American ways, we seem to provoke resentment in them, for they find it difficult to treat us as American.

"Ugly Americans" act the same way at home and abroad, wherever we may be. Many do not need a mask. We say what we think and are open about how we feel, since the kind of society we live in encourages this kind of disclosure, transparency and openness. We are free-spirited, without any baggage of historical traditions and customs, or burdensome bureaucracy with feudalistic remains that affect our daily lives. We are individualists and independent in our actions and thinking, the opposite of groupism.

Regarding cultural differences between United States and Japan and U.S.-Japan relations, the situation might be changing. Akihiro Takahashi, President of Orient Chemical Industries Co., which was founded by his father, offered to me a situation which was my one and only experience involving a combination of Japanese and American culture. I had known Akihiro since he was attending college. I represented Orient Chemical, a specialty chemical company, when his father was the president. His father was also a member of the Young Presidents Organization of Japan and we had occasion to meet and socialize.

In 1989, when Akihiro decided to be married to Haruko Maeda, we were invited to his wedding, but in addition to that he asked me to be his best man, a concept of American tradition. The wedding ceremonies took place at the Royal Hotel in Osaka on June 4, 1989. I was dressed in formal coat-tailed rental attire and Sarah had a raspberry colored gown, selected especially for the occasion. At first, Haruko was dressed in a typical Japanese outfit with an elaborate Japanese colorful kimono and coifed wig. She then changed four times. She wanted to wear her grandmother's and her mother's bridal outfits and, in addition, a traditional white bridal gown at the end. With each change, she modeled the outfit. The wedding ceremony was fairly simple with a Japanese Buddhist priest officiating.

When the Japanese ceremony was done, Haruko changed into a traditional western wedding gown, as was a popular custom to follow at the time, and Akihiro and Haruko headed for the banquet hall where several hundred well wishers waited to celebrate the occasion with a luncheon banquet. The bride and groom and I were seated on an elevated platform with a good view of the many guests who were there to celebrate Akihiro and Haruko's marriage.

It apparently was the custom in Japan for the guests to offer toasts to the bride and groom with a small cup of sake. At first, a few close friends came up to Akihiro and offered a toast. Before long, more came up and since I was sitting next to him, they also offered me a celebrative drink. I accepted most of the sake offered to me, but later I noticed that there was a bucket under the table and there the rest of the offertory sake went in.

Since then, Sarah and I have been celebrating the Takahashi family's wedding anniversary each year. I visit Japan once or twice a year and, depending on when I visit Japan, we have a celebration of their wedding anniversary in Osaka. The last anniversary in 2003 was the 14th and ivory was the traditional gift for that year. We presented them with ivory carvings from Liberia. The next is the fifteenth anniversary in 2004 and it is crystal for the occasion. They have three lovely children, the oldest: Hanako, 12, Hifumi, 10, and Kai, 7.

From this experience with the Takahashi couple of Osaka, it seems the modern generation may be becoming westernized and Japan will gradually change in the years to come.

DIVERSITY IN NEW YORK

When I first visited New York in 1944, while serving in the U.S. Army in Fort Snelling, there were only two Japanese restaurants in the whole city: one on 29th Street called Suehiro and another on 56th Street called Miyako. There were many Chinese restaurants, both in midtown and in downtown Chinatown. Many New Yorkers would go to a Chinese restaurant once a week, especially on weekends, as a variation from their regular diets. After the war, especially after the peace treaty with Japan was signed in 1952, Japanese restaurants began increasing in number. At one time, there were more than 125 in Manhattan alone. The Korean restaurants followed, then Malaysian, Vietnamese, Thai, Filipino, Indonesian and others. As Asian businessmen and United Nations diplomats arrived in New York, especially after the 1970s, their native cuisines became more prominent and available. As a result, many New Yorkers were able to sample Asian food more often. Japanese sushi bars became very popular, even among the younger set and among women who learned that sushi and sashimi were healthy and non-fattening. These additions to our diet have added new words to our dictionary.

Wedding of Akihiro and Haruko Takahashi, 1989

Today, New York has become a Mecca of foreign food from all continents. We now have a choice of cuisines that we never had 50 years ago when Sarah and I were living here. These changes are all to our benefit, as we become familiar with the food of different countries, we also come into contact with their people, learning about their culture and their language. We therefore understand and appreciate different people who have come to our shores to find a home. This will lead to a borderless culture that can thrive, just as a borderless economy has proved its value. Diversity in the cities and the communities in our country is the key to world peace. It is like a huge pot of stew with each ingredient retaining its individuality and contributing to the flavor of the final product.

MULTICULTURAL HAWAII

Just as New York has always been a city of great diversity, my native Hawaii has always been home to a wide variety of peoples, especially from Asian backgrounds, truly a multicultural society. Many Americans who are concerned about the large number of immigrants coming to our shores would probably not be so worried if they were mostly from Europe, since "they would be like one of us." The United States needs to recognize the drastic demographic changes that are taking place in various states, and look to the experience of Hawaii. Our 50th state has already reached multicultural pluralism, and it is better off for it. The rapid changes that took place after World War II made it possible for Hawaii to achieve this desirable stage of maturity. There, people of color are now a part of the dominant society in control of the government and exerting considerable economic leverage.

Many years ago, the situation was quite different in Hawaii, where many private luncheon clubs, golf clubs, and other social organizations were exclusively for the white mainstream and no "other" could ever have hoped to gain membership. In recent years, though, it has become a reality that these clubs just could not survive economically without membership of people of color. For example, the Oahu Country Club, Waialae Country Club, and the Pacific Club now have a large number of Asian Americans who sustain their viability. This is as a result of the demographic shift that has happened to Hawaii over the past 50-plus years, a total change from what it was like in 1945 when World War II ended. It is said that California has also changed in the same way in that a majority of the population is made up of people of color. This is all very good and it should continue for the good of the country. Unlike the United States, Australia has recognized this and it has decided to encourage the study of foreign languages, especially those of Asia, in order to be effective in its relations with fellow Pacific Rim countries.

JAPANESE AMERICAN NATIONAL MUSEUM

During the period of my later career, one of the most significant organizations I have been involved in is the Japanese American National Museum in Los Angeles, a cultural and educational center that united the efforts of Nikkei all over the United States. At first I had no initial interest in the Museum. It was on the west coast, and I was involved in many other issues and organizations, primarily on the east coast in New York. But things changed in 1989 when I had a discussion with Henry Y. Ota, who was an attorney in the office of Mori and Ota in Los Angeles. He came to New York with Siegfried Kagawa, president of Occidental Insurance Company of Hawaii; Irene Hirano, president and the Executive Director of the Museum; and Mo Marumoto of Washington, D.C., a well known Republican figure in the capital. Henry was the chairman of the Board of Directors of the Museum at the time. After an hour or so of discussion on its mission and future plans, I was greatly impressed and decided to join the board. There would be regular meetings four times a year in different parts of the country: in Hawaii, Chicago, New York, Los Angeles, and Seattle, and an annual meeting in Los Angeles. The initial goal was to raise sufficient funds to renovate the former Hongwanji building in Little Tokyo as the Museum's headquarters.

Plans for the Museum were initially conceived in 1985, when a few Nisei in Los Angeles got together and organized it with Bruce Kaji as its president. The idea was novel, but these founders had a vision and realized their dreams after many years of struggle. This vision is being supported by Japanese Americans throughout the country, and the Museum is now a reality, under the fine leadership of Irene Hirano, the President and Chief Executive Officer, who joined the Museum in 1988, and a staff unequalled by any other ethnic institution.

The mission of the Museum is to promote understanding and appreciation of America's ethnic and cultural diversity by sharing the Japanese American experience. The concept of a community-based museum is a critical part of the Museum's program development. With a targeted membership of 100,000 or more, it has become a truly national and international museum with members from all of the 50 states and from Japan and other countries.

After a successful fundraising campaign, the renovation of the Hongwanji building was completed and the Museum was formally dedicated in the spring of 1992, just as the Los Angeles riots were breaking out. For the occasion, former Japanese Prime Minister Kaifu was in attendance, and the dedication ceremonies took place under the leadership of Chairman Henry Ota.

In the spring of 1992, a meeting of the Museum took place in Hawaii, prior to which Henry had said that he would like to have me succeed him as chairman, who was the chief executive officer of the institution at that time. Henry had been chairman for three years and wanted to devote more time to the practice of law. From the start, I had been impressed with his demeanor and leadership in dealing with situations and resolving differences of views and opinions. For me it was a different situation: I had been born and raised in Hawaii and had been molded by the New York social and business world for nearly 50 years. I had traveled extensively around the world on business. My style of leadership was somewhat different as I was more inclined to the type of leadership that I knew in the Army, with strict discipline and order. I was not certain whether the board of the Museum would be amenable for the change from a collegial to a more blunt, straightforward and transparent leadership. To me, the good of the institution was of prime importance. As a postwar product, Henry Ota represented the third generation, while I was from the old, prewar school, but with a liberal and progressive outlook.

At the time when I was getting heavily involved in Museum business, I was at the height of my profession, working six days a week and many hours a day, sometimes 16 hours, but 12 hours regularly. I was also traveling extensively every year on business, visiting places I never thought I would go, crossing the Pacific and Atlantic, and to other parts of the world. On Henry Ota's recommendation, I was elected and served as chairman of the board of the Japanese American National Museum from 1992 to 1996. Then, Yoshio Uchida of San Jose, California, succeeded me as chairman of the board. The Museum was a national institution in name and our fundraising efforts extended throughout the country, and our membership grew tremendously from around the nation. To extend its scope and interest beyond our borders, we became more involved with the South American and Canadian Nikkei, a result of my extensive connections with the Pan-American Nikkei Association (PANA). The Museum sponsored a conference of North and South American Nikkei in Los Angeles for cultural and educational exchange. My international interest and connections in business had broadened my vision of any institution in which I served.

I realized that no prior study or research had previously been done on Nikkei of North and South America. This was confirmed by Dr. Richard Kosaki, retired Chancellor of the University of Hawaii, and then President of the Tokai University in Honolulu. Richard had been my classmate at the University of Hawaii, and we had volunteered together for the Military Intelligence Service in 1944. He confirmed that such a study or research project would be an interesting one for the Museum to undertake. I proposed the project to Dr. Akemi Kikumura of the Museum, an anthropologist, and she was willing to write a proposal to raise funds to undertake such a study on behalf of the Museum. Irene Hirano endorsed it and we moved ahead to raise funds. I approached the Nippon Foundation in Tokyo, which had been established by Mr. Sasagawa, a philanthropist of considerable reputation in Japan who was also managing a boat-racing operation in that country. Dr. Kikumura prepared the proposal and we submitted it, only to be rejected immediately, almost by return mail. I was personally convinced that this study and research project was a good one, so I resolved to pursue it further. On my next trip to Japan, I visited a Mr. Yamashita, who was director of the Nippon Foundation's International Department. We talked at length about the Museum, its mission, and the people involved. Though the institution was young, I explained to him that it was an ambitious project and one that would be a great credit to all Japanese Americans in the United States. By the close of our meeting, I noticed a glimmer of brightness in his eyes, indicating his interest in the project. We closed the meeting by arranging to meet again in New York when he would be attending a conference in the near future. At that time, he could visit the Museum in Los Angeles.

This whole exercise taught me another lesson about persistence and how a different style of negotiation was practiced in Japan. A number of years ago, I attended a group discussion by a number of Japanese business-men from that country that had visited New York to sell products and to explain about Japan and the Japanese. One thing that distinctly remains in my memory is the statement by the leader of the group that Japanese busi-nessmen, unlike Americans, are very persistent. He said that when Ameri-cans go to Japan and make a proposal that is rejected, they pack up and return home. But Japanese businessmen are different, he said: "When the Americans say 'no,' the Japanese then begin to negotiate." I remembered this discussion when Mr. Yamashita arrived in New York. We had lunch at The Sky Club. For an hour or two after lunch, we talked about the Museum and the people who were the leaders of that institution. No men-tion was made of the proposal or the request for financial support for the research project. At the end, Mr. Yamashita said that he would stop off in Los Angeles to visit Irene Hirano and some of the leaders of the Museum. Apparently, he was quite impressed, because after he returned to Japan, he asked that we submit our proposal again for consideration. At that point,

I knew that the International Nikkei Research Project would become a reality.

In due course, we received approval by the Nippon Foundation for a $1.5 million, three-year project to be financed incrementally at the rate of $500,000 per year, based on progress reports to be filed periodically. Dr. Kikumura's administration of the funds and direction of the research project made it possible to have the necessary scholarly work done in each country, for she would be selecting leading Nikkei scholars to do the work within the stipulated time. Dr. Kikumura traveled to South American countries where there were fairly large Nikkei communities and coordinated research work with the scholars. Everything went smoothly. The results of the International Nikkei Research Project were published in two volumes, both in English and Japanese. They were reported out at XI COPANI (the Eleventh Conference of Pan-American Nikkei) in New York in August 2001.

As a result of this grant, our international/global initiative has established a firm foundation for further research and study of Nikkei in the world, not limited to North and South America. The Museum developed a Nikkei Legacy Project and successfully received $1.5 million project funds, payable over three years in three equal amounts, and, in addition, a $3 million endowment fund from the Nippon Foundation in Tokyo. The centerpiece of this will be the Nikkei Legacy Project, which will serve as an international forum. It will be a resource databank and a portal where visitors will have access to information on and/or links to Nikkei collections and resources; institutions with holdings and interests in Nikkei history and culture; and "best practices" in collections management, preservation, documentation, and access. We will have "workshops on the web" on how to conduct audio/visual histories, how to preserve family albums, how to set up and manage archives, and so forth. We will feature some collaborating partners whose collections, resources, and activities will be enhanced with greater features, information, and visuals.

One collaborative partner of the Museum that should be mentioned is the National Japanese American Veterans Council in Washington, D.C. Its first Chairman was Fred Murakami of Virginia who was succeeded by Walter Ozawa of Hawaii. The National Council will be responsible for collecting, recording and preserving the stories and experiences of the Japanese Americans of all wars for the web site to be established by the Museum. The uniqueness of the Japanese American veterans in World War II is that many volunteered to serve their country from American concentration camps where they were incarcerated by their own government in violation of the constitution. In addition, these veterans who served in the Military Intelligence Service contributed much to the success of the occupation and democratization of Japan because of their superior knowledge of the language, customs, and the people of Japan.

Another Museum project that was of great personal interest to me was the story and history of the coffee farmers in my native Kona, Hawaii, the only location where gourmet coffee is grown commercially in the United States. The community also represents a unique culture different from the other plantation communities in Hawaii. The coffee farms there were initially operated by other ethnic groups, such as the Portuguese, but because of the hard times and depression of the 1930s, Japanese immigrants began to take over where the Portuguese left off. The Japanese had left the plantations after their contracts expired and gradually gravitated to Kona. Also, it was a haven for those who broke their contracts, ran away and escaped from their contractual obligations at sugar and pineapple plantations and found it a place of refuge.

Many of the Japanese immigrants to Hawaii had come from farms in Japan and, being accustomed to long and arduous work, the hardships they faced on the coffee farms were not a novel experience. The families were large, and having seven children was not uncommon. Our immediate neighbors had 11, and another family nearby had 16. Depending on the acreage of a farm, all hands in the family were necessary to harvest the coffee crop completely every season.

Following other regional exhibits done about Nikkei in Oregon and

California, the Japanese American National Museum decided to organize an exhibit called The Kona Coffee Story. I thought that this exhibit would impart an unusual cultural insight into the lives of Japanese Americans who are to this day the backbone of the coffee industry in the United States, producing a distinctly flavored gourmet coffee that is world famous. There is a distinct cultural characteristic of these coffee farmers, which may be true of farmers in general, who are the true capitalists in America. The coffee farmers are persistent, hard workers, individualists, stubborn in their ways and loath to give up until they succeeded in whatever they undertook.

The Museum organized The Kona Coffee Story under the able leadership and guidance of Dr. Akemi Kikumura. It was later exhibited at the Bishop Museum and other locations throughout Hawaii and finally in Sao Paulo, Brazil, where 1.2 million Japanese Brazilians live and are engaged in large-scale farming of coffee, which is exported throughout the world. However, there is one important difference: Kona coffee is gourmet quality, while Brazilian coffee is a regular popular blend. Dr. Kikumura has shown tremendous skill in working with local Japanese Americans, especially in Kona where many outsiders have not been able to win over the Kona farmers very readily because of their independence, individualism and stubbornness, unlike those who worked on plantations. As typical capitalists, they must plan, take risks of weather and market conditions, persevere, and persist in order to survive and succeed. As a result of Dr. Kikumura's skill in winning over the people of Kona, The Kona Coffee Story exhibition was a success and we now have a very large contingent of loyal supporters of the Museum from Kona. Also, James Morita, originally from Kona and one of the founders of City Bank of Honolulu, and his assistant, Wayne Miyao, were very helpful in raising funds to make the Kona Coffee exhibition possible.

During my watch as the Chairman of the Museum, we were also very fortunate to have had the Emperor Akihito and Empress Michiko of Japan visit the Museum when they stopped in Los Angeles during their tour of the United States in the 1990s. They showed great interest in the history of Japanese Americans in the United States and spent a considerable amount of time at the Museum looking through the exhibition.

As the first national ethnic Museum, it has been successful in attracting many supporters nationally from Japanese Americans and other national leaders such as Senator Daniel Inouye; George Aratani; George I. Azumano of Oregon; Henry I. Daty and Susan J. Onuma of New York; Glen Fukushima of Tokyo, former Vice Chairman of Japan-US Friendship Commission and President of the American Chamber of Commerce of Japan; George. H. Takei, actor of *Star Trek* fame, Manabi Hirasaki; Dr. Frank L. Ellsworth, current President of Japan Society in New York; Steven Arai; Mark Fukunaga; Ernest Y. Doi; Elaine Y. Yamagata; Thomas M. Yuki; R. Thomas Decker; Leslie K. Furukawa; Rena Miwako Havilland; Bill Hughes; William H. (Mo) Marumoto; Margaret Y. Oda; Paul N. Shishima; Dr. Robert H. Suzuki; Hon. Nao Takasugi; Graham Y. Tanaka; Robert D. Volk; Yoshihiro Uchida; Guy Watanabe and Gordon T. Yamate; Harry Fukuhara; John N. Fuyuume; Thomas Iino; Tomio Ito; Raymond E. Inouye; Hon. Helen Kawagoe; Hon. Walter Kirimitsu, Vice President and General Counsel of the University of Hawaii; Dr. Richard H. Kosaki, former Chancellor of the University of Hawaii and President of the Tokai University in Hawaii; Akemi Kurokawa; Dr. Takashi Makinodan; Chip Mamiya; Dale Minami; Warren Minami; Tomio Moriguchi; Steven Nagata; Margaret Nakano; Peter K. Okada; Scott D. Oki; Peter M. Suzuki; Dr. Richard J. Wood; and Aya Yamakoshi.

PHILANTHROPY AND THE SOGI FOUNDATION

In 1980 Sarah and I established The Sogi Foundation. We made generous annual contributions to it, so that scholarship grants could be given to graduates from Konawaena and Kealakehe High Schools, from the former of which we had both graduated in 1941. These scholarships were designed for students who had excelled in their studies so they could further their education. We also started to assist those who were needy, even though their high school academic performance was not good but sufficient to enable them to attend an institution of higher learning.

In addition, since 1997, we have funded two summer internships at the Japanese American National Museum to do Museum studies and training. This enables students from Dean Judith Hughes College of Arts and Humanities at the University of Hawaii to gain Museum experience. A recent report from the University indicated that it has proven to be an important learning opportunity for their students. A number of the students who participated in the program are now working in museums.

Also, we established a summer internship in New York at my law firm, Kelly Drye & Warren, so a second-year law student at the University of Hawaii Law School can spend the summer there and train in a large law firm.

Finally, Sarah and I established the $225,000 Francis Y. and Sarah M. Sogi Asian Pacific American Studies Fellowship at the Smithsonian Institution in Washington, D.C. for a student from the University of Hawaii's College of Arts & Sciences, Ethnic Studies program. Under the auspices of Dr. Franklin Odo, who is director of the program, this Fellowship enables a student to train and study in the Asian American Studies Program for a semester, with credit.

We hope to continue with grants and scholarships for education and research aimed at a better understanding of Asian Americans in our country, as well as for the betterment of students in Hawaii who have much to gain by broadening their education and experiences outside of insular Hawaii. In 2004, we made a grant of $150,000 to the University of Hawaii Foundation for scholarships. In establishing these scholarships, I was very aware that education had established the basis from which Sarah and I were able to realize so much more than we had ever dreamed. In making funds available to enable a new generation to further their educational endeavors, I think back on my long and eventful life and reflect on how the Kona wind has carried me to heights unimaginable. It is in this spirit that we provide for young people who are just beginning their own journeys in life.

Sarah M. Sogi with her tulip-tree sculpture, "Hokusai Wave"

"17th Century Courtesan,"
alabaster sculpture by Sarah
M. Sogi in Kaigetsudo mode

After graduating from law school and passing the New York bar, I did not have any difficulty in getting employment as a lawyer in a respectable and well-established law firm. My career as a lawyer was strenuous but very lucrative and enabled Sarah and me to give back to society what it gave us.

PAN-AMERICAN NIKKEI ASSOCIATION (PANA OR APN)

During the early 1980s, at board meetings of the Japanese American Association of New York, I began hearing about the Pan-American Nikkei Association (PANA). It was formed by a group of Japanese Americans from San Francisco under the leadership of Chuck Kubokawa, a member of the Japanese American Citizens League (JACL), and a group of South Americans under the leadership of Carlos Kasuga, a businessman from Mexico. The first biennial conference of PANA took place in Mexico in 1981, then in Lima, Peru, in 1983. When the 1985 conference was scheduled for Sao Paulo, Brazil, Sarah and I registered for it and attended with a number of Japanese Americans, primarily from California. A number of Peruvian Nikkei settled in the United States, having been released from an American concentration camp, after the war when they were not permitted to return to Peru. During the war the Japanese and Japanese Peruvians had been relocated en masse and placed in concentration camps in Crystal City, Texas, to be used for exchange of prisoners of war with Japan. After the war ended, they were rejected by Peru and prevented from returning to their country. The U.S. Government paid a paltry sum of $5,000 as compensation to each of the Peruvians, while U.S. citizens received $20,000. It was quite a revealing experience meeting so many Nikkei from various parts of South America, most of them not speaking English, but who were fluent in Spanish. We could, however, communicate in understandable Japanese.

Most of the countries in South America during this time were under some form of dictatorial government, and democracy was not too familiar to the Nikkei who attended the COPANI (Conference of PanAmerican Nikkei). PANA itself was a loose form of association of Nikkei, with a president, vice president, and other officers. The first president was Carlos Kasuga. Chuck Kubokawa was also an officer at the Brazil conference, but afterwards he resigned from PANA. The information was that the Brazilian government wanted to cancel the conference since a civil rights group was involved in PANA. The military rulers of Brazil were apparently unhappy about welcoming such advocates into the country, but the conference took place without incident, and we developed many friends and contacts in South America.

By the time we attended the Brazil conference, I had been to most of the South American countries in connection with the US Aircraft Sales Company and their sale of YS-11 aircraft. Chile was an exception. Subsequently, COPANI was held in Argentina, Paraguay, Mexico, Peru, Chile, as well as in Los Angeles, Vancouver and New York, all of which I attended informally, representing the East Eoast Nikkei. In 1999, at the COPANI held in Santiago, Chile, New York was designated as the site of the 2001 conference, known as XI COPANI. By then, I had formed Pan-American Nikkei USA East, Inc., as a non-profit, tax-exempt 501(c)(3) organization with regular officers and directors.

We embarked on the preparations for hosting XI COPANI, though we had no financial resources except for my own bank account. I ended up advancing and eventually contributing more than $40,000 to pay for expenses that could not be covered by the income we derived from the convention. Our group was composed of people who were working for a salary; many had families and hardly any financial means to make substantial contributions to a non-profit, tax-exempt organization for tax purposes. It fell upon me to make the advances and to cover certain expenses if the conference was to succeed. After many meetings, XI COPANI took place and it was fairly successful. Our granddaughter Kimberly Makiko Sogi, who worked with us in our office in New York, contributed much to the success of the conference with her administrative skills on the computer for registration and in recording massive details and information on hundreds of participants.

JAPANESE AMERICAN ASSOCIATION OF NEW YORK

From 1983 to 1986, I served as President of the Japanese American Association of New York, which is one of the oldest Japanese organizations in the country. It was founded in 1907 as a welfare organization to look after and care for newly arrived Japanese immigrants. It is now a mixed group that includes Japanese newly arrived after World War II and those Japanese Americans who came from all over the United States after the war, including those released from the American concentration camps. During my term as president, I attended many functions sponsored by the Japanese Consulate in New York, including those surrounding the visits of many government officials and politicians from Japan. In my involvement with various organizations, I was privileged to meet two Presidents of the United States, two Prime Ministers of Japan, and the Emperor of Japan. When Akihito was enthroned, I was invited to represent the Japanese Americans from the East Coast. For a complete report of these proceedings, see the Appendix .

ASIAN AMERICAN FEDERATION OF NEW YORK

Asian American Federation of New York (the "Federation") is a non-profit leadership organization created to help unite the City's diverse Asian American communities by providing community services and identifying their critical needs. Its mission, among others, is to promote better understanding, cooperation and coordination between Asian Pacific Americans and other communities.

At the invitation of Chairperson Dr. Setsuko Nishi, who was a professor at City College of New York, and Cao O, the Executive Director, I joined the Federation's board of directors and served for three years. It was a new experience to me to be involved in this type of social service for all Asian Americans. Because of the large population of Asian Americans in the New York area, the Federation served the many needs of the community and I was able to support and participate in its activities. I continued to support the Federation in various ways although I had left the board after my term of office expired.

Much to my surprise, I was informed that the Federation was honoring me at a dinner at the Water's Edge Restaurant on the East River waterfront with a number of other Asian American leaders, such as Yoko Ono, who was unable to attend but was represented by her daughter. Her father was the Chairman of the Bank of Tokyo Trust Company in New York, which Hunt, Hill & Betts incorporated. I also knew him well since I served as the Acting Secretary of the Trust Company and attended their regular monthly board meetings and prepared the minutes of the meetings. At the banquet, there were over 150 members, guests and honorees present on a floating restaurant, and Senator Daniel Inouye was the Master of Ceremonies for the evening.

After dinner, the honorees were introduced to the gathering. I was the first to be introduced and the Senator said: "Frank Sogi comes from a place that is not even on the map of the United States." He was right. In response, however, I said:

"Lanihau/Keopu is not on the map of the United States, but I would like to mention four people from where I come from who are nationally and internationally known; they are: Astronaut Ellison Onizuka, my neighbor, who was killed on his second flight to outer space and is honored with monuments in Hawaii and in Los Angeles; Hon. Masaji Marumoto, the first Asian American to graduate from Harvard Law School and to be appointed as Justice of the Supreme Court of the Territory and later the State of Hawaii; Harold Sakata, our famous Olympic champion weightlifter; and Sgt. 1st Class Rodney Yano, a recipient of the Medal of Honor who died in the Vietnam War."

It was a happy occasion for me to have the Senator open the door for me to be able to expound the virtues of Lanihau/Keopu and Kona in general at this prestigious gathering. The Kona wind has definitely carried these gentlemen from Kona to soaring heights and they have served their country well and I ride on their coattails.

CHAPTER ELEVEN

Seven Times Around the World

RUDYARD KIPLING (1865-1936) wrote in "The Ballad of East and West": "Oh, East is East, West is West, and never the twain shall meet." So long as we are Eurocentric in our thinking and approach to human relationships, the East occupied by the Asians will be totally different from the West occupied by Europeans. But in a certain cultural sense, there may be a place of meeting. Art, music, and science are borderless realms that can offer people in all parts of the globe a commonality in knowledge and appreciation. The East and the West can and should coexist especially when the whole world is becoming interdependent. I believe it is pride and lack of understanding that prevents any nation or people from refusing to recognize the truth of this global phenomenon. As we move into the 21st century, it is apparent that there is no longer an American product, or Japanese product, or German product, or Korean product. Many nations and peoples of this world are, in some way or other, involved in the production and marketing of a product until it gets into the hands of the consumer because, more and more, outsourcing will be the trend of the future.

Wouldn't it be more economical and prudent to have a nation that is best fitted to do something to do it for the benefit and enjoyment of others? This assumes, of course, that harmony and order prevail in the world community. There is no predominant nation in the world anymore, although the United States would like to believe that it is so. On close analysis, and if we are honest with ourselves, we see that even a rich and powerful nation like ours is dependent on other nations. We are a debtor nation and rely on the credit of other countries. Also, I understand that much of the technology that went into the sophisticated equipment used in the Gulf War came from Japan. The people of the nations of the world must understand each other, accept others for what they are and are capable of doing, and coexist with mutual respect.

I came to this conclusion after having traveled around the world on business seven times. During the early days I would go on propeller planes to the West Coast from New York then to Hawaii for another refueling stop. From there we would proceed to Midway and stop in Guam sometimes, depending on the airline and its flight schedule, before landing in Japan at Haneda Airport, which was relatively close to Tokyo. The return trip was the reverse of this route, and required many hours, if not a day or two considering the time difference between New York and Tokyo.

When jet aircraft came into operation, we first stopped in Anchorage or Fairbanks for a refueling stop, approximately seven hours out of New York and another seven hours to Tokyo. I usually returned to New York via Hawaii to visit relatives and friends, and, especially if it were winter, to enjoy some warm sunshine. I usually made two or three of these trips every year.

When Pan Am was at its height as a major airline, it offered a 10 percent discount for circling the globe on their regular scheduled flights and I took advantage of this and circled the globe seven times. Three of these trips were through Europe, Moscow and Tokyo, returning through Hawaii. Four of the other trips were from New York to Tokyo, returning through Asia, the Middle East, Southern Europe and New York. Actually, the distance over the Pacific Ocean to Tokyo and back to New York may be longer than the distance around the world, which is 25,000 miles, since the time difference between New York and Tokyo is 14 hours.

On three globe-circling trips through Europe and Moscow to Tokyo, the first was from New York to London to visit a shipping client that I had represented for many years and then came an overnight stopover in Moscow in the midst of the Cold War. Customs and other travel procedures getting through Russian security were cumbersome and deliberate. It was time consuming, but I did not complain, lest I be placed in a cold cell somewhere. After a long wait, I was cleared and took a taxi with a fully paid round trip receipt before leaving the airport. The hotel was also prepaid. I stayed at Moskva Hotel with no frills and simple furnishings, worn-out towels and a gloomy room. One evening, at the bar in the hotel, I ordered the best vodka martini standing up and the hefty lady behind the bar poured the vodka generously into a large tall glass and started to pour orange juice into it and I tried to stop her, but she continued. A few guests from Canada sitting next to me at the bar chuckled and said: "Whatever you order with vodka, it will be with orange juice," or what we call a screwdriver.

Next day, I rose early and toured the city but I felt as though someone was always watching me. The moment I put my foot onto the street to cross, against the red light, someone invisible to me blew a whistle and yelled in Russian using a bullhorn. The Russian I learned in Hokkaido from one of the many White Russians during my time with the Occupation Forces in Japan was not sufficient at all.

That evening, I left for Tokyo and arrived there at 10 a.m. the next day. The advantage of arriving in Japan from Europe or Moscow was the fact there was less traffic on the highways and not as many international arrivals in the morning at Narita Airport. Going to Japan across the Pacific was difficult as the flights arrived during the early afternoon and after completing security and custom and immigration procedures, I would be at the airport at a time when the highways became very congested and slow. After Narita Airport opened, it was a good one-and-one-half hour ride by bus. The return trip from Japan was relatively simple. There was a stop in Hawaii and then at one time there used to be a flight directly to Kennedy Airport in New York from Hawaii.

On my second global trip through Europe, I stopped in our affiliated law office in Paris to attend to pending matters involving a Japanese public relations company with international connections. From there, I headed for Tokyo via Moscow, which was a refueling stop. Our Tokyo Office was very active representing many Japanese and foreign companies doing international business. Our partner, Tai Tsuchiya, was bilingual and bicultural, and was comfortable in communicating in English and Japanese. At one time, we were located in the Yamaguchi Building, a block or two away from the Imperial Hotel. On my return trip, I stopped in Hawaii for R&R for a few days in the bright warm sunshine to visit family and friends.

On the third trip around the world through Europe, I visited a shipping client in London and then stopped in Brussels, Belgium, where we had established an office after our relationship with our Parisian affiliate terminated. Like many European law firms, it was a relatively small office, but we handled many substantial international transactions involving sophisticated arrangements. From there I headed for Japan, but stopped off in Warsaw where a new Marriott Hotel was built that had a casino. I had never been to that city and had heard much about Poland during World War II and thereafter, in connection with the extermination camps established by Germany. The Warsaw Marriott Hotel was like any other in the United States with the usual American amenities. Coincidentally, the name of the city is quite popular in the United States, there is a city named Warsaw in Indiana, Kentucky, Missouri, New York, North Carolina, and Virginia. My return trip to New York over the Pacific Ocean included the usual stop in Hawaii.

Of the four global trips from New York to Tokyo over the Pacific and return through Europe, the first started with a stop in Fairbanks or Anchorage. Later, non-stop flights from New York to Tokyo shaved traveling time by a couple hours. On the average, I visited and worked in our Tokyo office two or three times a year. From the Yamaguchi Building, we moved to the Daiwa Bank Building, across from the Iino Building, close to government offices. There we had Tai Tsuchiya, Sumio Takeuchi, and Hideo Yoshimoto. Masao Migita had established his solo practice in the Marunouchi area. After working in the Tokyo office for a week or so, and on some trips longer, introducing new clients to the office, I returned home to New York through Asia, the Near East, and Europe.

On the first of the four trips through this route, I stopped in Hong Kong where I had a few clients, including YKK and Hiraoka Co. Ltd, a trading company with a substantial office in New York. After a few days, I stopped off in Beirut, Lebanon and en route, there was a refueling stop in New Delhi. Beirut had been advertised as a famous resort for Europeans and Near Easterners where the wealthy spent their vacations on the Mediterranean. It is located north of Israel and west of Syria. The city was made up of all conceivable colors of people from almost everywhere. Many had the proverbial beards or mustaches. The hotel was comfortable and the service was first-class because of the type of clientele it attracted.

From Beirut, I stopped over in Rome to look at the ancient remains and took in the tourist attractions. Conversion of currency was not easy because there is the official rate and an unofficial rate that moneychangers on the streets offered. It was dangerous to assume that everyone was honest and that transactions were fair. From Rome, I headed back to New York.

On the second trip to Tokyo and return to New York through Asia, the Near East and Europe, I visited Hong Kong as usual and headed for Cairo, Egypt via New Delhi, which was a refueling stop. But we were delayed for eight hours because the engine sprang a leak and it was necessary to fly over new parts of the engine from another city in India. With the compliments of Pan Am we toured a museum and other tourist areas. Close to a museum, a person came up to me and offered to sell me a small 3" x 4" book, which appeared to contain some pornographic pictures of olden days. It was only $5, but I refused and just about said to him: "Go away and don't bother me." When I returned to New York, I saw that one of the bookstores in New York was selling the same book for $20 as classic art.

I finally made it to Cairo, but my plane arrived at about 4 a.m. and I could not check in until 7 a.m. so I waited in the lobby. The hotel would not bend its rules for me. So as tired and sleepy as I was, I boarded the tour bus after I checked in at the front desk and visited the Pyramids and

Sphinx as well as parts of Cairo. The Sphinx had its nose broken because General Rommel of the German Army during World War II ordered his troops to fire a cannon at it. I climbed the Great Pyramid. The steps were very narrow, but wide enough for a person to walk up or down without turning sideways. Only one group could go up or come down at a time. The guide led the way up and there was an opening from where we could see quite a distance. On the way down, the guide led the way and before we reached the bottom, he had his hand out for a tip from each one of us. I hate to think what might have happened if we did not tip him.

Later in the day, I walked the streets of Cairo and, as I saw in movies and pictures at home, all men wore a white tunic, which resembled a pajama to me. Since the movies I saw showed many of them with a dagger under their garment, I imagined that every one of them carried such a weapon. Thus, I formed false and often damaging characterizations. From Cairo, I returned to New York.

On my third global trip, after spending some time in my Tokyo office, I visited Taipei where we had an affiliation with Min Shen Lin who had trained with us in New York at Miller, Montgomery & Sogi for about a year. He specialized in trademarks and patents in Taipei and had established a substantial staff to do the work in his office. From Taipei, I stopped off in Rome to meet a fellow investor in a British Virgin Islands trust company before returning to New York.

My fourth and last global trip was to Tokyo from New York and then to Taipei, Hong Kong, Beirut, and finally home. The stopovers in Taipei and Hong Kong were somewhat business-related. On every trip I made, if at all possible, I tried to arrange to visit a client's office or visit a potential client on the trip so that there was an element of business involved.

One interesting thing I noticed on these travels was that many Americans would stare at Asians when they appeared at a gathering, theater, restaurant, or other public places, such as the streets of New York. In the foreign countries I visited, it was quite different. In Asia, of course, this did not happen, as was the case in Eastern Europe (Hungary, Poland, and

Czechoslovakia), or in the rest of Europe I visited, such as Norway, Denmark, Holland, Italy, Greece, Switzerland, Spain, Portugal, and Belgium). Having come from Kona, where there was implicit trust, respect, and loyalty among friends, neighbors, and in the community, I was not sensitive to the attention we attracted in the United States. Deep inside, I was confident and strong in the belief that we were as good as the next person, as human beings, and this was all that mattered.

TRAVELS IN EUROPE

Biarritz, France To celebrate our son Jim's graduation from Hackley School in 1971, we offered him a trip to Europe to visit cities that I had visited in connection with my professional work. He said that he would like to go surfing in Biarritz and enjoyed doing so on the west coast of France, near the northern part of Spain, close to the Basque country. Through the kindness of one of my clients, Jim's cumbersome surfboard was shipped to France. But thereafter we had to worry about getting it here and there. At other times, Jim had to lug it everywhere. We stopped first in Copenhagen, Denmark, where Sarah and I stayed in a hotel and rented a BMW. I still remember clearly that the steering wheel was heavy and I have never liked the car ever since. Jim stayed in a camping community and unexpectedly met Alan Silverberg, a friend from White Plains. The next stop was in Holland. In Amsterdam, Jim again camped out in a large park set aside for this purpose.

Since we had an affiliation with a French law firm, we visited Paris and stayed at a fairly prestigious hotel with a concierge who was attired in full tuxedo with a gray high top hat and white gloves. He was very solicitous when he saw us but when he saw Jim with a tie-dyed shirt and wrinkled trousers and shoes, he frowned and shook his head back and forth, as if to say under his breath: "What great misfortune do we have here?" While Jim loved camping out and did so most everywhere, he often visited us in our hotels to bathe and clean up and enjoy a good solid meal.

We did not spend too much time in Paris since our primary interest was Biarritz. However, we stopped off in Geneva where I had visited a number of times on client business so that Sarah and Jim could see the snow on the mountains, even during the early summer. Southeast of Geneva was Chamonix and Mont Blanc, steep mountains that were excellent for skiing during the regular ski season. There was a credible amount of snow at the top of the mountain that can be reached only by a cable car that operated from 10:00 a.m. to 2:00 p.m. Jim and Sarah went up on the cable car to see the mountains and peaks covered with snow. Sarah said that it was cloudy and foggy and she could not see anything, but suddenly, it cleared like magic for about 15-20 minutes and they could see vast mountainous peaks all around them. Just below the platform on which they stood, a mountain climber had just made it to the top of a peak, and Sarah was able to capture the moment with a picture. It turned out to be a prize photo shot.

Next, we headed for Zurich, where we rented a car, and then drove to Biarritz through country roads. There were no regular hotels, but only old smelly barns converted to countryside inns. The hotel in Biarritz was like the one in Paris and Jim did not impress the concierge with his surfboard and tie-dyed attire. Since I was scheduled to go to our Tokyo office, I took leave after a couple of days and went to Japan, and Jim and Sarah found their way home to New York.

Brno, Czechoslovakia On another occasion, after a convention in Geneva, we traveled to Czechoslovakia to visit Jirina Pospicholova, Sarah's friend from Columbia Presbyterian Medical School where they were classmates in Occupational Therapy studies. This trip first took us to Budapest, Hungary; Vienna, Austria; and Prague and Brno, Czechoslovakia, before it was divided into the Czech Republic and Slovakia.

We stopped off in Budapest for several days and saw the two old cities of Buda and Pest as they existed in the old days, facing each other across the river. It was a hilly city and quite compact and picturesque in the ancient parts of it with cobblestones in some areas.

Photo by Sarah M. Sogi

Mont Blanc, Chamonix, eastern France

Then, we headed for Vienna where the international conference was being held. We saw many parts of the old city and the modern area with many of the international shops that you would see in any large European city. It was noted for Sacher Torte, a special dessert made of chocolate, but on tasting it, we were not impressed. We attended a symphony at the Symphony Hall, and it was impressive to sit in a place where Mozart, Straus, and other famous composers had been. After three days in Vienna, we headed for Prague on the Orient Express and had all of the required papers to enter a communist country. On the train, a stern looking and a very heavy-set woman conductor looked us over and told us to put our heavy baggage on the shelf above the seats, and we struggled and managed to do so. We were not going to argue with her and end up in a cell, cut off from the civilized world. An unpleasant incident involved Sarah who had taken a few camera shots out the train window. The officials at the border, for some reason, knew she had taken pictures and she quickly took out the whole roll of film from the camera to expose it. That satisfied the officials, who then walked away while she shook in fear.

Jirina Pospicholova had attended Columbia Presbyterian Medical School under a World Health Organization scholarship from the United Nations and had returned to Brno after she graduated. She told Sarah that she joined the Communist Party, while her husband, Jaryn Pajtlova, did not choose to and neither did her two children, Helena and Martin. Being a party member, she had many advantages in her life.

We stopped off for a day in Prague, the capital, and visited many of the tourist spots with a tour group since our time was limited. The goods in the stores were plain and simple, especially the clothing, with no fancy, or frilly, or designer styles. The market was simple and the vegetables were not fresh and looked somewhat wilted.

We finally arrived in Brno and Jirina and Jaryn were at the railroad station to greet us with their car. They invited us to their apartment. We talked from about 3 or 4 p.m. to after 10 p.m., catching up on their lives after Jirina had left New York for home. We munched on cheese and other snacks and enjoyed a fine dinner with what was delightful raw red wine with no labels that Jirina was able to get for the occasion. It must have been quite good quality wine, since I had no hangover although we must have consumed quite a number of bottles. After we finished most of the wine, our hosts took us back to the hotel and we stopped off at a disco on the top floor of the hotel where Sarah tried to take more pictures but was again stopped. The place was packed full of people dancing and enjoying themselves.

The next day, our hosts drove us around Brno and we saw quite a prosperous-looking industrial town with modern apartment buildings and many parks and recreation facilities of which Jirina was very proud. It was a wonderful visit and our hostess never mentioned a word about communism, except to say that she was a communist party member and quite active in it. We left via train to Prague, from where we flew back to New York.

Lisbon, Portugal On the way to the International Bar Association convention held in Madrid, Spain, we flew to Lisbon, Portugal. We wanted to visit that relatively small country because we knew many Portuguese in Hawaii on the sugar and pineapple plantations who were usually the lunas, or foremen, riding on horses and cracking whips to perk up the laggards. From Lisbon, we drove south to a seaport where we learned that fishing boats came in with large catches of sardines to be delivered to the factories. Having eaten sardines only in cans since we were children, we headed there looking forward to having the fresh variety.

After driving for about two hours, we arrived at the port at about 11 a.m., where there were many fishing vessels docked at the pier and local restaurants lined the streets nearby. We watched the fishermen unloading their catch of thousands of silvery shiny sardines. The system was hardly automated and the workers carried large quantities of sardines in slatted wooden boxes, balanced on their heads, across shaky wooden planks. They wore large sombrero-like hats with very wide brims turned upward to catch any water or drippings from the containers. As they walked back to the ships across the planks, they all tipped their hats to empty the water and drippings from the boxes they had loaded on the trucks nearby. Then the sardines were hauled away to the factory for canning.

We could not see anything like this in the United States and it was quite a sight. We were now ready for the fresh sardine lunch that we had traveled so far to enjoy. When we saw the menu at the restaurant, there was nothing that resembled a sardine dish and, when we inquired, we were informed that no fresh sardines were served anywhere since all of the catch went to the cannery for canning. We were disappointed but the trip was worth it.

Madrid, Spain   In Madrid, we attended the convention with lawyers from many countries, including the United States, and visited many tourist spots in the city, old and new. We realized how ignorant one can be and how wrong one can be when we went into a Spanish restaurant with no English on the menu. We guessed what each item might be and when we saw *pojo,* or what we translated to be chicken, we ordered it. Lo and behold, what came were two pieces of small birds that looked like sparrows, cooked somewhat crisp with not much meat on them. It was certainly not fowl as we had thought. Also, at one of the museums there was an interesting exhibition on the Spanish Civil War, all in Spanish, except one piece of paper in English that some visitor had prepared and left, which enabled us to follow generally what had happened during that war. We had also driven quite far to see especially one of the popular museums, only to learn that it was siesta time in the afternoon and no place was open, and as a result we missed seeing some of the classics of Spain.

Berlin   After visiting Lisbon and Madrid, we proceeded to Berlin, Germany before returning home, since there was much news in the media about divided Germany. We checked in at a reasonably comfortable hotel in Berlin and the next day took a tour to East Berlin. We had our required papers and expected considerable delay at Checkpoint Charlie, the entrance to East Berlin, but it was relatively simple compared to the procedure I went through in Moscow. While West Berlin had department stores and markets filled with products and produce, East Berlin's stores were sparse and not as affluent and prosperous-looking. It was apparent from what we saw that a communistic regime is unable to provide its citizens the basic essentials in the same way as a capitalistic country. The Berlin Wall still stood ominously thick and tall, dividing Germany in two, but eventually it came down. The wall we saw at that time was covered with graffiti. There were vendors everywhere and the place was full of tourists. At Checkpoint Charlie, the guards looked under the buses with long handled mirrors and in the bathrooms for anyone they thought was escaping from East Berlin. We were warned not to carry any books when we first began the trip.

Dusseldorf, Germany It might be interesting to mention my travel to Dusseldorf, Germany, because of the circuitous route through which I traveled to reach my destination. I was in my Tokyo office working on some legal matters when on relatively short notice I was informed that an important meeting was scheduled in Dusseldorf about the German interests which controlled LIAC and LISCO of Wologisi Iron Ore Project in Liberia. My clients requested that I attend the meeting and I always gave high priority to any request from my clients. I left Japan one evening and arrived in Anchorage the next morning and then changed planes to fly directly to Dusseldorf over the polar route, arriving later on the same day. Flying over a frozen mass of ice and snow for hours I saw something I had never seen before. It was not comparable to the massive glaciers in Alaska.

The meeting between the Japanese Group, the American interests, and the Germans in control went well, but eventually the control of LIAC and LISCO and the Wologisi Iron Mine returned to our clients and we continued it until President Tolbert was assassinated by Master Sergeant Doe who then declared himself the head of the Republic of Liberia.

Vaduz, Lichtenstein On one of my travels around the world with Pan American Airways, I stopped off in Vaduz, Lichtenstein, a protectorate located in a mountainous area with Vaduz as its capital, located east of Zurich and west of Innsbruck. I was much interested in knowing about tax shelters and tax havens for my many clients. By establishing an *Anstalt* in Lichtenstein, individuals could shelter their assets since an *Anstalt* does not reveal who is the principal involved. I called on a local attorney who handled hundreds of *Anstalts* for his clients from England and European countries. It did not fit the requirements of our clients and I did not pursue this legal tax-saving practice.

The Concorde On one of my many travels to London and to other parts of Europe, I flew on the Concorde from London to New York and took advantage of the speed of Mach II Supersonic travel, barreling along 1,350 miles an hour, 10 to 11 miles above sea level. Time is money, but only up to a point.

For 27 years, the name Concorde had summoned images of an exclusive supersonic clientele: supermodels thumbing through magazines that may feature them on the cover; Ambassadors who insist on being seated in 1A or 1B; and businessmen to whom time is certainly money. It flew high enough to see the earth's curvature, and it beat the clock by arriving in New York an hour or two earlier than it had left London or Europe. The ride was fast but not all that comfortable with a fairly narrow aisle and two rows of seats on either side. I recall the pilot saying over Newfoundland: "Attention, please, fasten your seat belts, we will be landing shortly." We landed in five or 10 minutes, having priority over all other flights into Kennedy Airport. But the dozen Concordes are not in operation anymore since this means of travel was discontinued by Air France in October 2003. It was the end of a short era.

CHAPTER TWELVE

Social Clubs

T hroughout the years, in order to make my social and professional circle grow, I found it necessary to join many clubs and associations. What follows is a brief, description of some of them.

Tokyo American Club As a result of my work for this Club in its claim against the Japanese Government in 1953 for compensation for prewar assets confiscated by the Government, I was made a Life Member without any dues. Whenever I visited our Tokyo office, I used it frequently and, in recent years, once or twice a year. It has an extensive library, a pool and email facilities that members could use. I also entertain at the Club because of its fine cuisine at reasonable prices.

The other advantage of the Club is that it has extensive reciprocal arrangements with many clubs in the United States. In New York, through this service, I could use the Yale Club, New York Athletic Club, and University Club. In Hawaii, reciprocal arrangements are available at the Pacific Club and the Outrigger Canoe Club where I regularly entertain current and former clients who pass through Hawaii.

The Nippon Club I was responsible for reinstating the active status of this Club in New York State at the request of Mr. Morita, Agent of Sumitomo Bank who was the first President of the Club. His title was Agent because, in 1953, foreign banks were allowed only to establish an Agency, without full banking privileges. While the Club was dormant during World

War II, it was reinstated in 1956. The Club was organized in 1905. Postwar, it was first located on 96th Street in the former residence of Prince Obolensky, and it later moved to 57th Street, the present location, across from the Carnegie Hall. The Club was later rebuilt and now has over 20 floors with an exhibition hall, reception and meeting rooms, dining rooms and other facilities. Many cultural activities take place here, as well as business seminars and lectures that are scheduled regularly. When Prime Minister Nakasone visited New York a reception and dinner were held here. I have been using the new facilities and its cuisine has been excellent under the capable management of Tsutomu Karino.

The Club is celebrating its centennial in 2005 and Mr. Karino is busily preparing for it One of the exhibits that will be highlighted at the centennial celebrations is about John Manjuro, well known in New England as the first Japanese seaman that was rescued by an American whaling vessel and brought to the United States. I introduced to Mr. Karino the name of Joseph Heco, another seaman, who was rescued by an American whaling vessel and brought to the United States. He is not too well known, but he is reputed to be the first Japanese who became an American citizen. A group in Hawaii headed by Dr. Joe Muratsuchi and Dr. Samuel N. Mukaida have collected and prepared an exhibit about Joseph Heco that The Nippon Club will display at the exhibition, together with information about John Manjuro.

The Sky Club This Club is located on the 56th floor of the Met Life Building, the former Pan Am Building above Grand Central Terminal, located at 200 Park Avenue in New York City. The Club was formerly the private dining room of Juan Tripp, founder of Pan Am Airways, and it now occupies just about the entire floor. I have been a member since 1974 when Miller, Montgomery & Sogi moved into the building. I am now a member of 80/20, which is equivalent to a Life Member, similar to my membership at the Tokyo American Club.

The Saint Andrews Golf Club As the name indicates, this is a golf club, not a luncheon club as in the case of others. It is located in Westchester County in New York about 15 miles north of New York City, via the Taconic Parkway. It is the oldest golf club in the United States, having been organized in 1888, with members the likes of Andrew Carnegie, founder of U.S. Steel, whose old portrait hangs in the lobby of the clubhouse. His summer home during the horse and buggy days was converted to a clubhouse by the swimming pool. The course was renovated by Jack Nicklaus and has a very respectable slope rating of 137 with postage stamp greens.

Because of its Scottish influence very early in its history, the Club operated a curling rink on which the winter sport was played by sliding on ice a 40-pound stone with a handle on top of it. It was similar to bowling, except there were no pins. Since I lived ten minutes away, my partner Boardman Spalding, nephew of A.G. Spalding, the sporting goods manufacturer of the same name, asked me to join this prestigious and exclusive Club. The processing of my application moved very slowly and was time-consuming since I was the first Asian, and even Jews and Italians were not generally admitted. It was strictly a WASP club. There was a lawyer on the admission committee that I happened to know who worked behind the scene quite extensively and I was admitted in 1972.

Saint Andrews is an unusual club in that it has limited its members to 250 regular members, and there is no starting time as such. Whoever comes first is allowed to tee-off, and if a player is alone, he is paired up with another member or other members to make up a foursome. This is a fine way to get to know other members of the Club and this is encouraged as a matter of tradition. The Club emphasizes sociability and camaraderie.

Honolulu Country Club One of my clients of long standing and a former member of the Young Presidents Organization from Japan was an original member when a Japanese built this Club on the island of Oahu. Unfortunately, he passed away at a rather young age and I was asked by the family to purchase his membership, which I did as an investment.

Japan Golf Clubs I invested in two additional golf clubs in Japan, also on the recommendation of clients who were affiliated with them. The system worked in this manner. The initial payment is considered a loan and after ten years it is returned if the golf club is able to do so financially and, if not, it had the privilege of extending it for another ten years. No interest is paid on the loan, but it gave the lender all of the privileges of membership to utilize the club. The first club that I joined under this arrangement for twenty million yen was the Central Golf Club in Ibaragi with 36 holes. I used it extensively whenever I visited Japan. After the first ten years, the loan was extended unilaterally.

The other loan that I made under the arrangement that I have mentioned is the Glen Oaks Golf Club in Chiba Prefecture, for eight million yen in 1995. Because of the adverse economic conditions in Japan for the past decade, both golf clubs are on the verge of bankruptcy and may be liquidated. The only salvation is that the exchange rate when I made the loans was much weaker and the yen has appreciated considerably since then.

CHAPTER THIRTEEN

Redressing the Injustices of the Past

T HE REDRESS MOVEMENT occupied a central position in the Japanese American community during the 1980s and later, uniting (and sometimes disuniting) many thousands of Nikkei all over the country. More than 120,000 Japanese Americans were forced into American concentration camps during World War II. It was not until 1988 that the U.S. Government formally apologized for this miscarriage of justice and paid token compensations to the survivors and their families. The internment went into force with Executive Order 9066, issued by President Franklin D. Roosevelt in early 1942. The order broadly authorized the Secretary of War, or any military commander to prescribe military areas from which any or all persons may be excluded. However, martial law was not declared on the West Coast, the writ of habeas corpus was not suspended, the civil courts were in full operation, and anyone charged with espionage or sabotage could have been brought to trial. It should also be remembered that of the 1,100,000 nationals of enemy nations living in the United States in 1942, fewer than four percent were Japanese nationals.

As a result of Executive Order 9066, Japanese Americans had to leave their homes, in many cases with only a few days' notice, and could take only what they could carry with them. Property had to be hurriedly sold, abandoned, given away, left in insecure storage or unpredictable trusts. Crops were left un-harvested. Many lost titles to homes, businesses, and farmlands because taxes and mortgage payments became impossible to pay. Most bank accounts had already been frozen or confiscated as enemy assets, and there was little source of income within the camps to which the Japanese American population had been confined.

Over the years, Japanese Americans commenced legal actions against the United States Government, claiming damages, but regrettably, judges and even justices of the Supreme Court were not immune from the prejudices of the times. The judicial system shamefully failed in its constitutional responsibility to protect citizens against abuses by the executive and legislative branches.

Eventually, after considerable effort by the Japanese Americans and their supporters, the U.S. Government recognized the wrong that it had committed against its own citizens, apologized, and made redress payments to those who were placed in the American concentration camps during World War II. However, the real issue is to acknowledge the injustice and to be certain that such injustice will never happen again in our country.

In rescinding Executive Order 9066 in 1976, President Gerald R. Ford said: "An honest reckoning must include a recognition of our national mistakes as well as our national achievements. Learning from our mistakes is not pleasant, but as a great philosopher once admonished, we must do so if we want to avoid repeating them."

As the Japanese Americans have been doing, and as the Jewish community is doing continuously, we must remind Americans that placing people in concentration camps in violation of our Constitution should never happen again. Also, we must be alert to any move to deny constitutional rights to any group because of ethnicity or religion.

The National Japanese American Memorial Foundation, of which I was a member of the board of directors, established a monument in Washington, D.C. It commemorates the experience of the Japanese Americans in American concentration camps during World War II, honors the veterans who served their country nobly and with bravery in extreme adversities, and celebrates the success in legal actions against the U.S. Government.

VETERANS: SERVING THOSE WHO SERVED

Advisory Committee of Minority Veterans, Veterans' Administration After my discharge from active duty in May 1947 from the Counter Intelligence Corps (CIC), I was connected with the Territorial Guard in Hawaii and the active reserve in CIC in New York, receiving training once a week at the Armory in Hawaii and on Governors' Island in New York, where the First Army Headquarters was located. Also, to keep current, I attended two weeks of military training at Camp Drum in upstate New York, Fort Holabird where the CIC School was located in Maryland, and Camp Zama in Yokohama, Japan, when I practiced law in Tokyo. I continued with this training until I was relegated to the retired reserve as a Captain, in order to receive a nominal but helpful financial support for my schooling in Hawaii and in New York. This training also exempted me from recall to active duty in 1950 for the Korean War.

Since my retirement from active reserve status, I joined veterans' organizations wherever I lived, but primarily in New York. The leaders there were Kelly Kuwayama, the late Bill Kochiyama, the late Tooru Kanazawa, the late Irving Akahoshi, Hiroshi Kaku, the late Richard Itanaga, Jimmy Konno, the late Chris Ishii, and John Suzuki from the 442nd RCT, 100th Battalion, and MIS. My military service has served me well throughout my active and reserve status because of the continuous education I received and constant exposure to the changes that were taking place in the military. Also, the discipline helped me a great deal in my life.

In my later years, I have gotten involved with a number of organizations designed to recognize the achievements of World War II veterans, many of them members of ethnic minorities like the Japanese Americans. In Hawaii, as a member of the MIS Veterans Club, I have renewed friendships with many classmates and fellow veterans of the Military Intelligence Service Language School in Camp Savage and Fort Snelling, Minnesota. As an officer of the MIS Veterans Club, I am involved with the members of the 100th Veterans Club, 1399th Engineers, and 442nd Veterans Club, and I participate in many programs and events that occur annually in Hawaii. Also, as one of the founders of the National Japanese American Veterans Council in Washington, D.C., I get invited, and attend regularly, ceremonial events at the USS Missouri, Punchbowl National Cemetery, and Fort Shafter. In addition, there are many banquets, reunions, luncheons, and social events at which we can renew friendships and enjoy camaraderie on a regular basis.

By legislation of Congress, the Veterans Administration established the Advisory Committee of Minority Veterans under the Center for Minority Veterans to advise the Secretary of Veterans Administration, a member of the President's cabinet. In 1993 I was appointed to this Advisory Committee by Senator Akaka of Hawaii and served for three years with 16 other members from groups including African Americans, Native American Indians, Puerto Ricans and other Hispanics, two women, and a white male.

At the first meeting at the VA Office in Washington, Secretary of Veterans Administration Jesse Brown spoke to the group, welcoming us and asking us to assist the Veterans Administration in serving the veterans of all wars and make the Department's services and benefits available and accessible to all veterans. We were also requested to study various reports and make recommendations to the Department. With this mandate, Willie Hensley, the Director of the Center for Minority Veterans, proceeded to elect the chair of the Advisory Committee. There were nearly nine African Americans out of the 16 members on the Committee, and I immediately became concerned that if the chair was assumed by one of them, all of the other minorities would have been ignored. I surmised their concern would primarily be for African American veterans and their view of the problem would strictly be black and white, while our minority view was quite the opposite, wanting to introduce multiculturalism to the Committee so that every veteran would be important and that his or her problem should be of concern to all.

Willie Hensley, as Chairman, asked each one of us to introduce ourselves with a short resume of our background and experience in the service or as a civilian. After having heard all of the members, we took a recess and

I immediately conferred with Thomas Kaulukukui, who was also a member from Hawaii, and asked for his cooperation on a plan to elect someone other than an African American to chair our Committee. Another member from Hawaii, a Vietnam veteran named David Cooper, was a retired Brigadier General who lived in the Washington, D. C. area. Everyone concentrated on explaining his experience in the Army to show his leadership ability. David Cooper mentioned the fact that he had experience in business and education after retiring from the Army. When the recess was over and the Committee reconvened, I nominated David E. K. Cooper for the chairmanship of the Committee and Tommy Kaulukukui quickly seconded the nomination. I said that everyone seemed to have exceptional qualities of leadership and experience in service, but that David was the only one with a combination of rank in service, and experience in both business and education. The group was either stunned or agreed with me. There was complete silence. No other name was nominated, and so David Cooper served ably as our Chairman for three years.

Our main mission was to make all of the services and benefits available and accessible to all veterans. As we began our deliberations, many stories began to come out from various reports and from among the members of the Advisory Committee. They are stories we have all heard in one form or another. Some of the members were directly involved within their respective states in providing the kinds of services and benefits we were trying to guarantee for all veterans. One member from a Native American tribe related the many problems that his group had faced in accessing these services. According to his account, some of his group lived in very remote, rural areas where the nearest telephone was an hour away.

There was a study made in my own state of Hawaii called the Matsunaga Report, which concluded that many veterans there did not take advantage of VA benefits and services because of certain cultural peculiarities that VA personnel assigned to Hawaii did not understand. As an example of this, some Asian American veterans might have a sense of shame in revealing the fact that they are suffering from Post Traumatic

Stress Disorder (PTSD). Also, if the Asian American was a prisoner of war (POW), this might be an additional source of shame that non-Asian veterans and VA personnel might not realize. Sometimes, these situations are not revealed until many years later, unless elicited by someone at the VA facilities with cultural sensitivity. Then the veteran can be assisted in regaining his pride at having served his country and avail himself of the services and benefits that the VA offers. As time went on, many more similar problems involving ethnic and cultural differences emerged. I had realized early that, in a larger sense, many social issues have been categorized as either black or white and that other minorities and ethnic groups were ignored or were not a problem. No single paradigm or model for the black and white issues could be applied to everyone. I suggested to the Committee that its members must first understand all the other minorities, and that we spend some time having each representative speak of his or her own situation.

Since I was the only Asian American in the group, I spoke on behalf of my ethnic minority, and others did the same. At least this approach insured that the Committee as a whole would hear of all the minorities represented, thus becoming aware of the enormity of the problem or at least made aware of its existence. I suggested that multicultural Hawaii requires that an agency such as the VA should have personnel who understood or who were willing to reach out to veterans of many different backgrounds, including native American Pacific Islanders, Native American Hawaiians, Asian Americans, Europeans, African Americans, Portuguese, and Hispanics. In addition to respecting the peculiarities of each group, this mixed community presents a different culture with pidgin English as one means of communication.

With this in mind, the Advisory Committee for Minority Veterans strongly recommended that directors of any VA facility in the United States should have a good knowledge and understanding of the cultural and ethnic mix of the veterans in his or her region so that they can be served fully and effectively. The example that I am most familiar with is the VA

Center at the Tripler General Hospital in Hawaii where the Spark Matsunaga Center is located. We urged the VA to appoint someone familiar with the cultural and ethnic makeup of veterans in Hawaii. David K. Burge, a senior official at the VA in Washington, emerged as a candidate, and he was appointed Director. As a result, a great change took place at Tripler's Matsunaga Center. In his new position, David Burge reached out to all of the veterans' groups throughout the state and established offices on each major island. He and his assistant, Ronald Yonemoto, who also came from the VA in Washington, attended all VA functions throughout the year, of which there were many in Hawaii because of its proximity to Pearl Harbor, Punchbowl National Cemetery, and other military and naval stations situated within the state. It has been reported that veterans in Hawaii availing themselves of the services and benefits of the Veterans Administration increased considerably after these changes were made, based on the recommendations of the Advisory Committee for Minority Veterans. The Director of the Center for Minority Veterans in Washington, D.C. has also been keenly interested in these issues and has gone out of his way to respond to questions, particularly by including minority veterans in his monthly telephone conferences. He has responded promptly to any inquiry and has been a willing supporter of minority veterans by providing materials and information requested.

Five Star Council of Veterans History Project, Library of Congress After having served my three-year term on the Committee, I was appointed by the Library of Congress to the Five Star Council of Veterans History Project. Some members of the Council are notables from public and private life. Among the members are news anchors Walter Cronkite and Tom Brokaw; Senator Daniel K. Inouye and other members of Congress; Secretary Anthony J. Principi of the U.S. Department of Veterans Affairs; the Hon. Everett Alvarez, Jr., former Deputy Administrator of that Department; and Sheila Widnall, former Secretary of the United States Air Force. On October 27, 2000, Congress passed legislation (Public Law 106-380) establishing this project in which the American Folklife Center at the Library of Congress would collect and preserve audiotaped and videotaped oral histories of America's war veterans, along with documentary materials such as letters, diaries, maps, photographs, and home movies. In so doing, Congress recognized the urgency of collecting wartime memories, which become more precious as the veteran population dwindles by 1,500 every day. Congress also saw the value of engaging the American public in its own history. The Veterans History Project encompasses veterans of World War I, World War II, and the Korean, Vietnam, and Persian Gulf Wars. All services are included, and the first priority is to focus on the most senior veterans and those who served in support of them as the Project is intended to encourage the entire family, including grandchildren, to participate in this effort.

I have been campaigning among the Asian American veterans, especially the Japanese Americans, to contribute their stories. At my request, a Veterans History Project of Hawaii was organized. It is located at Tripler General Hospital and is under the direction of David Burge. The MIS Veterans Club of Hawaii has been very actively taking oral histories of its members under the capable leadership of James Tanabe and Ted Tsukiyama, who is also the official historian of the 442nd Veterans Club, which celebrated its 60th Anniversary from April 3-6, 2003 in Hawaii.

Because of its uniqueness in American history, the National Japanese American Veterans Council (NJAVC), which I was instrumental in organizing in 1996 at one of the national conferences of Japanese American veterans, with Fred Murakami of Washington, D.C. as chairman, has taken an active role by having its members record their experiences during World War II. How many veterans have served while their families were placed in concentration camps, and how many veterans volunteered or were drafted from such camps after having their constitutional rights summarily denied or taken away from them? It is said on official records that the Japanese American soldiers who served in the Pacific Theater in the Military Intelligence Service shortened the war by two years, thanks to their invaluable service as translators and interpreters, thus saving at least a million American lives. Our National Council has established a committee in Hawaii with David Burge as its Chairman and General Irwin Cockett (retired) as Co-Chairman, ably assisted by Ron Yonemoto of the Veterans Administration. Its members include the Oahu Veterans Council, 442nd Veterans Club, MIS Veterans Club, 1399th Engineering Construction Battalion, and Korean War and Vietnam War veterans. In Los Angeles, the Council has met with many of the veterans' organizations in that area in order to introduce itself and encourage them to become a part of this Veterans History Project. The Council's newsletter will publicize and promote the Project through the director of the board of each major area in the United States represented on the Council.

As a part of this project, my wife Sarah's sister, Ai, donated a collection of more than 350 letters that her husband, the late Chaplain Masao Yamada, the first chaplain of Japanese American descent in the U.S. Army, had written to her and to General John J. McCloy and many other officers and friends during his time in service with the famous 442nd Regimental Combat Team from 1943 to the end of the war. Chaplain Yamada served with Nisei soldiers in Mississippi and later in Europe. His letters, offering years of stirring war memories from the front lines, were published in a book entitled *Captain Masao Yamada (April 10, 1907 - May 7, 1984), Chaplain, 3rd Battalion, 442nd Infantry Regiment, Collection of World War II Letters*. One volume of this is on display at the Library of Congress, according to a recent report.

The history of the Japanese American military contributions to the winning of World War II in Europe has been well documented. The role of Japanese American soldiers in battling the enemy in the Pacific has not been as well known and publicized although they are reputed to have helped in shortening the war and saving American lives. With no restrictions existing now, part of the history of the Military Intelligence Service (MIS) describing their role during World War II, written by Dr. James C. McNaughton, Command Historian of the Defense Language Institute, will be published.

Although the MIS history covers the entire war period, given the enormity of the project, it will cover only the first three months of the occupation of Japan. Since the MIS played an important role in the successful occupation of Japan, the National Japanese American Veterans Council (JAVC), under the former Chairmanship of Fred Murakami, has developed a plan to add to and complete the history of MIS.

NJAVC announced plans for the sponsorship of a contest inviting MIS veterans, or their families, to provide personal stories and experiences about the part they played in the occupation of Japan after World War II. Because of their language ability, knowledge of, and familiarity with the culture of Japan, MIS personnel were able to engage, in addition to their official duties, in many community activities and to assist the Japanese in recovering from the devastation of World War II. These stories will highlight and publicize the various ways in which Japanese American MIS personnel contributed to the successful occupation of the country.

Eventually, these stories of the veterans will be included in the web site that is being developed by the Japanese American National Museum under the able leadership of Dr. Akemi Kikumura, in partnership with NJAVC. In addition, the stories will be submitted for inclusion in the Veterans History Project of the Library of Congress, making these stories available and accessible to the general public. These stories will also be included in the programs that will be developed by the Library of Congress and broadcast over the media and they will highlight and publicize the various ways in which Japanese American MIS personnel contributed to the successful occupation of a country. They might also serve as a reference for similar operations in the future by American forces.

There are many oral histories that have been recorded and preserved by many MIS organizations, but they have not been made known, or available and accessible to the general public. This is an important part of our American history and a heritage that can serve us well in the future.

Like the most beautiful music or symphony played in a forest where no one hears it, these stories will not be appreciated or valued unless they are gathered, collected, and published. The Japanese American National Museum and the Library of Congress will preserve and present to the public this rich history of our veterans through exhibitions, publications, public programs, and their web sites. Asians generally avoid self-reference, but we cannot follow the Japanese cultural practice of avoiding the nail that sticks out just because it will be pounded down. We must make known our contributions in the making of America and not be forgotten as a part of American history by our own benign neglect. This is exactly as Thomas Gray wrote in his "Elegy Written in a Country Churchyard" in the late 18th century:

> "Full many a gem of purest ray serene,
> The dark unfathomed caves of ocean bear,
> Full many a flower is born to blush unseen,
> And waste its sweetness on the desert air."

Bridging the Cultural Gap

Japan-US Friendship Commission Over the years, I have been involved in several organizations designed to bridge the cultural gaps between the United States and Japan. One of the most important of these is the Japan-US Friendship Commission, an independent federal agency that supports training, education, and information management to help prepare Americans to meet the challenges and opportunities of the relationship between the two countries in the 21st century. Created by an Act of Congress in 1975, it was provided with an initial substantial fund plus an additional sum in Japanese yen It works through providing grants to cooperating nonprofit entities involved in the following projects: Japanese studies in the United States, policy-oriented research, public affairs/education, the study of the United States and Japan, the arts, and infrastructure building.

I was appointed to the Commission in 2002 for a three-year term, succeeding George Takei, former chairman of the board of directors of the Japanese American National Museum. The group is made up of elected and non-elected federal officials, scholars and others from the private sector, and meets twice a year in April and September. About $1 million in grants are made at each meeting, based on a critical analysis of each proposal that comes before the Commission.

US-Japan Bridging Foundation One of the goals of the Foundation is to increase the number of American undergraduates studying in Japan. There are currently more than 47,000 Japanese students in the United States every year studying at American universities, but only 2,000 American students in Japan. In 1988, the Commission established the US-Japan Bridging Foundation, a charitable organization that provides individual student scholarships. Scholarship recipients are not intended necessarily to be Japan experts. Instead, the Foundation aims to nurture a new generation of professionals in policy, academics, business and the arts and prepare them to deal effectively with their Japanese counterparts, without the stereotyping that all too frequently distorts professional and personal relationships between Americans and Japanese. However, very few Japanese Americans take advantage of these opportunities.

The Japanese American National Museum may be an excellent institution for the US-Japan Bridging Foundation to collaborate with and promote programs to attract potential candidates for the scholarships offered by the Foundation. Also, the Museum has built an infrastructure of programs and expertise in both American and Japanese cultures. Heretofore, U.S.-Japan relations have not been viewed through Japanese American eyes. The time may be arriving when the views of Japanese Americans will be considered by those involved in U.S.-Japan relations. Both the Museum and the Center for Preservation of Democracy established next door to the Museum have much to offer to America and Japan in maintaining good relations. There are many leaders in the Museum who can assist directly the Commission and Foundation's efforts to improve U.S.-Japan relations. One well-qualified example is Glen Fukushima, who has had an illustrious government career and is now in the private sector in Japan, and who has emphasized the role that Japanese Americans can and should play. Glen was a member of the Japan-US Friendship Commission and served also as a vice chairman of the Commission.

White House Banquet

In 1998, on the occasion of the visit of Prime Minister Obuchi of Japan to Washington, President Clinton held a formal official banquet at the White House. Many Japanese Americans from throughout the country were invited. It was a formal black-tie affair with hundreds of dignitaries and guests. Sarah and I received invitations and we checked in at a nearby hotel and took a cab to the White House entrance at the appointed hour for the reception. President and Mrs. Clinton greeted us on the receiving line, and their welcome was warm and gracious. At the reception, we met Tomio Moriguchi, a leading businessman from Seattle, and his daughter. Since we were somewhat early and many guests saw Sarah with a cane they all urged us to move ahead of the line. At about that time, the television cameras were recording the event and when we returned home to New York a neighbor said: "We saw you on television."

After the reception, we were led to the banquet hall and Sarah was given a card with the number "4" on it and I had number "34." Sarah nudged me and said: "I guess I will be sitting close to the President and Prime Minister's table and you will be somewhere in the back of the room." When we entered the huge banquet hall with chandeliers on the ceiling, a marine soldier took each of us by the arm and led us to our respective tables. As we separated, I noticed that there was a podium with a microphone and I was headed in that direction and Sarah was headed somewhere in the back of the room and seated in the corner somewhere. My assigned table was two tables away from the podium and next to the table where Prime Minster Obuchi, Mrs. Clinton, Senator Daniel K. Inouye, and other dignitaries were sitting. On the other side of the podium was the table for President Clinton, Mrs. Obuchi and others. At our table we had Thomas Foley, Ambassador to Japan, (the former Speaker of the House) from Seattle, Washington; Scott Oki, a substantial entrepreneur from Seattle, formerly of Microsoft; Senator Torricelli of New Jersey; and others whose names escape me now.

We later received a number of photographs of the occasion from the White House photographer. One of Sarah's artist friends, Emiko Ozawa, who formerly lived in Kahala, saw one of them and did a large painting of us being greeted by President Clinton, which hangs in our study at home.

REFLECTIONS ON A LIFE OF SERVICE

All of these reflections have been very pleasant and enjoyable. We celebrate the past achievements of our veterans by commemorating them on Memorial Day. Many other events extol the virtues of the Japanese American veterans and the great contributions they made in the Pacific and European theaters during World War II, the Korean War, and the Vietnam War. This

President Bill Clinton greets Sarah M. and Francis Y. Sogi
at the White House, 1999

is fine, and the veterans certainly deserve all of this, but my concern is what all of this has done to America. Has it contributed to the making of America? The answer is obviously a positive one. We have advanced America forward and eliminated many of the ills of the past. We established a historical precedent when the President of the United States apologized to the country and to the world for the placing of Japanese Americans in the concentration camps (the term used by President Roosevelt) noting it was both a mistake and a violation of our Constitution. The conclusion is that this should never happen again to anyone in our country. But this story and experience must be told and retold to remind America, since it is so easy to forget in times of crises.

The Japanese American veterans in Hawaii have achieved wonders in changing the life of that state to what it is today. They have made great strides forward socially and in the community, and they have opened many doors that were closed tightly shut a generation ago. General Eric Shinseki has contributed much in this respect, moving ahead to new opportunity levels in the military, going beyond the glass ceiling that was there only a few decades ago. With education, training, and ability, the younger generation can be assured that our country offers a future potential for their advancement and progress.

We have honored the past of our veterans, which they certainly deserve. As the inscription on the National Archives Building in Washington, D.C. reads, "What is Past is Prologue," we must look to the past to see the future and plan for it. It may have different meanings to different people. For example, a passenger in a taxi passing the building asked the driver what the inscription meant. Without hesitation, the driver responded: "It means, you ain't seen nuttin' yet." And that is what I see in the past of the 100th, 442nd, MIS, and 1399th Engineers, veterans of the Korean, Vietnam, and Gulf wars. Their service is also a prologue of what is to come. The veterans opened many doors of opportunity and their beneficiaries have entered these doors with a bright future ahead of them.

The older generation of Japanese Americans took stock of their situation after World War II and strived ahead, seeing the gate of opportunity open, and made many changes, improvements, advancing in all aspects of life to where they are today. The younger generation might do the same and forge ahead and improve America in the next 50 years so that it will be a greater country for everyone.

After I retired from the active practice of law in 1993, Sarah and I returned to Hawaii in 1996 and established residency in our former home state while maintaining an office at Kelley, Drye & Warren in New York City with clerical staff and a home and a car in White Plains, New York. I return to the mainland quite often to attend board and other meetings in Los Angeles, New York, and Washington, D.C. Once or twice a year I visit our Tokyo office, which I still manage. Also, Sarah and I visit New York for five or six weeks each year in the spring and fall to enjoy the flowers and autumn foliage in Westchester County where we have lived for nearly 50 years, a truly eventful half-century in our personal lives.

In all of these activities, I am reminded of the importance of working with others toward common goals that benefit our local community, our nation, and the world. Looking back on a life that began many years ago in Kona, I am grateful to have had so many experiences and connections all over the world that have enabled me to make my own contribution to the human enterprise. But in the final analysis, it was Sarah who has been a helpmate through it all.

Epilogue

KONA SIGNIFIES HARD WORK with determined stubbornness and perseverance over a number of generations. This has been the case since the first Japanese immigrants arrived to develop the Kona coffee industry, which faced a great economic depression at the time, with some farms being abandoned by other ethnic groups who preceded them. Ultimately, through sheer determination, mutual respect, and cooperation, the community thrived. One great difference from any mainland village, town, or city was the multiethnic makeup of the community in Kona. While the Japanese were dominant, there were Portuguese, Filipinos, Chinese, Irish, Polish, and English.

Most of the families were engaged in coffee farming, although as time passed, many engaged in developing macadamia nut farming which proved to be a lucrative industry because of the ideal climate. There were also ranchers who owned large parcels of land on the slopes of Hualalai Mountain and Maunaloa. They were rugged and stubborn in character and could withstand long hours of work tending their farms and ranches to eke out a living and give their children an education. There was a sense of independence among the people, plus trust, respect, and freedom in life, with each one his own boss. Living was hard, but they were strong and resolute and bravely faced adversities in life and in the environment, including the vicissitudes of the market place.

Going out into the world from this life situation, drifting with the Kona wind, I felt strong inside and was able to deal with whatever adversities and challenges the future might blow my way.

It has taken me a number of years to write my memoirs and I have tried to include as much information as I could recollect and verify with sources available to me. Hopefully, any reader who reads this book will learn or acquire some knowledge that he or she was not aware of. It has been my great fortune to have met and befriended so many wonderful people with far more education, experience, and insight than I was ever able to acquire. I continuously poached on their knowledge and experience and learned much from them and, at times, retold it as my own. I wish to thank everyone for having been a part of my life, even just as a reader.

Interview with Mrs. Nami Sogi

THIS INTERVIEW was conducted on May 30, 1975 at 3412 B Paalea Street, Honolulu, Hawaii, by the Rev. Charles Hasegawa and the Rev. Seiko Okahashi of the Honpa Hongwanji Mission of Hawaii.

Mrs. Nami Sogi came to Hawaii in 1912 to join her husband who was working at the Aiea Plantation on the island of Oahu.

Q. When you came to Hawaii in 1912, you first went to Aiea, didn't you?
A. Yes

Q. How many years did you stay in Aiea?
A. I left there when I was 24 years old, so it was 4 years.

Q. Will you recall those days and tell us all about it? First of all, your husband was already here when you came, wasn't he?
A. Yes, he had come 10 years earlier.

Q. As you mentioned previously, it was a picture marriage, wasn't it?
A. His picture was sent to me in Japan and I was married there before I came to Hawaii. I went to Hakata to have my eyes checked before coming to Hawaii, and that is where I first saw an ocean. There were many black spots scattered far apart on a blue Japanese mat-like place, and I wondered what they were. I was told they were boats and I was to go to Hawaii on such boats. I was frightened and thought of giving up the idea of coming to

Hawaii. Then my father told me that it was going to be a bigger boat so I finally decided to come.

Q. Did you have relatives in Hawaii?

A. No. My husband came to Hawaii with his sister and brother-in-law. He didn't want to live with them, so he moved out of their home and lived alone. He didn't want to be a bother to his sister. They lived in Maui but when I came, my husband was at Aiea plantation.

Q. You came on the Shinyo Maru, didn't you.

A. Yes.

Q. Did you arrive in Honolulu?

A. Yes.

Q. About how many years did you live in Aiea?

A. I left there when I was 24 years old so we stayed for 4 years.

Q. Will you tell us about those days.

A. I came to Hawaii in 1912; my husband came here 10 years before me. I was a picture bride. I arrived in Honolulu and was married at the immigration station by a Mr. Katsunuma. All the brides-to-be who came from Japan were gathered at the immigration station grounds and all the husbands were there to meet us. We women were lined up alternately with the men and Mr. Katsunuma made us shake hands. That was our marriage vow. Then the husbands took their brides to where they lived on a hack (buggy).

When we reached Aiea with my one wicker trunk, my husband said, "This is our house." I was shocked. Bachelors lived in houses built with 1" x 12" rough lumber and the outside was painted with white lime. In a room, there was a narrow one Japanese-mat-sized platform built a little bigger for sleeping. My husband lived with another person but because I came the other person left. There was only one door and no windows. In the evenings, we were annoyed by mosquitoes.

I rested for about one week and went to ask for a job. I got a *hoe-hana* (weeding with a hoe) job. We were so ignorant when we were in Japan, we used to hear stories as though money grew on trees in Hawaii. We were very anxious to earn lots of money quickly and to go back to Japan, but when we heard that we would be paid five cents an hour, I was shocked. On rainy days, if we should ever stop our work and go home before 4:30, we wouldn't get our hour's pay of five cents. No matter how hard it poured, we had to work with our raincoats on. Then when a whistle was blown, it was the signal to stop work.

In the mornings we used to get up at 4:00 a.m. and at 5 o'clock, when the first bell rang, we would gather in one place where we were counted. Then we would go to our working place on the train. It made us very happy about coming to Hawaii but it turned out to be a cane-hauling train. We rode on a box car with only a board on the sides so we were very scared. Some people were so disappointed that they regretted coming to Hawaii. One day a woman committed suicide. We used to go as far as Pearl City to work. One day, on the way, there were several valleys and bridges and this woman jumped from the train. I didn't notice when she jumped from the train. I was so scared and trembling but went to see her with the others. She couldn't die so she cut herself with a knife and died. We were so scared thinking she might appear as a ghost so I didn't want to go to work. With all the good stories she had heard in Japan about Hawaii she became too depressed with actual conditions in Hawaii. It was about six months after she came here that this happened.

The boat fare when was $75.00. My husband worked in the mill and I worked in the field. I used to cry every day after the day's work. When working on high places, we could see boats sailing which reminded me of my family in Japan.

After I got used to the work, I did *happaiko*, carrying bundles of burnt cane on the shoulders and dropping them into the rail car we used to ride to work. When we filled one car we were paid $1.05. Because this was better pay than the hoe-hana, I worked but I couldn't continue. It was such a hard job for a woman. My husband worried about me because I talked so much about Japan and he tried to discourage me from going to work.

One day, when I had fever, in my delirium, I talked about how happy my father would have been if I had worked as hard as I do now. Neighbors worried about me, thinking it might be some other sickness. They suggested that I go to a doctor. I didn't remember but my husband took me to a plantation doctor. The plantation doctor told me that I could go to work because it was just a slight sickness. The luna came to get me the following morning to go to work and told me that if I didn't go, I would be discharged. If I were to be discharged from work, we couldn't afford to live (eat) so I went to work. My sickness got worse and I lost my first baby by miscarriage.

Married people were given a little larger house. A room about 12 feet by 12 feet and a yard about six feet by six feet at the back of the house. I continued to work for about three years. I was pregnant with my second child. I would need a lot of money to have a baby so I worked hard. My grandmother wanted my husband to take me back to Japan so that I could recover. I wanted to go back as soon as possible so I tried to economize on food by eating wild grass grown in the cane fields. My husband was very angry with me when I served him wild grass. The grass grew nicely in the fields because we gave fertilizer to the cane. I would go and pick the grass and boil or cook it with dried fish for better tasting. One day my husband got angry and threw down the dish and said, "don't mistake me for a rabbit." He lived in Hawaii for over ten years so he was used to good food. Since my home in Japan is a farm and I used to eat only vegetables, I didn't mind. He was sometimes very mean to me. I went to work until my last month of pregnancy.

Wages for hoe hana (weeding) was $15.00 a month but if we worked as *mizukake* (one who gives water to cane) we were paid $17.00 a month because we worked on Sundays, too. When working as a mizukake, one day, I slipped and fell and suffered pain in my stomach for three days and three nights. The baby was born but he was dead. His brain was mushy. Not long afterwards I became pregnant again. A baby girl was born safely because I took good care of myself this time. I couldn't go out to do field work but I was anxious to earn money and was in good health so I started to sew Japanese kimono for people. In those days people used to wear kimonos at home. I used to sew all day till late at night. Because I was so busy, I didn't notice my baby's face was getting yellow. We took her to a doctor and were told it was already too late, that she had pneumonia. The doctor told me to change from breast feeding to bottle but my baby wouldn't suck the nipple. After changing her feeding, she lived for only about three weeks. That day, before I went down to prepare dinner, I called for my baby, "Fusae, Fusae," and she smiled at me. Because it was time for her medicine I went upstairs and found her cold; and she was not breathing. I should have taken her to a doctor once more but we couldn't afford the train fare so I didn't. I felt as though I had killed her.

Q. Was she three years old?
A. No.

Q. Did all the three babies before this die?
A. Yes.

Q. Fusae was the third child, wasn't she? How many months was she when she died?
A. 100 days. It was during her most cute days. Then my mind became

funny. In Aiea, a country district, a dove would chirp early in the morning and it sounded as though I was hearing it calling, "mother, mother." On the day of the funeral, when Fusae was being put into a box and covered, I saw a man nailing on the cover. I told the man not to hit it too hard because it would hurt Fusae, and pushed him away. After the funeral a neighbor told my husband to hide, give away, or burn all the clothing belonging to Fusae because if I saw Fusae's things I would think about her and become insane. All the clothing was disposed of but somehow I found one.

When the dove chirped I imagined Fusae was calling me and so I took her kimono and nipple with bottle plus a hoe to the grave. I thought of digging the grave up to put the kimono on Fusae. My husband found me standing by the grave. I didn't know what I was doing.

The doctor told my husband that I couldn't be cured unless he took me back to Japan. The doctor suggested that I be taken out to parks but I didn't enjoy this because everything I saw or heard made me sad.

One day, a woman who owned a restaurant told my husband to send me to her place to work. While working in this restaurant she suggested to my husband about taking lessons in dressmaking.

When I was 23 years old my fourth child, Chiyoko, who is now married to Mr. Kinoshita, was born. I worked in the restaurant, and my husband worked in the mill. I had a babysitter for Chiyoko and worked hard so we were able to save money.

Because we had children, I couldn't work in the field any more so my husband and I decided to buy a store in Honolulu and to start a business. We came to Honolulu to look for a store when my husband's relative, a second cousin named Kumagai, told us that he would find the store for us. He felt that we should start our business in a good location where many people lived. He told us he found one and wanted us to make a deposit so that the owner would hold the store for us. We trusted him and gave him half of our savings to be deposited. Later when we went to see the store, the owner said he didn't know of such a person. We went to the place where he lived but were told that he had not come home for two to three days. As a result, we couldn't buy the store and lost our savings, too. We found out that we had been cheated by our husband's cousin. My husband was a very honest person. He trusted others, believing that others were the same as he. Of this experience, my husband said that it was all right: we didn't cheat, we had been cheated.

We had to do something so we decided to buy a fourth acre of land in Kaimuki on which was located an old house. My husband worked as a carpenter and I planted vegetables. I pushed the cart my husband made for me and sold vegetables from Sixth Avenue in Kaimuki to as far as Waikiki where a fountain was located. I used to leave my daughter Chiyoko at my neighbor's home and left my baby son in the hammock. He was the son who died in World War II.

One day after selling all the vegetables except one bunch of burdock, I went to a camp where Japanese people lived to sell it. I had lima beans and other vegetables for white people but they didn't buy burdock. When I came home late that day, I heard my baby crying and found him about to fall from the hammock. I felt so sad that I couldn't help but think ill of the man who cheated us. If he hadn't cheated us, I thought, we could have been all right with our business by now. Just because of him we still had to work so hard.

About this time the child I bore when I was 24 years old was four years old. We found another one-half acre of land so we bought it. Believing we would be successful this time, we made a down payment and paid the balance in small installments. No matter how hard my husband worked, our affairs did not turn out as well as we expected. We had a lot of debt and finally lost everything.

We couldn't stay in Honolulu any longer so we decided to move to Kona. We left with our three children and a few possessions as if we were running away. The price of coffee then was very low and Kona was in an economic depression. There was no work. In Kona raising coffee was the only means for living. Because of my pregnant condition and the fact that we had three children, our friend would not let us stay with them. There was an old house which was vacant for a long time so we rented it. The place was so filthy that at night "dew snails" crawled into the house and came even to our pillows.

My husband was asked if he would like to enter into a contract to clear a five-acre piece of land. He accepted it. In those days, cleaning one acre of land brought only $2.50 but it was big money then. He worked hard and saved enough to pay our debts.

My baby was born after two weeks. But because I had suffered so much, my body, face and eyes were so swollen that I couldn't see. There was a good medicine called *mikkasan* for after birth but we couldn't afford to buy it. One day, my husband said that he had a friend some distance away so he would go to borrow some money. Unfortunately, his friend was not at home. He went on a car but had to walk coming home. He was unable to borrow the money. He came home around two o'clock in the morning. He was looking at his feet with the lamp so I asked him what was the matter. I noticed that both his feet were bruised and covered with blood and that the skin of the soles of his feet had been rubbed raw. He had walked with his shoes on but because his feet hurt after walking for such a long distance he had to take them off and walked barefeet instead. He said, "Please forgive me for returning without the money," but I told him that I should apologize for giving him so much trouble.

Fortunately all of my children grew up with no trouble. We didn't help them to grow but they got their education entirely by themselves. When they started to go to high school I would ask them to pick one bag of coffee before going to school every morning. When they came home from school they would have their snack and then go out into the fields to pick coffee. If we hired people to pick, we had to pay them. My children used to say, "Mother doesn't wake us up early during school days but she wakes us up very early on Saturdays and Sundays." Now, I have nothing to say except "thank you" and "I am sorry I subjected you children to so much hardship when you were young." But the children would only say, "No, Mother, that hardship has done us good." Fortunately I have never let them go hungry.

It was about seven or eight years after we left Honolulu, the price of meat was 15 cents a pound. One bag of Waimea cabbage cost 25 cents. The children used to say that they thought it was better to call the soup "cabbage soup" instead of "beef soup."

Q. Let's go back and talk about the time you first came to Aiea. When you lost your three babies. I imagine it must have been your most painful experience.

A. Yes, it was so painful that I almost became insane.

Q. Was your pay 15 cents a day?

A. No, we got 50 cents for working 10 hours. It was 5 cents an hour.

Q. How much did your husband get?

A. He received $18.00 a month and I got $15.00

Q. How much did the luna (supervisor) get?

A. Lunas were white people so I had no idea how much they were getting. Besides, I was too young to know about their wages. Instead of worrying about our wages, people were afraid to be dismissed so some people used to bribe them. My husband hated the idea of bribing so he never did it. He would say "*Bushi wa kuwane do takayoji*"—the proud samurai (warrior) pretends he has eaten by using a toothpick even if he hasn't, if only to show that he is not of lowly mind. The head luna used to watch us working from far away with binoculars and would come and line us up, pick out the one who was standing around and dismiss him. When we were dismissed, we used to feel as though our heads had been chopped off. We were very scared of him.

Q. If you were dismissed, you couldn't go back to Japan but just stayed at home without working because you were still under contract? Even if you had enough money, they wouldn't let you go back, wasn't that it? That was the arrangement between Japan and the U.S.?

A. I was not on contract so I was free but my husband came 10 years earlier so he was on contract.

Q. The Japanese government sent its people to Hawaii on contract. These immigrants were Japanese nationals and had no U.S. citizenship. Wasn't there a Japanese Consul then?

A. Yes, there must have been a Consul General.

Q. As an American citizen myself, I wonder why the people didn't complain about their mistreatment to the Consul General?

A. I think the people were afraid. They had no guts.

Q. In those days Japan was considered a first-class country. Through letters from the immigrants to their families, and rumors, the Japanese government must have known about the conditions in Hawaii. It would seem the government should have sent an inspection committee to see for themselves how their people were being treated. When I hear about such cruelty, as an American citizen, I want to reproach the American government.

A.   The Chinese were not treated like the Japanese. Only the Japanese were mistreated.

Q.   I wouldn't say positively but it seems the Japanese government had deserted their own people. As long as there was a contract between the two countries, both governments had the responsibility to see that everything went well. For instance, if I should go to Japan now and marry a Japanese national, I wouldn't have the right to vote and would have to report to our American Consulate every three months while I'm in Japan. That means our government is taking care of me. I wonder what kind of policy it was to ignore those who were having trouble in a strange country. I think the Japanese government should have checked on the situation.

We are now taping this fact to let the current Japanese Consul General know how their people had suffered so during the early emigration days. To the American government, too, it was an unforgivable act to permit human beings to be treated like animals.

A.   Yes, we were treated like animals. Now when I see how well the chickens and pigs are fed, I do not think we had such good food. We were inferior to the chickens and pigs of today.

Q.   Why was it necessary to bear all those mistreatments when there were many other places one could go to live? Both governments are to be blamed for being so irresponsible.

A.   Even if the Japanese took a case to court we knew we would not win the case because we couldn't speak English to make ourselves understood. We just had to bear the suffering even if it was unreasonable. That is why no matter how poor we were financially and we had to borrow money, we were determined to send our children to the Japanese language school. When the children were in high school they wanted to quit Japanese school because it was too much work to attend both English and the language school. I told them they must not quit because they will, in the future, have to work together with the white people and with only English they will certainly not be able to compete with them. That they will have a better opportunity if they were good in the Japanese language as well. I also told them to at least complete high school since it will help in the future. One might say one will study later but this may be too late for by then you may have a lot of gray hair.

Because I was so strict with my children, they often wondered whether or not I was their stepmother. They would often say that other parents would listen to their children and let them quit school, and that their father would listen to them and say "all right, " but their mother would always say "No! No!"

In sending our children to the language school we had to pay tuition which was lots of money then. If we let them quit, it would have been easier financially on us but the duty of parents to our children is not accomplished. Parents who do not think of the future of their children cannot be called true parents. As long as we are in America, we must give them enough education so that they would be able to work equally among the American people.

I am ashamed to mention it but we finished paying our debts just before our son graduated from law school. My husband would say to me, "You don't have to work too much because our children will pay our debts when they grow up." I would say, "How could we let the children pay our debts? We have no right to expect them to pay." I argued with my husband.

My son, who is now an attorney, has been to Japan two or three times already. When he went to Europe the first time, he wrote to me saying, "Forgive me, Mother, for thinking you were my stepmother. Because you made me live a disciplined life during childhood, I was able to travel as an adult without shame." I was very, very happy to hear that. When children grow up, they'll realize. But when they were young they didn't like to go to the Japanese language school because the Portuguese children called them Japs.

We gave all our five children a good education and spent a lot of money. When attending school they would study till late at night—sometimes until midnight. At 2:30 a.m. my son would get up and deliver more than 100 newspapers. Our children all worked their way through school. We did not help them much. I used to tell my husband we must not tell the children that we are still paying our debts. We haven't done anything for them to feel obligated.

We were not on contract but people who were here on contract were treated cruelly by being threatened with a whip when working. During the contract period, the plantation knew that the people could not leave, so the lunas did not hesitate treating us in a cruel manner.

Q.   Did they really beat you with a whip?

A.   No, they just made a whip noise behind us and they would say, "Go ahead, go ahead," meaning "Work, work."

Q.   Is that when you were doing hoe-hana in the field?

A.   Yes, that was done to the people who were under contract.

Q.   Did your husband work in the field?

A.   No, at Kenkairo, where the cane is dropped from the car into a place where the cane juice is extracted. Aiea mill was the only mill where the sugar was refined. Waipahu and Ewa plantations brought their sugar to Aiea to be refined. In the mill, there was work for women to sew sugar bags. In order to get the job, people had to bribe the luna. My husband didn't like to bribe so he never did it.

Q.   What kind of social gatherings did you people have? Did you cele-

brate the Emperor's birthday? Did you gather at the church for such occasions?

A. At Aiea, we lived near the Hongwanji church and there was a
Japanese school on the grounds. It was a spacious ground so we used to
have the gathering there. In those days, the boss used to allow us to celebrate. On Coronation Day, we all gathered at the boss's home. We used to
celebrate the Emperor's birthday every year until the first World War
started. When my youngest son was still attending Japanese school they
used to sing the Japanese national anthem, "*Kimigayo*," and they would
receive cookie boxes which cost about ten cents.

When I went shopping on hot days I wanted to drink soda water but on
second thought I always thought of my children and would buy marble
candy or a package of chewing gum instead. With five cents I could buy five
marble candies and give one to each of my children. Gum was five cents,
too, so each child could have one.

In those days in Kona, a pair of Japanese straw slippers cost about 15
cents. I used to wear them to go out to places, but for home wear I used to
make my own slippers. On rainy days, I used to unravel the string from the
fertilizer bags and weave them.

In Kona, I was fortunate to live near the church. On occasions at the
church, everybody brought all kinds of vegetables from their homes and
prepared a feast. On *Gotan-e* (Buddha's birthday) or on *Hoonko* (memorial
service for Shinran Shonin) we did not have to buy anything for the feast
except flour for *manju* (bean cakes). Many women worked in the kitchen
and prepared the food. My children would come to find me by looking at
my feet among many women there. I was the only one who wore homemade slippers so my children would call me by looking at my feet. When I
asked them how they found me they used to say, "by looking at your feet."
When I took my children to such occasions when food was prepared, they

naturally wanted to taste the food, especially the bean paste for the manju. If I gave them a little and there wasn't enough to make even one manju, I would feel bad should someone say that it was because I had given them to my children, so I tried not to take my children to such events. I remember when I arrived in Hawaii I ate a pancake made of flour and salt. It tasted so good I couldn't forget about it.

Q. That must have been what nowadays we call *malasadas*.
A. I think so.

Q. In those days, what kind of food was considered a treat, a feast for a special meal or daily meal?
A. I think it was when we were able to get beef. Even the small dried fish (*iriko*) in miso soup was also considered a good meal. I used to pick out two or three fish from the soup and give them to my children. The children enjoyed them. You can more or less tell what kind of life we lived. When I cooked soup with beef and cabbage there was more cabbage than beef so the children used to say it was "cabbage soup." I picked out all the beef and gave them to the children so I had no chance to taste beef.

Q. What is *tamana*? Is it a powder?
A. No. It is a vegetable. Round or head cabbage.

Q. How was life in Japan in those days? What kind of food did you have daily, especially in the country?
A. We had more vegetables. We used to make our own tofu with soyu beans grown in our garden. We had a big place to farm so it wasn't like the life we had in Hawaii. At home, we hired people to help with our farming.

Q. Did you think about home when you had to work ten hours every day in Hawaii?
A. Yes, I used to think if I had worked at hard at home as I have to in

Hawaii how happy my father would have been. I used to think so much about it that I even talked about it when I was delirious during my illness. But, by comparison, people who came to Hawaii earlier on contract endured greater hardships than I did.

Q. That much, the plantation was strict.

A. Yes, it was. Kyushu (southern tip of Japan) people are said to have violent temper. One day that all got together and beat the luna because he treated them cruelly.

Q. Japanese people have so much pride that it was an insult to them to be mistreated.

A. Japanese people treasure boys so much that they bring them up with special care—more than the girls. That is why men have pride and won't stand for insults. When one of the men started to beat the luna the rest of them joined in. The luna had enough of a beating but there was a fellow who joined in last and said, "let me beat him too." He instructed the others to run away and said he would take the blame himself and go to prison if necessary. Since he had no family he didn't mind going to jail. He gave the last extra pounding a good and hard one and said, "I feel good." This incident was told to my son when he came from New York to see his father who was stricken with cancer.

To comfort his father, my son said, "Father, you must be in pain." To which my husband answered, "No, it isn't too painful." When my son said, "Father, will you tell me all the stories and incidents which happened during your early days?" his father asked, "What will you do by learning my story?" My son said, "I must let my children know how their grandparents suffered when they were young." I heard my husband talking to our son in the hospital. Some of our children want to hear about the past, but others do not care to know about it.

Q. I guess they don't want to hear about it because it is painful?

A. I guess so. I experienced scanty living when I was young to I cannot waste anything. I talk about not wasting so the young people don't like me. Once I talked to my daughter-in-law about my past—about how we worked hard. When working in the fields on rainy days, we couldn't leave the work place in the field and go home even five minutes earlier. If we did, we didn't get our one hour's pay so we had to work until 4:30 p.m. exactly. We had to work from 6:00 a.m. to 4:30 p.m. It sounds foolish now to work for only five cents an hour. My daughter-in-law said, "Things must have been very cheap then. Nowadays, things are very high." But I said, "Compared with prices of today, wages are high too."

A bag of rice cost $3.50. Rice was grown in Hawaii but it didn't taste good. It was called *to-mai* and the Chinese used to eat them. The Chinese people eat only hot rice so it must have been all right. They drink only hot tea too, so for their lunch, instead of taking their lunch with them in the morning, the lunch was prepared just before lunchtime and was brought to the working place for the group. We Japanese used to take our own lunch in the morning and leave it where we started the work. A water-boy would bring us water for mid-morning and mid-noon, and he would take care of our empty lunch bags and take them back to the place we left.

Q. Didn't you people have some pleasures, like entertainment in general?

A. There wasn't any. After my daily work in the field, I used to wash clothes for people. I would come home at 5:00 p.m. on the train, then prepare our dinners. After dinner, I would do my laundry by lantern light. I used one-half of a 50-gallon wine barrel to wash and the other half to rinse the clothes. I washed for seven people—all bachelors. I had to finish the laundry by Saturday. For working clothes, handkerchiefs, and stockings, I used to charge 75 cents a person.

Q. Did you iron too?

A. Yes, wash and iron. Even mending torn clothes.

Q. What kind of iron was it? Was there a fire in the iron?

A. Yes, we used a charcoal iron. Using regular charcoal was expensive so I used charred wood left after cooking rice. I economized by not using expensive charcoal. That is why we were able to save some money little by little.

We had a thing called *tanomoshi-ko* (saving fund). About ten or so persons would get together and deposit $3.00 or $5.00 each month. And that was very big money. The one who bid the highest interest would get the month's collection. Sometimes it was only $1.00 a month but we tried not to take it in order to earn the interest. People who needed money badly were willing to bid a high interest offer. So the person who waited until the last received lots in interest. When we got our tanomoshi-ko money, people used to sing a song: "Shall I go back to Japan or go to Maui?"

Q. Do you remember the song?

A. Yes, I do.

Q. Will you sing it for me?

A. *Joya kuwa kireta shi, tanomosha toreta, yukoka, Maui no Spreckelville. Hore hore pari pari.* (Our contract is over, I got my tanomoshi money, shall I go to Spreckelsville in Maui to work *hore hore*? (*Pari pari* was in reference to the sound of peeling the old leaves of the sugar-cane stock.)

Q. Did everybody use to sing?

A. Yes, the luna didn't like us to talk because we didn't work while we talked. The luna encouraged us to sing because we would be working with the rhythm of the song.

Q. So you people used to sing while working? It was like *taue-uta* (rice planting song)?

A. Yes, like *Ocha tsumi uta* (tea picking song).

Q. Don't you remember any other songs?

A. *Nihon deru tokya yo, futa oya sama ni, kane o okuru to yuute deta ga.* (When I left Japan, I told my parents I'd send them the money.) We thought of sending money to our families in Japan but now that we have our own children to support, we couldn't afford to do it.

Q. Did everybody who came to Hawaii experience the same kind of hardships you had?

A. Yes, but in those days Kabuki players used to come once in a while so those who used to go and see the performance enjoyed their life. I never went to see such performances. It used to cost about 50 cents to 75 cents a show. We had to work so hard to earn 50 cents. I used to think if I would send that 50 cents to my grandmother who brought me up, how happy she would be.

Q. Did you send some money?

A. Yes, several times. I sent $1.00 each time and sometimes $2.50. I received a letter saying that grandmother was very happy. She had a cold and was in bed when she received the money so mother bought beef and served her. Instead of meat and vegetables as usual, she cooked only meat so grandmother was very happy. Grandmother had bad eyes but her eyes got well after eating the meat, she said.

I think people nowadays cannot bear the kind of hardships we used to have. I used to tell my children that it's easy to change from a hard life to an easy life but to go from an easy life to a hard life is difficult. I used to tell my children, "experience hardships when you're young even if you have to buy it, because it is worthwhile." When I came to Hawaii, all the people surrounding us were strangers who came from different parts of Japan. I missed my family so much that I really worked hard to save money to go back to Japan as soon as possible. Because I was so anxious to go back to Japan, I tried my best to economize as much as I could. When I served wild grass for dinner, my husband would get angry and tell me not to mistake him for a rabbit.

Q.   Wasn't there anything all the people could do together?

A.   If we weren't so anxious to save money and go back to Japan soon, I think we would have been successful.

Q.   Were there many people who made lots of money and went back to Japan?

A.   No, not so many. People who didn't have children were able to go back. Parents wanted to give their children a good education so that they wouldn't be treated like animals. We were so ignorant, and not being able to understand English, when the English people said, "I'll kill you," we would just say, "Thank you, thank you."

Q.   Wasn't there an interpreter when you couldn't understand?

A.   No, even the luna himself didn't understand English well. Most of the lunas were Portuguese and Puerto Ricans who came to Hawaii earlier. The Portuguese were good lunas. They were mostly water lunas and hoe-hana lunas.

Q.   Were all women in one group and was the luna a woman?

A.   No, it was a man luna. Lunas were assigned to take care of different groups.

Q.   What happened to the luna who was beaten up?

A.   The last man who beat him took the blame and was sent to jail.

Q.   Was he in the jail for many months?

A.   Yes, I think so. People used to take food to him in the prison. He shared the food with prisoners of other nationalities so I heard he was very popular and happy. This is only one incident but there were many more. The Japanese were really slighted—"taken cheap."

Q.   Did the Portuguese have better jobs than the Japanese?
A.   Oh yes, Other nationalities used to call us "yellow." I guess because our skin was yellow.

Q.   Weren't there any strikes?
A.   Yes, there was a strike once.

Q.   When was that?
A.   I don't remember too well but it was when we were in Kaimuki after we left Aiea. I heard there was another one before that.

Q.   When you gave birth, did the midwife help you?
A.   No, neighbors used to help each other. I had experienced the cutting of the umbilical cord of babies many times. It wasn't a good feeling.

Q.   Weren't there any midwives?
A.   Yes, there were but we couldn't afford to pay her.

Q.   Until how many days before you gave birth did you work?
A.   Some people worked until the last moment. One woman had her labor pains on the train and was rushed to the hospital. We had to give birth by ourselves quietly without any help. I was told by my grandmother that it was a disgrace to moan or cry out when having labor.

Q.   Why is it a disgrace?
A.   You won't understand me. To fuss, to depend on others, to mention pain is a shameful thing.

Q. Such a way of thinking is interesting.

A. When pain came, I would lay an old raincoat on the floor in the corner of a room and put some old clothes on top and use it as a mattress. I would leave a bag of rice in front of me and hold on to it when I needed strength.

Q. Did you do it too?

A. When I was in pain for three days and three nights I couldn't lie down.

Q. Did you go to church often when you were in Aiea?

A. Because I lost my babies, I used to go to church often. Mr. Oi was the priest then. When he read the *Hakkotsu no gobunsho* at my baby's funeral, I felt very, very sad. Since then I used to go to church so often that my husband said, "People are saying your are a church maniac."

Q. Do your parents belong to the Shinshu sect?

A. Yes, all my ancestors. My grandmother used to say that if I went to church I would be able to meet my true mother. The church was Mangyoji in Hakata. All the young girls used to go to regular sewing school but I was sent to this Mangyoji temple to learn sewing.

Q. That means you had been going to church from a very young age when you were in Japan?

A. All my ancestors used to serve at the church as *Sodai* (elders of the church). When I used to suffer mentally and spiritually, I always recalled what my grandmother said about the church.

Q. In what way was the church important to the plantation people?

A. [NOTE: this answer was left blank in the original transcript.]

Q.   Did the church have sermons several times a month?

A.   No, there weren't any.

Q.   Then, the church was used only on funerals? Did they have weddings at the church? Didn't they have regular services?

A.   No such things. Everybody worked even on Sundays so we had no time to go to church. People who didn't work on Sundays used to gamble. My husband gambled too. He wouldn't say anything when he lost but when he won, he would give me $10 or $5 gold money. But I refused to take it. I told him I didn't want dirty money and that I would take it only when it was honest money earned by hard work. After realizing it wasn't worth it, he stopped gambling.

Q.   When you went to Kona, did you go to the Hongwanji first?

A.   Yes, the priest then was Rev. Iida. I lived near the church so on annual Buddhist Services, I used to attend church. Whenever I was suffering hardships, I would recall what my grandmother used to say. Something in our fate has brought us together as stepmother and stepdaughter. At times, we were both bitter. My grandmother would say, "You must understand her. Until I meet my natural mother, I would never understand," she would say.

I used to tell my grandmother, "You are a liar, because no matter how many times I went to church, I was not able to see my natural mother." My natural mother was not dead. I found out later when I met her. For many years, I hated my stepmother until I heard the *Okikase* (Shinran's teaching). I realized then that I was wrong. Instead, I should have thanked her for being my stepmother. I was very anxious to go back to Japan and apologize to her.

If it weren't for my stepmother, I didn't have to come to Hawaii and suffer this much. I really hated her. I could understand now what my grandmother had been saying. Later I went back to Japan to ask for forgiveness of my stepmother. But my grandmother had already died.

Q.   What year did you go home?

A.   Thirty-five years after I left Japan. I think it was in 1941, just before the World War started. I was in a dangerous situation. On the return journey to Hawaii, three days after the boat left Japan, a telegram came to tell us we had to return to Japan. After about two days in Japan, we were allowed to sail home. When we reached Honolulu, the inspection was very strict because Japan and America [were] at war.

As soon as I returned to Kona, my daughter who had a dressmaking shop in Honolulu wrote to me saying that since she was very busy and she needed my help. I came out the morning of December 7, 1941. Pearl Harbor was so bright and many airplanes were flying above the battleships. We thought they were having maneuvers. Later we found out that a Japanese submarine had attacked Pearl Harbor and war had started.

Q.   Where did one of your sons die?

A.   In Okinawa. He volunteered to go to Okinawa so that he would be close to Japan where his grandfather was. He was very anxious to meet him and relay that we in Hawaii were safe. Just before the war ended, he was in a plane that crashed in Okinawa, and died. The base in Okinawa was located between mountains so the plane hit the side of the mountain. The island of Okinawa was then blacked out.

Q.   That means you lost four children?

A.   Yes, I had a miscarriage with the last child. I gave birth to eight children. During the war three of my sons served in the U. S. Army. Two of them volunteered for the interpreters and one for the 442nd RCT.

This is the end of the interview with Mrs. Nami Sogi.

Report on the Ceremonies of the Accession to the Throne of His Majesty, the Emperor Akihito
November 12, 13, 14, 1990

ALTHOUGH I WAS not able to attend the *taiso no rei* (funeral services) of Emperor Showa [in 1989], I was happy to be invited by the Japanese Government through the Japanese Consulate General of Japan in New York to attend the Ceremonies of the Accession to the Throne of His Majesty the Emperor on November 12, 13, and 14, 1990, representing the Japanese Americans on the East Coast of the United States. It was a singular honor as, I understand, there was some pressure to limit the number of Japanese Americans from North, Central, and South America. The final number was 28 from Canada, the United States, Mexico, Venezuela, Colombia, Peru, Bolivia, Brazil, Paraguay, Argentina, and Uruguay. In this group, our Vice President Quayle was 19th in the order of seating for the Enthronement Ceremony.

The United States was represented by me from the East Coast; Ralph Fujimoto of Chicago; Takeshi Ikeda of Tacoma, Washington; George Azumano of Portland, Oregon; Sadako Tsubokawa of Arvada, California; Yukio Sekine of San Francisco; Noritosi Kanai of Los Angeles; and George Ariyoshi, Fujio Matsuda, and James Morita of Hawaii. Also, there were

Emperor Akihito greeting Francis Y. Sogi and other guests at the Imperial Enthronement, Tokyo, 1989

Kings, Queens, Prime Ministers, Crown Princes, Vice Presidents, and other dignitaries from 157 countries and two international organizations.

In preparation for the Ceremonies, I received from the Japanese Consulate General of Japan in New York various instructions and schedules to be followed on each day of the three-day program. Again, on the eve of the Enthronement, we received further information and guidance from officials of the Ministry of Foreign Affairs who kindly invited the entire Japanese American contingent for dinner. We were told that cameras were prohibited in the Imperial Palace grounds.

On November 12, 1990, all of us in tail coats (those with Imperial awards were encouraged to wear them, displaying them prominently), appeared at the Ministry of Foreign Affairs by 10 a.m., the appointed hour.

After further instructions and a list of do's and don'ts, we left sharply at 11 a.m. for the Imperial Palace by bus with senior officials of the Foreign Ministry, some retired and inactive, fully decorated and bemedaled for honorable past service to their country.

We entered the Palace Grounds through the entrance north of the twin bridges, or Nijyuu Bashi. We proceeded into the Imperial Palace with buildings surrounding a square unpaved and graveled courtyard. Apparently, we rated fairly highly as we were in the second row, facing the court and to the right of the main building in which the Matsu-no-ma or the Pine Room is located and where the imperial thrones were situated.

The Imperial Palace, located in Central Tokyo, where the Enthronement Ceremony was held, is surrounded by a beautiful moat. The grounds of the Imperial Palace occupy the site of Edo Castle, which served as the Shogun's residence for nearly three centuries. The total area of the grounds is about 1.15 square kilometers. The original palace was completed in 1888. Some of the present ferroconcrete structures were built in 1969, after the destruction during World War II in 1945.

The Palace consists of seven buildings, surrounding a square courtyard, which are connected by galleries and corridors. Rooms such as he Matsu-no-ma, Seiden, Homeiden, and Chowaden occupy the central part of the Palace. It is simple and charming rather than solemn and majestic. Excessive decoration is avoided.

The Imperial Palace does not serve as the residence of the Emperor and Empress. It is used for important ceremonies of State and for welcoming State guests from overseas.

Seventy-four ceremonial attendants, in traditional garb, entered bearing swords and bows. There were also Imperial banners, many of them colored blue, yellow, red, white and purple, and a number of halberds.

In prior enthronement ceremonies, there were banners bearing a crow and a golden kite, animals linked with the myths about Emperor Jimmu's conquest of Japan. They were here replaced with a chrysanthemum crest to avoid the mythical overtones of the Enthronement.

Instructions were given in English and Japanese to the effect that no further announcements would be made during the ceremony except that the audience would rise with the beat of the drums and sit with the ringing of the bells.

At 12:55 p.m., the procession of the Imperial Family appeared in the hallway to our right. It was led by Crown Prince Naruhito, followed by Prince Akishino, his wife Princess Kiko, and Princess Nori, youngest daughter of the Emperor. They were followed by six ladies-in-waiting in beautiful traditional attire.

While waiting at the Imperial Palace for the Ceremony to begin, there was conversation going on in the audience around us, but in subdued tones. The only noise of any consequence was the cawing of the crows, several of which were flying around our buildings. In the clear blue skies with sun streaking into the Palace courtyard, the sound of the crows was very loud and clear. However, immediately after the announcement on the public-address system, the entire area became absolutely quiet except for the light thumping sound of the procession given off by the wooden footwear or shoes worn by everyone in the ceremony as they walked along the hallway of the Matsu-no-ma.

During the entire procession and ceremony there was no music or sound of any kind except for the proclamation read by the Emperor and the congratulatory message of Prime Minister Kaifu on behalf of the people of Japan.

Another aspect of this ceremony that struck me as significant was the fact that there was no flag of Japan, the Hinomaru, or Rising Sun, anywhere in the Palace grounds. There were flags displayed here and there outside of the Palace grounds and along the roads where the Imperial Motorcade passed on the way to the Akasaka Palace.

The traditional symbols of Imperial authority are the sword, jewelries, and the Sacred Mirror, the replica of the one supposedly used by the Sun Goddess Amaterasu Omikami. However, the Sacred Mirror was omitted from the Enthronement Ceremonies because it was deemed too much of an object of worship for the State occasion under Japan's postwar Constitution.

Following the Imperial Family, several officials presumably from the Imperial Household appeared, bearing the sword and jewelries, followed by ten others, each bearing some item.

The procession appeared from the hallway to the right of the Matsu-no-ma where the thrones were situated. This was immediately to the right of where the foreign Nikkei delegation was sitting.

At 1 p.m. sharp, the Emperor appeared to the right and facing us, then he turned the corner of the open hallway and headed for the Matsu-no-ma. The Emperor wore traditional 7th century attire that is worn only by the Emperor. The robe was dyed a dignified shade of yellowish red-brown using materials from trees. On his head, the Emperor wore the *ryuei no kanmuri*, a coronet with a pennant of silk gauze standing at the back; on his feet were the *gosokai*, which are wooden shoes (*asakutsu*) with embroidered covers. In his right hand, he held the *onshaku*, a wooden baton.

The Empress followed immediately behind the Emperor. She was wearing a robe consisting of five layers made of silk damask and embroidered with floral patterns. This attire is popularly known as the *jun-hitoe*, the ceremonial dress of ladies of the court. In her hand, the Empress held a ceremonial fan called an *onhiogi*. Her hair was tied at the back and hung down in the traditional *osuberakashi* style. As a hair ornament, the Empress wore a *saishi*, a kind of small mirror with crystals. She was followed by six ladies-in-waiting.

The Emperor first ascended the Takamikura and then the Empress ascended the Michodai. In the Matsu-no-ma, two thrones, one larger than the other, sat side by side. These were dismantled in Kyoto and brought to Tokyo. The Emperor's throne is called Takamikura and the, other, Michodai, is for the Empress. They are both eight-sided canopies ornately decorated with artwork of birds and animals. The Michodai, which was initiated in the Meiji era, and not used prior to that time, has one phoenix standing on the roof with no other adornments there.

The Takemikura, on the other hand, has a much larger phoenix sitting at the center and on top of the roof of the throne. In addition, there are smaller phoenixes in gold at each of the eight corners.

At about the time the Imperial Family entered the Matsu-no-ma, the representatives of the different branches of government had entered; they included Prime Minister Toshiki Kaifu, the Speaker of the House, the Speaker of the House of Councillors, and the Chief Justice of the Supreme Court of Japan.

The drums sounded and everyone stood up. The curtains concealing the thrones on three sides were opened. Their Majesties were sitting in their respective chairs. The drums sounded again and the audience bowed.

The Emperor read his speech, saying:

"Having previously succeeded to the Imperial Throne in accordance with the provisions of the Constitution of Japan and the Imperial House-hold Law, I now perform the Ceremony of the Enthronement at the Seiden and proclaim my Enthronement to those at home and abroad.

"On this occasion, I pledge anew that I shall observe the Constitution of Japan and discharge my duties as symbol of the State and the unity of the people, always wishing for the well-being of the people, in the same spirit as my father, Emperor Showa, who, during his reign spanning more than 60 years, shared joys and sorrows with the people at all times, and ardently hope that our country, through the wisdom and unceasing effort of the people, will achieve further development and contribute to friendship and peace in the international community and the well being and prosperity of mankind."

Prime Minister Kaifu, standing in the Matsu-no-ma, without stepping down 18 steps to the courtyard as prior Prime Ministers had done, gave his congratulatory message. Concluding his message, Prime Minister Kaifu said: "*Sokui wo Shukushite. Banzai, Banzai, Banzai.*" The foreigners present, except a few Nikkeis, joined in the Banzai.

The Prime Minister led three cheers for the Emperor in the same room as the Emperor. This was designed to clarify that he was the Chief Repre-sentative of the people, not the Emperor's "subject" as before. In previous Enthronement Ceremonies, the Prime Ministers led the cheers in the courtyard after stepping down from the elevated floor, to the Emperor, who was the "sovereign."

Also, Prime Minister Kaifu added, "Cheers for His Majesty the

Emperor to celebrate the Enthronement" instead of just "Cheers for His Majesty the Emperor" to identify the purpose of the cheers.

The bells then sounded and the audience sat down and the Imperial recession started leaving the Matsu-no-ma from the opposite hallway and along the Take-no-ma.

At 1:24 the bells rang. A 21-gun salute started at 1:26 p.m.

A Constitutional Monarch

With 2500 guests present, the departure from the Palace grounds required over an hour, but all in all it was a novel and memorable experience that I would like to share with as many as may be interested. What is important is not so much the ceremony itself but how the entire Emperor system affects Japan, among the Japanese themselves, and in the international community where they have difficulty being understood, let alone appreciated, for whatever they do.

Immediately after the Enthronement Ceremony on November 12, 1990, critics noted and discussed on television and in newspapers some differences in the pledge of the Emperor made at this ceremony and in his first address after accession on January 9, 1989. At that time, he said, "I shall observe the Constitution of Japan with you and discharge my duties in accordance with it." This was in reference to the Prime Minister and other top government officials present. He deleted this reference on November 11.

Also, in 1989 he said, "I also express my earnest desire that our country continue to prosper, and the peace of this world and the welfare of mankind be furthered."

The Emperor seemed to qualify his pledge to observe his Constitutional duties as the Symbol of State and the Unity of the People, rather than just observing the Constitution, as in the speech last year.

This is the first time that an Enthronement Ceremony was held in Tokyo. It was an indication of the change or break from the past under present Japan's postwar Constitution. Also, the elimination of the Sacred Mirror at the Ceremonies shows a change to the modern. Another change involved the banners in the courtyard. A pair of the leading banners in the courtyard usually indicated or showed the Rising Sun, but on this occasion, this was changed to the words "Banzai" or ten thousand years.

There was absolutely no music of any kind during the entire Enthronement Ceremony. The National Anthem was not played. No flag of Japan was shown anywhere in the Imperial Palace. Along the road where the Imperial Motorcade passed in the afternoon of November 12, 1990, the Rising Sun flags were displayed prominently on almost every lamppost.

To meet a growing trend among the Japanese people concerning the Emperor of Japan, but at the same time satisfying the demands of the Emperor System supporters, certain changes were made from the traditional ceremonies.

The religious connotation of Sokui-no-rei dates back only to the Meiji Era. In pre-Meiji times, Sokui-no-rei was basically Chinese in form. The Emperor dressed in bright red attire embellished with Chinese symbols of authority.

With the Meiji Restoration, all elements considered foreign in origin were discarded, and religious interpretations were added.

Although the *Kimigayo* and *Hinomaru* are de facto National Anthem and Flag, in the months before the Enthronement, they had become quite controversial throughout Japan. During the Seidennogi, the central ceremony in the Emperor's Enthronement Rites, the National Anthem was not played and the National Flag was not hoisted although this was the nation's most important national ceremony.

The Enthronement law, established in 1881 and scrapped after the war, was used as a basis for the Seidennogi. The law does not mention the playing of the Kimigayo or raising the Hinomaru and, therefore, they were not included in the Ceremony. The Government Committee responsible for the Enthronement Ceremony tried to be in line with the Constitution while respecting the traditions of the Imperial Family.

There appears to be a distinct difference between an Enthronement and Coronation. First, there is no Japanese Crown over which competing dynasties have fought wars since time immemorial. Whoever won did not assume the title Emperor or grab a crown, or start a fresh Imperial Dynasty.

In Japan, the Imperial Family line has not been broken since 660 B.C., when the legendary Amaterasu, the sun goddess, proclaimed to the first Emperor, her grandson Jimmu to rule Oyashima, or the eight islands of which Japan consisted at that time. Also, there was no one who could place a crown on the Emperor's head unless it be the Emperor himself. And hence he ascends to the throne and proclaims himself the Emperor of Japan.

Although we still wore formal morning outfit, the second day, November 13, 1990, was more informal and casual because it was a reception at the Akasaka Imperial grounds, adjoining the Akasaka Imperial Palace and the State Guest House. The grounds were beautiful, with lakes and pine trees surrounding them and with walking paths meandering around each lake. The lawn area was immaculately manicured. Our reception tent, only for the 28 Nikkei representatives, was set aside from the main tent for service of snacks and beverages. We freely mixed with the other guests who were primarily from the diplomatic corps in Tokyo and foreign delegates, and talked to a number of them in their tent.

Immediately in front of our area was a garden with chrysanthemums in full bloom in all their fall colors and splendors. Many of them were shaped into conical, round, or pear-shaped trees, and others were huge blossoms standing three or four feet tall, something you always see at a Kiku-Ka-Ten, a chrysanthemum exhibition.

At about 4 p.m., the Emperor and Empress appeared and we formed a receiving line to greet them and meet them on the open lawn. The Emperor looked tanned, walking upright and wearing a well-tailored morning outfit, unlike our rentals, while the Empress walked a few steps behind him in charming grace.

As I shook his hand, I mentioned that I was attending the Enthronement Ceremony as the representative of the Japanese Americans from the East Coast of the United States, and congratulated him on the occasion of the Enthronement. I spoke in Japanese. I also mentioned the fact that I had met him in New York in the Temple of Dendur of the Metropolitan Museum when we sponsored a reception in his honor about three years ago. Finally, in passing I mentioned that I also had the pleasure of meeting the Crown Price at the official residence of the Consulate General of Japan in New York, when a reception was held in his honor. He was returning to Japan after completing his education at Oxford University.

At our previous meeting, the Emperor was more expressive and asked a few questions, but on this occasion he merely nodded and smiled. The Empress, on the other hand, said that she was very happy to see so many of us.

Concluding the three-day affair for us, on November 14, 1990, our group entered the Imperial Palace grounds by bus with the officials of the Ministry of Foreign Affairs. The State Banquet Hall (Homei-den) is situated immediately behind our seating area for the Enthronement Ceremony. There was a head table, with 22 other tables occupied by about 800 guests in neatly arranged rectangular format.

The courtyard is a Heian period design. It was in this period, which lasted from the 8th century to about the 12th century, that Japan wanted to shed the extensive Chinese influence in its culture, religion, and education.

In preparation for lunch, we were all seated at about 11:45 a.m. Promptly at 11:50 a.m. for some unknown reason and without any signal or sound of any kind, the hall became absolutely silent and quiet as during the Enthronement Ceremony. Again, promptly at 12 noon, the Emperor and Empress with their immediate family entered and sat at the head table.

The Emperor read a short message of welcome to the guests, followed by a short responding message on behalf of all the guests. For the first time, the Kimigayo was played, and then after "*kampai*" was offered, lunch was served.

The menu consisted of a typical Japanese *ozen* on a lacquer tray, and included *chawan mushi, kama meshi*, soup, *yasaimono*, fish, *kamaboko*, and pieces of candy. We were invited to take home a container of fish and other foodstuffs, together with the Imperial-crested *sakazuki* cup and a silver-covered container bearing the Imperial crest in gold, all wrapped up in a white *furoshiki*. All in all, it was a simple and very pleasant lunch. It also gave us an opportunity to meet a number of other guests and to get to know the other members of our group better.

FINAL REFLECTIONS

Japanese scholars agree that although the Emperor system may undergo changes on the surface, its essence as a social and ideological apparatus will remain the same.

The Emperor's democratic and educational background will exert its influence in the daily life of the Imperial family. The core of the Emperor System will not change.

In the same evening, the Overseas Japanese Society of Japan invited our group to an informal dinner at the Japan Press Club in Tokyo. We were able to exchange ideas and convey our message, at least from the Japanese Americans' standpoint in the United States, that we are striving to educate Americans about the contributions made by the Japanese immigrants and the Japanese Americans during the past century or more. We were able to tell how the Japanese American National Museum, then slated to open in Little Tokyo in Los Angeles, would tell the Japanese American experience in American history. Through this National Museum, it was hoped that we would firmly be a part of American history and accepted by the dominant society in the same way as in Brazil.

By promoting better understanding of the Japanese and Japanese Americans among other Americans in general, we are certain that it will inure to the benefit of Japan in becoming a member of the international community and one of the leading countries in the world.

Many members of the Overseas Japanese Society were not aware of the National Museum and I took this opportunity to inform them of the efforts of those supporting this important undertaking. At every opportunity, I mentioned the activities of the Japanese Americans in the United

States and the establishment of the National Museum as a development of considerable consequence to all in this community.

I am grateful to the Japanese Government for inviting me to the Enthronement Ceremony and giving me the opportunity to be part of a major event in history for Japan and the Japanese. The opportunity to carry a simple message from the Japanese Americans in the United States to Japan was equally gratifying. It is to be hoped that this experience will enable me to be truly international and global in my thinking and continue to exert my efforts in building a better country for all of us to live in.

Names Index